ABRAHAM LINCOLN THE ORATOR

Abraham Lincoln delivering his "Gettysburg Address." "The world will very little note nor long remember what we say here," said Lincoln. Courtesy of the Illinois State Historical Society.

ABRAHAM LINCOLN THE ORATOR

Penetrating the Lincoln Legend

Lois J. Einhorn

Great American Orators, Number 16

Bernard K. Duffy and
Halford R. Ryan, Series Advisers

Greenwood Press
Westport, Connecticut • London

Library of Congress Cataloging-in-Publication Data

Einhorn, Lois J., 1952-
   Abraham Lincoln, the orator : penetrating the Lincoln legend /
Lois J. Einhorn.
     p   cm.—(Great American orators, ISSN 0898-8277 ; no. 16)
   Includes bibliographical references and index.
   ISBN 0-313-26168-7 (alk. paper)
    1. Lincoln, Abraham, 1809-1865—Oratory. 2. Political oratory—
United States—History—19th century. 3. United States—Politics
and government—1845-1861. 4. United States—Politics and
government—Civil War, 1861-1865.   I. Title.   II. Series.
E457.2.E46 1992
973.7'092—dc20   91-46971

British Library Cataloguing in Publication Data is available.

Library of Congress Catalog Card Number: 91-46971
ISBN: 0-313-26168-7
ISSN: 0898-8277

First published in 1992

Greenwood Press, 88 Post Road West, Westport, CT 06881
An imprint of Greenwood Publishing Group, Inc.

Printed in the United States of America

The paper used in this book complies with the
Permanent Paper Standard issued by the National
Information Standards Organization (Z39.48-1984).

10 9 8 7 6 5 4 3 2 1

This book is dedicated with love and affection

To my "adopted" Daddy, Eric Loeb, who is "among the better angels of our nature,"

      and

To my mentor, Carroll C. Arnold, who lives "with charity for all."

Contents

Illustrations ix

Series Foreword xi

Foreword xv

Preface xvii

Acknowledgments xix

PART I: A RHETORICAL ANALYSIS OF 1
  ABRAHAM LINCOLN'S SPEAKING

Introduction 3

1. Lincoln Speaks about Speaking 11

2. Did Lincoln Practice What He Preached? 23
 Characteristics and Development of Lincoln's Speeches

3. No Laughing Matter: Lincoln's Use of Humor 43
 as a Rhetorical Device

4. Lincoln's First Inaugural: Peace <u>and</u> Sword 55

5. Evolving Rhetorical Stances on Emancipation 71

6. Lincoln's Gettysburg Address: 93
 Immediate Failure and Lasting Success

Conclusion: The Making of a Legend   113

PART II: LINCOLN SPEAKS OUT: **117**
            TEXTS OF SELECTED SPEECHES

"Lyceum Address"   119

"Address Before the Washington Temperance Society"   127

"House Divided" Speech   135

"Second Lecture on Inventions and Discoveries"   143

"Cooper Union Address"   151

"Farewell to Springfield"   167

"First Inaugural Address"   169

"Gettysburg Address"   177

"Second Inaugural Address"   179

Notes   181

Chronology of Selected Major Speeches   193

History in Motion: Selected Bibliography on Lincoln   197

Index   219

Illustrations

The "tousled" Lincoln in this photograph is consistent with the contemporary reports of how he presented himself. 2

Daguerreotype of Lincoln. 10

Lincoln speaking in one of seven debates against Stephen Douglas. 22

Cartoon from *Harper's Weekly* depicting Lincoln's humor. 44

Political cartoon of Lincoln's First Inaugural Address. 54

Lincoln reading the Emancipation Proclamation. 70

Lincoln Address Memorial honoring the Gettysburg Address. 92

The Lincoln Memorial in Washington, D.C. 114

Photograph of Lincoln used for the engraving on the five dollar bill. 196

Series Foreword

The idea for a series of books on great American orators grew out of the recognition that there is a paucity of book-length studies on individual orators and their speeches. Apart from a few notable exceptions, the study of American public address has been pursued in scores of articles published in professional journals. As helpful as these studies have been, none has or can provide a complete analysis of a speaker's rhetoric. Book-length studies, such as those in this series, will help fill the void that has existed in the study of American public address and its related disciplines of politics, history, theology, sociology, communication, and law. In books, the critic can explicate a broader range of a speaker's persuasive discourse than reasonably could be treated in articles. The comprehensive research and sustained reflection that books require will undoubtedly yield many original and enduring insights concerning the nation's most important voices.

Public address has been a fertile ground for scholarly investigation. No matter how insightful their intellectual forebears, each generation of scholars must reexamine its universe of discourse while expanding the compass of its research and redefining its purpose and methods. To avoid intellectual torpor, new scholars cannot be content simply to see through the eyes of those who have come before them. We hope that this series of books will stimulate important new understandings of the nature of persuasive discourse and provide additional opportunities for scholarship in the history and criticism of American public address.

This series examines the role of rhetoric in the United States. American speakers shaped the destiny of the colonies, the young republic, and the mature nation. During each stage of the intellectual, political, and religious development of the United States, great orators, standing at the rostrum, on the stump, and in the pulpit, used words and gestures to influence their audiences. Usually striving for the noble, sometimes achieving the base, they urged their fellow citizens toward a more perfect Union. The books in this series chronicle and explain the accomplishments of representative American leaders as orators.

A series of book-length studies on American persuaders honors the role men and women have played in U.S. history. Previously, if one desired to assess the impact of a speaker or a speech upon history, the path was, at best, not well marked and, at worst, littered with obstacles. To be sure, one might turn to biographies and general histories to learn about an orator, but for the public address scholar these sources often prove unhelpful. Rhetorical topics, such as speech invention, style, delivery, organizational strategies, and persuasive effect, often are treated in passing, if mentioned at all. Authoritative speech texts often are difficult to locate, and the problem of textual accuracy is frequently encountered. This is especially true for those figures who spoke one or two hundred years ago or for those whose persuasive role, though significant, was secondary to other leading lights of the age.

Each book in this series is organized to meet the needs of scholars and students of the history and criticism of American public address. Part I is a critical analysis of the orator and his or her speeches. Within the format of a case study, one may expect considerable latitude. For instance, in a given chapter an author might explicate a single speech or a group of related speeches or examine orations that comprise a genre of rhetoric such as forensic speaking. But the critic's focus remains on the rhetorical considerations of speaker, speech, occasion, and effect. Part II contains the texts of the important addresses that are discussed in the critical analysis that precedes it. To the extent possible, each author has endeavored to collect authoritative speech texts, which often have been found through original research in collections of primary source material. In a few instances, because of the extreme length of a speech, texts have been edited. But the authors have been careful to delete material that is least important to the speech, and these deletions have been held to a minimum.

Because of the disparate nature of the speakers examined in the series, there is some latitude in the nature of the bibliographical materials that have been included in each book. But in every instance, authors have carefully described original historical materials and collections and gathered critical studies, biographies and autobiographies, and a variety of secondary sources that bear on the speaker and the oratory. By combining in each book bibliographical materials, speech texts, and critical chapters, this series notes that text and research sources are interwoven in the act of rhetorical criticism.

May the books in this series serve to memorialize the nation's greatest orators.

Bernard K. Duffy
Halford R. Ryan

Foreword

I take for my text John I:46 wherein Nathanael asked concerning the Christ: "Can anything good come out of Nazareth?" Unlike Nathanael's rhetorical question, which signaled disbelief, this book is an affirmation, for we contemplate the oratory of a man who was lowly born in Hodginville, Kentucky, in 1809, and ponder the measure of a critic who would treat his rhetoric.

The sixteenth President of the United States of America delivered several speeches. However, a senatorial campaign address, some debates with the Little Giant, a Presidential campaign speech, two inaugural addresses, plus a very short speech delivered at a cemetery, comprise the accepted canon of his great speeches. Yet, Abraham Lincoln's speeches are the apotheosis of American addresses, orations of the first water.

Consider his craftsmanship. No president since John F. Kennedy's Inaugural Address in 1961, and before him Franklin D. Roosevelt's Inaugural Address in 1933, has attained such Olympian heights in investiture oratory as Lincoln did in 1861, and especially so in 1865. The so-called campaign debates of the late twentieth century have as their archetype the Lincoln-Douglas debates of 1858. And as for the genre of ceremonial oratory, his Gettysburg Address, with its prayer-like tones, has yet to be surpassed by any president of the United States.

But what of the critic who would treat Lincoln's rhetoric? Like Nathanael, one questions: Have not others so trod the oratorical path that little awaits explication? Have not all of the major addresses been attended at length? Have not the significant speeches been anthologized in countless places?

Nevertheless, much good comes from examining Lincoln's oratory, especially when Professor Lois Einhorn is the critic. A patient researcher, a proven writer with a critical acumen, Einhorn has produced her *magnum opus.*

Halford Ryan
Co-Editor, Great American Orators Series

Preface

But we can help turn the legend of Lincoln into the living reality of the man by looking at the words with which he clothed his thought and conviction.

Theodore Blegen, author of *Lincoln's Imagery*

William Jennings Bryan, himself a famous orator, said in a speech celebrating the 100th anniversary of Lincoln's birth, "Lincoln's fame as a statesman and as the Nation's Chief Executive during its most crucial period has so overshadowed his fame as an orator that his merits as a public speaker have not been sufficiently emphasized." Henry Clay Whitney, a lawyer who rode with Lincoln on the circuit of Illinois, argued that Lincoln's rise from a circuit lawyer to the presidency "was achieved entirely by oratory. He held no office; had no position where he could act; had no publication in which to air his views; no way to reach the public except by speeches."[1]

This book examines Lincoln as an orator, the public man communicating to listeners. It combines rhetorical analysis of important aspects of his speaking with transcripts of some of his important speech texts. His speeches show him in a wide variety of roles. By studying Lincoln's rhetoric, we gain insights into him as an orator, debater, jester, lawyer, statesman, leader, and president.

Acknowledgments

I could not have written this book without the help of many people. First I wish to acknowledge my debt to Abraham Lincoln, the subject of this study, whose rhetoric continues to fascinate and inspire me.

I thank Halford R. Ryan and Bernard K. Duffy, Co-Editors of the Great American Orators Series, and Mildred Vasan, Senior Editor of Social and Behavioral Sciences, and Julie LeGallee, Production Editor, at Greenwood Press.

I acknowledge with pleasure the many librarians at the Cornell University Library and the Library of Congress who helped me locate materials. I am especially grateful to the numerous librarians at the State University of New York, University Center at Binghamton. They helped me in more ways than I can list. I extend my appreciation to Sidonie Smith, then Dean of the College of Arts and Sciences at SUNY-Binghamton, for awarding me a Research Semester to conduct research and begin writing. My special thanks go to the Department of English, General Literature, and Rhetoric at SUNY-Binghamton and to the University itself for constantly supporting and encouraging me to pursue my research interests. Special thanks go also to my students, who have allowed me to test ideas on them. I hope I have touched their lives a little; I know they have touched mine a lot.

I extend particular gratitude to historians Gabor S. Boritt, Robert C. Fluhrer Professor of Civil War Studies and Director of the Civil War Institute at Gettysburg College, and Don E. Fehrenbacher, William Robertson Coe Professor of History and American Studies Emeritus at Stanford University, for giving me valuable feedback on the book's proposal and for enthusiastically supporting my efforts. Professors Boritt and Fehrenbacher also are among the sixteen Lincoln scholars whom I thank for allowing me to test out some of my ideas at the Colloquium on "Liberty in the Works of Abraham Lincoln," Gettysburg, April 1990.

Lincoln wrote, "The better part of one's life consists of one's friendships." I thank my friends for supporting me and sharing ideas with me. I especially extend my appreciation, admiration, and affection to the two people who have contributed most to this book and to my life: Eric Loeb, my "adopted Daddy," for always being there for me with unconditional love and continual nurturing, and Carroll C. Arnold, my mentor, for his incisive criticism on drafts of the manuscript and for his constant direction, encouragement, and love.[1]

I

A RHETORICAL ANALYSIS OF ABRAHAM LINCOLN'S SPEAKING

The "tousled" Lincoln in this photograph is not the Lincoln most Americans know, but the way Lincoln looks here is consistent with contemporary reports of how he presented himself. Although so much scholarship exists on Lincoln, there is still more to learn. Lincoln Museum, Fort Wayne, Indiana, a part of Lincoln National Corporation.

Introduction

One always has his tongue with him, and the breath of his life is the ever-ready material with which [speech] works.

Lincoln in his "Second Lecture on Inventions and Discoveries"

Throughout history people generally have dealt with disagreement in one of two ways--by force and by rhetoric. Rhetoric is discussion in the human forum. It deals with people's choices and, unlike force, it depends on the free will of others to accept or reject ideas. Rhetoric is the foundation of civilization. As a process, it existed from the moment humans began to communicate. As a study, it was one of the first humanistic disciplines, humanistic because it concerns an activity that is uniquely human: the use of symbols to influence the beliefs, values, and/or actions of other people. Lincoln seemed to recognize the relationship between rhetoric and force. In his "Lost Speech," he supposedly said, "The ballot is stronger than the bullet," and at the end of his "Cooper Union Address," he spoke the now-famous line, "Let us have faith that right makes might, and in that faith, let us, to the end, dare to do our duty as we understand it." Lincoln understood the importance of rhetoric; he seemed to agree with the advice of Mentor Graham, his tutor in elocution, who said that "the right words will guide the world."[1]

Like all arts, the art of rhetoric has changed through the centuries. In the middle of the nineteenth century, the ability to speak effectively was a prerequisite for leadership. In his introduction to *Abraham Lincoln: A Press Portrait*, Herbert Mitgang wrote, "Abraham Lincoln entered public life nearly a century and a half ago--long before the selling of cosmetized Presidents in televised packages--when the force of a man's mind and the power of his lungs still counted." Journalist Horace White made a similar comment: "When Lincoln was preparing himself unconsciously to be the nation's leader, the only means of gaining public attention was by public speech. The Press did not exist for him. . . . If a man was to gain any popularity he must gain it by talking into the faces of the people."[2]

Given the importance of rhetoric in the mid-nineteenth century, and given that Lincoln delivered most of his speeches during a critical period in American history, it is not surprising that his oratory affected the actions and reactions of so many people. Commenting on Lincoln's verbal battles against Stephen Douglas in 1858, historian Roy Basler said, "It would be difficult to find in all history a precise instance in which rhetoric played a more important role than it did in Lincoln's speeches of 1858." Basler's comment applies to Lincoln's speaking in general. As a leader, Lincoln is remembered as much for what he said as for what he did.[3]

A plethora of books and articles on Lincoln exists. Many examine his oratory, but almost all of these works are historical and biographical. There is a surprising dearth of scholarly study on Lincoln's speaking by rhetorical scholars. The *Index to Journals in Communication Studies Through 1985* lists only thirty-seven articles on Lincoln published in communication journals before and through the year 1985. Many of these are not even recent, as the following breakdown of publication dates shows: 1920-1929 (two articles), 1930-1939 (seven), 1940-1949 (one), 1950-1959 (four), 1960-1969 (twelve), 1970-1979 (nine), and 1980-1985 (two). Of course, rhetorical scholars have published articles on Lincoln in journals appearing outside the field of communication, and they have written a few books and book chapters about his speaking (see Bibliography). Still, in view of the above facts, there is room for a study focusing entirely on his rhetoric. Accordingly, in what follows I shall combine rhetorical analysis of important aspects of Lincoln's speaking together with transcripts of some of his important speeches.[4]

Lincoln as a subject for rhetorical inquiry is not exhausted and probably never will be, in part because almost every aspect of his speaking consists of contradictions. He was plain yet profound, simple yet complex, funny yet serious. He mingled mirth and melancholy in a somewhat mysterious manner. He identified with people and spoke of his faith in them; yet, while speaking he seemed to detach himself from his listeners. Winston Churchill once made a comment about Russia that applies to almost every aspect of Lincoln's rhetoric: "It is a riddle wrapped in a mystery inside an enigma."[5]

In many ways Lincoln becomes increasingly mysterious as new studies of him appear. A problem with many of the rhetorical and historical works on Lincoln is that they are so pro-Lincoln that it is difficult to separate the man from the myth and fact from fiction. This book attempts to present Lincoln as a life-like not God-like speaker, complete with strengths and weaknesses, consistencies and contradictions. I shall attempt to penetrate the Lincoln legend by examining Lincoln's own words. The testimony of eye-and-ear witnesses will be used primarily as supplementary support.

For each speech in my "Selected Speeches" section, I have tried to locate the most accurate, word-for-word record of what Lincoln actually said as opposed to what he had prepared to say or what he wished he had said. Almost all books that include some of Lincoln's speeches print the official versions, which he usually edited after delivery. Since rhetorical inquiry is concerned with how a speaker adapts to an immediate audience and how that audience perceives the speaker's message, it is important to use a text that most accurately reflects what listeners actually heard. To paraphrase Herbert A. Wichelns, rhetorical criticism is concerned not only with permanence or beauty. It is concerned primarily with effect. It regards a speech as a communication to a specific audience and holds its business to be the analysis and appreciation of the methods used by orators to impart their ideas to their hearers.[6]

From the beginning of his oratorical career, Lincoln prepared his speeches so carefully that the differences between variant texts are few. Still, some important differences exist. For example, none of the drafts of the "Gettysburg Address" in Lincoln's handwriting include the phrase "under God." Lincoln apparently added this important phrase while in the process of speaking. In editing his "Cooper Union Address" for what was to become the official version, Lincoln corrected a factual error. Listeners, of course, heard the speech with the inaccurate information.

For each speech, when more than one text was available, I compared the variant texts. These comparisons revealed that Lincoln frequently made the following types of editing changes after delivery: clarifying referents, adding parallel structures, placing subject and predicate together, deleting split infinitives, and adding repetition. Lincoln's listeners, of course, did not have the benefit of these changes; neither did newspaper readers at the time. Most official versions of Lincoln's speeches are full of quotation marks and italics that do not appear in newspaper accounts, making it doubtful that Lincoln said, "And I quote. . . . " Listeners, of course, cannot hear quotation marks or italics.

For each speech presented here, I have checked the original source and verified every word and every punctuation mark. For Lincoln's early speeches, *The Collected Works of Abraham Lincoln* printed the newspaper versions since no other speech texts were available. For these speeches I examined the microfilms directly. Where the editors of the *Collected Works* corrected grammar or punctuation, I present the account of the speech exactly as it appeared in the newspaper. **I PURPOSEFULLY HAVE KEPT**

<u>MISSPELLINGS, TYPOGRAPHICAL ERRORS, PECULIAR SPELLINGS, AND PUNCTUATION ERRORS</u> in order to let Lincoln's personality and the style of the time come through as clearly as possible. When Lincoln emphasized a point in a text, I am using italics. When I am emphasizing a point, I am underscoring.[7]

A limitation of my choice of texts is that stenographic reports are not always accurate. Other limitations naturally arise from analyzing printed speeches. Before printing Lincoln's "Cooper Union Address," the *New-York Daily Tribune* noted, "We present herewith a full and accurate report of this Speech; yet the tones, the gestures, the kindling eye and the mirth-provoking look, defy the reporter's skill." In his article "Lincoln the Speaker, 1830-1837," Earl W. Wiley elaborated on the difficulty of capturing in print the symbiotic relationship between speaker and audience: "But a speech once uttered vanishes like a bubble, and cold ink fails to rekindle in us the glow of the man in the focus of the crowd. Speech always denotes the articulate man in conscious contact with men. It implies the nearness of an audience and the vitality of an occasion." Any critic of past speeches works with an incomplete past because of missing evidence, and all critics work with an incomplete picture because they are human beings who approach their critical objects with different sets of assumptions and critical tools and with different expectations and perceptions.[8]

The audiences for Lincoln's speeches consisted of more than just his immediate listeners. His audiences also included people who read his speeches in newspapers. It is worth remembering that newspaper readers usually skim rather than read articles and usually look at articles only once. It is important to realize also that the rate of illiteracy was relatively high in the middle of the nineteenth century. Frequently people gathered to hear someone read the newspaper to them. Thus, another audience for Lincoln's speeches consisted of people who could not read his words themselves but who listened to others read newspaper accounts to them; these people also constituted a <u>listening</u> audience.[9]

In what follows I shall begin by discussing Lincoln's rhetoric about the art of rhetoric. In speeches, recorded conversations, letters, and other oral and written messages, Lincoln expressed definite ideas about the qualities needed for effective speaking. To the best of my knowledge, these ideas have never been collected. Considered together, his ideas on speaking are remarkably consistent and coherent. Examining them provides information needed to answer the question raised in the next chapter: Did Lincoln practice what he preached?

Chapter 2 shows that Lincoln did practice what he preached. There I discuss characteristics of his speaking that spanned his career, qualities of his rhetoric that remained constant throughout his years as a stump speaker, debater, and president, as well as specific ways in which his speaking changed as he moved from a stump speaker and debater to president. I argue that Lincoln's speeches changed from an oral to a written style.

An important characteristic of Lincoln's speaking was his use of humor. In Chapter 3 I contend that for Lincoln humor was not a laughing matter, but usually was rhetorically purposeful. Humor helped him prove his points and refute the points of others. The chapter examines the roots of Lincoln's humor, characteristics of his humor, and the influence of his humor on evaluations of his speaking effectiveness.

I begin Chapter 4 by examining Lincoln's strategic silence between his election in November 1860 and his inauguration in March 1861, and I discuss how this rhetoric of silence affected his "First Inaugural Address." Most of the chapter consists of an in-depth analysis of this speech, explaining why most Northerners viewed the speech as conciliatory while most Southerners considered it a declaration of war.

Chapter 5 examines Lincoln's rhetoric on slavery and racial equality. I show that Lincoln abhorred slavery, although he did not advocate complete equality between the races, and I argue that the person associated with one of the most radical reforms in history was not a reformer by nature.

My final critical chapter offers an in-depth analysis of Lincoln's "Gettysburg Address." Examining the speech from both a literary and a rhetorical perspective helps explain why the speech was not considered great in 1863 but is considered great today. I argue that many of the factors that make the "Gettysburg Address" a literary masterpiece are precisely the factors that prevented it from being an immediate success.

In concluding the "Rhetorical Analysis" section, I examine the transformation of Lincoln from a man-like to a God-like speaker. I contrast how Lincoln was perceived by his contemporaries with how he is perceived today.

Part II, "Lincoln Speaks Out: Texts of Selected Speeches," contains the most accurate word-for-word record I could find of what Lincoln actually said in some of his important speeches. The content of his "Lyceum Address" and "Temperance Address" contained the seeds of views he espoused in later speeches. According to rhetorical critic Michael Leff, Lincoln's "House Divided" Speech "permanently altered perception of the slavery controversy. It crystallized public opinion about what had happened before and about what was to happen later, and the lens of Lincoln's terminology still focuses our vision of the 1850s, a decade known as the era of the house dividing." Lincoln's "Second Lecture on Discoveries and Inventions" dealt in detail with his views on the nature of speaking and writing. This is the only speech included in Part II that was considered a failure in its day (1859) and is still considered a failure today. The speech also featured Lincoln in the role of popular lecturer rather than politician. Lincoln's "Cooper Union Address" represented the culmination of ideas he had expressed in his "House Divided Speech" and his series of formal debates with Stephen Douglas. This speech gave Lincoln national prominence, introducing the prairie politician from the West to the sophisticated citizens of the East. Even Lincoln admitted that this speech helped to put him in the White House. In February 1861, Lincoln bid "Farewell to Springfield" in a brief but eloquent speech as he began his journey to Washington D.C. to assume the presidency. To some critics this brief speech represented the beginning of Lincoln's last phase as a "literary artist," a phase where prose and poetry merged into "lofty eloquence." Lincoln's "Gettysburg Address" and his first and second inaugural addresses have secured permanent places in rhetorical literature. Although they were not considered great speeches by many people at the times of delivery, all three speeches today are considered among the best speeches of all time.[10]

Choosing which speeches to include in this collection meant choosing which speeches to exclude. The Lincoln-Douglas Debates are my most obvious omission. I have chosen to omit excerpts from these debates because there is no way to capture the give-and-take of a debate by presenting the speeches of just one of the participants, and there is no way to portray twenty-one hours of debate (seven debates each lasting three hours) in ten or twenty pages. Thus, rather than including excerpts, I cite several examples from the Debates in the critical chapters.[11]

Lincoln's rhetoric consisted of words, actions, humor, and even silence. From analyzing his rhetoric, we gain insights into general rhetorical processes and into the making of the Lincoln legend. Contrasting reactions to Lincoln's speeches at the times of delivery with reactions to those speeches today illustrates more than just the historical record. The contrasts help refine the differing criteria used in judging immediate and historic rhetoric and the different criteria that need to be applied in judging oral versus written excellence. In general, examining the strategies and techniques Lincoln used in various rhetorical situations and before varying kinds of audiences yields insight into how and why he became an important national orator.

Like all rhetors, Lincoln both shaped his world and was shaped by his world. Analyzing his rhetoric contributes to our knowledge of this critical point in American history. A better understanding of the public dialogue of the past can shape our present and our future. In the foreword to the *Collected Works*, Roy Basler, the primary editor, wrote "that the record of past human effort, in failure and in success, in error and in truth, is the chief source from which mankind can

draw an understanding of the present and the hope of the future."
Lincoln's speeches provide such a record: Through them he continues
to speak to the present generation and to generations to come. Join
now in "listening" to Lincoln speak and in interpreting his rhetoric.[12]

Lincoln with pencil and spectacles in hand. In his "House Divided" Speech, Lincoln said, "If we could first know *where* we are, and *whither* we are tending, we could better judge *what* to do, and *how* to do it." Regarding his own speaking, Lincoln presented himself as knowing "where he was and whither he was tending." Photo courtesy of the Library of Congress.

1

Lincoln Speaks about Speaking

If we could first know where we are, and whither we are tending, we could better judge what to do, and how to do it.

Lincoln in his "House Divided Speech"

The relationship between words and essences did . . . occur to Lincoln as a problem.

Rhetorical theorist Richard Weaver

We have seen that Lincoln recognized rhetoric's power to influence people's actions and reactions and that his speaking ability helped him rise to the presidency. Almost all biographical sketches of Lincoln tell of his persistent passion to improve his communicative skills. He clearly spent much time trying to determine "where he was and whither he was tending" and trying to learn more about "the relationship between words and essences." His personal reflections on the art of rhetoric gave him definite ideas about the qualities needed for effective oratory.[1]

Lincoln never explained his views on the art of rhetoric in one speech or one essay, but several of his speeches, recorded conversations, letters, and other written messages contain bits and pieces of his ideas on speaking. This chapter collects these ideas. My thesis is that Lincoln's rhetorical judgments were remarkably consistent and coherent; usually people's ideas about communication contain many more inconsistencies, idiosyncracies, and changes over time. Throughout his life Lincoln's attitude toward communication was utterly pragmatic and deliberate. Beauty had little place in his judgments of what to say or how to say it, an especially unusual attitude toward communication at a time when aesthetic, hortatory, emotional speeches were the norm. Lincoln's rhetorical conclusions seemed to evolve from predisposition and from rational, consistent extrapolations to rhetorical practice. Because his natural tendencies were greatly influenced by his childhood environment and by his legal training and practice, I begin by examining these two influences.

THE INFLUENCE OF LINCOLN'S CHILDHOOD ON HIS IDEAS ABOUT SPEAKING

Lincoln's ascent from a log cabin to the White House has become part of the Great American Dream. Frontier life offered him little formal education or culture. In an "Autobiography" written in 1860, he indicated that he "went to A.B.C. schools by littles," with the "littles" totaling less than a year. Most of his education was other than formal, but he learned by observing, listening, reading, and discussing. He learned by experiencing more failures than victories. His realistic and pragmatic attitude may have stemmed in part from the harshness of life on the frontier.[2]

Lincoln was not content to stay in the raw, rustic environment of his youth. He disliked physical labor, preferring instead to think, read, talk, and debate. He considered the American form of government a "political religion" that allowed all people, no matter how poor, to better themselves. As he said in a speech in 1860: "When one starts poor, as most do in the race of life, free society is such that he knows he can better his condition; he knows that there is no fixed condition of labor, for his whole life."[3]

Education, including the study of communication, was Lincoln's route to "better his condition." Early in his life he wrote, "That every man may receive at least, a moderate education, and thereby be enabled to read the histories of his own and other countries, by which he may duly appreciate the value of our free institutions, appears to be an object of vital importance." Twenty years later he said that "one can scarcely be so poor, but that, if he *will*, he *can* acquire sufficient education to get through the world respectably."[4]

For Lincoln, communication constituted an important part of education. Throughout his life he purposefully experimented with words--how they work and how to adapt them to different kinds of settings, subjects, and audiences. He consciously experimented with various styles. As a boy he frequently heard itinerant preachers and went into the woods afterward to put what he had just heard into his own words. Eager to practice speaking, he did so before neighborhood boys and even before cornfields and pumpkins. Later, he spoke on stumps and platforms, in stores, mills, and polling places, and at socials and barn raisings--wherever he could gain experience. His speeches contain numerous instances of plays on words; the following, from an early speech, is but one example: "He *in*vaded Canada without resistance, and he *out*vaded it without pursuit" (Lincoln's emphasis).   Throughout his life, he also liked to mimic others, perhaps because it allowed him to try an assortment of styles.[5]

Lincoln experimented not only with using different styles but also with expressing points precisely. He frequently tried to phrase ideas in several different ways until he thought he had stated them as clearly as possible. Francis Carpenter, an artist who lived for six months at the White House, recorded Lincoln explaining how his childhood experiences related to his penchant for clarity:

I can remember going to my little bedroom, after hearing the neighbors talk of an evening with my father . . . and trying to make out what was the exact meaning of some of their, to me, dark sayings. I could not sleep . . . when I got on such a hunt after an idea, until I had repeated it over and over; until I had put it in language plain enough, as I thought, for any boy I knew to comprehend. This was a kind of passion with me, and it has stuck by me; for I am never easy now, when I am handling a thought, till I have bounded it north and bounded it south, and bounded it east and bounded it west.

William Herndon, Lincoln's law partner, also wrote of Lincoln's passion for finding the right word: "In the search for words Mr. Lincoln was often at a loss. He was often perplexed to give proper expression to his ideas . . . because there were, in the vast store of words, so few that contained the exact coloring, power, and shape of his ideas."[6]

With precision as a major goal, it was natural that Lincoln specially prized writing and meticulous planning of formal addresses. He was fond of practicing speaking, but in actual situations he often purposefully chose silence. Throughout his life, he wrote down memorable passages, relied on writing for the expression of important ideas, carefully prepared speeches, and often edited his speeches up until the moment of delivery. All of these behaviors demonstrate his striving for clarity and precision.

In his "Second Lecture on Discoveries and Inventions," Lincoln reflected on the nature of speaking and writing and on the relationship between these two means of communication. His reflections focused again on clarity and precision, but they focused here, too, on efficiency and accuracy. In his discussion of speech, Lincoln said, "You can count from one to one hundred quite distinctly in about forty seconds. In doing this two hundred and eighty three distinct sounds or syllables are uttered, being seven to each second; and yet there shall be enough difference between every two, to be easily recognized by the ear of the hearer." Speech alone, though, he continued, "valuable as it ever has been, and is, has not advanced the condition of the world much. . . . When man was possessed of speech alone, the chances of invention, discovery, and improvement were very limited." To illustrate "the wonderful powers of the *eye* in conveying ideas to the mind from writing," Lincoln returned to his example of counting from one to one hundred:

Take the same example of the numbers from *one* to *one hundred* written down, and you can run your eye over the list, and be assured that every number is in it, in about one half the time it would require to pronounce the words with the voice; and not only so, but you can, in the same short time, determine whether every word is spelled correctly, by which it is evident that every separate letter, amounting to eight hundred and sixty four, has been recognized, and reported to the mind, within the incredibly short space of twenty seconds, or one third of a minute.

In more general terms, Lincoln called writing "the great invention of the world . . . great, very great in enabling us to converse with the dead, the absent, and the unborn, at all distances of time and of space." In another speech he called reading "the key, or one of the keys, to the already solved problems" and something that "gives a relish, and facility, for successfully pursuing the yet unsolved ones."[7]

What books did Lincoln read in his youth and why did he choose them? His early favorites were *Aesop's Fables* named after an ex-slave named Aesop, and the *King James Bible*. He liked these books especially because they are full of parables, stories, and figurative language. That Lincoln was specifically interested in the details of language is further attested to by the fact that the following books were among others he chose to study: William Scott's *Lessons on Elocution*, Samuel Kirkham's *Grammar*, Thomas Dilworth's *Spelling Book* and *New Guide to the English Tongue*, and Noah Webster's *Spelling Book* and *The Kentucky Preceptor*. He also was fond of the plays of William Shakespeare, especially *MacBeth*, and of the works of Oliver Wendell Holmes and Robert Burns. He enjoyed reading Mason Weem's *Life of Washington* and David Ramsey's *Life of George Washington*, both of which included moral lessons. He read at least part of John Bunyan's *Pilgrim's Progress*, Daniel DeFoe's *Robinson Crusoe*, William Grimshaw's *History of the United States*, and the humorous writings of Artemus Ward, Petroleum Nasby, and Orpheus Kerr. He also read the *Revised Statutes of Indiana*, which included a copy of the Declaration of Independence and the Constitution.

For Lincoln, a meditative boy, reading was not a passive activity. Rather, reading meant questioning, probing, analyzing, and evaluating both the content and the form of words on a page. Herndon recorded a story told to him by Russell Godby, who frequently hired the young Lincoln to do farm work. Godby said he once asked Lincoln what he was reading, to which Lincoln replied, "I'm not reading. I'm studying." Apparently this attitude toward the written word was lifelong, for Herndon declared, "His powers of concentration were intense, and in the ability through analysis to strip bare a proposition he was unexcelled. His thoughtful and investigating mind dug down after ideas, and never stopped till bottom facts were reached."[8]

Although Lincoln read books intently, it is not clear that he always read them in their entirety. "The truth about Mr. Lincoln," said Herndon, "is that he read less and thought more than any man . . . of his standing in America, if not in the world." Consistent with his unusual attention to detailed meanings, Lincoln purposefully read aloud. He once explained, "When I read aloud two senses catch the idea: first, I see what I read; second, I hear it, and therefore I can remember it better."[9]

THE INFLUENCE OF THE LAW ON
LINCOLN'S IDEAS ABOUT SPEAKING

The legal profession provided Lincoln a way out of his frontier environment and a way to foster his belief in education as a lifelong process. In an article on Lincoln's imagery, James Hurt explained that Lincoln's choice of the law was itself a disavowal of frontier beliefs and values: "To men of Thomas Lincoln's background [Abraham Lincoln's father], the law was the instrument of the rich and powerful who could use its complexities to outwit the common man and to do him out of his property . . . Lincoln came to see the law not as trickery . . . but as the instrument of reason and justice, a way of bringing order to the entanglements of human affairs."[10]

Lincoln explained how he had studied law in a letter of advice: "When a man has reached the age that Mr. [John H.] Widmer has . . . my judgment is, that he reads the books for himself without an instructor. That is precisely the way I came to the law. Let Mr. Widmer read Blackstone's Commentaries, Chitty's Pleadings--Greenleaf's Evidence, Story's Equity, and Story's Equity Pleadings, get a license, and go to the practice, and still keep reading." Significantly, in his own training for law Lincoln did not confine himself to purely legal logic. In pursuit of the art of reasoning he also read Euclid's six books on logic. All of these works stress logic, order, precision, and rationality.[11]

Probably Lincoln's legal training was responsible for his understanding of the concepts of presumption and burden of proof. Regardless of his source for this information, he showed he was as acutely aware of how these concepts function in argumentation as was Richard Whately, the rhetorician who first introduced the concepts into rhetorical theory in 1828 in the first edition of his *Elements of Rhetoric*. Both inside and outside of the courtroom, Lincoln frequently stipulated the technical burdens of arguers, as he did in debating Stephen Douglas: "A man cannot prove a negative, but he has a right to claim that when a man makes an affirmative charge, he must offer some proof to show the truth of what he says."[12]

The legal profession stresses the value of thorough research, coherent thought, clear definitions, and precise expression. It prizes logic and reason and urges the conscious restraint of emotion. However, Lincoln was not unaware of the importance of rhetorical appeal. Chauncey M. DePew, a fellow lawyer, recorded Lincoln discussing what he had learned from riding the circuit:

He said that, riding the circuit for many years and stopping at country taverns where were gathered lawyers, jurymen, witnesses and clients, they would sit up all night narrating to each other their life adventures, and that the things which happened to an original people, in a new country, surrounded by novel conditions, and told with the descriptive power and exaggeration which characterized such men, supplied him with an exhaustless fund of anecdotes which could be made applicable for enforcing or refuting an argument better than all the invented stories of the world.

Interestingly, DePew did not report that Lincoln studied people to learn how to sway audiences--why many speakers have studied human nature--but to acquire material for proving and refuting points.[13]

GENERAL IDEAS ABOUT SPEAKING

Collectively, Lincoln's ideas on speaking form a coherent rhetorical theory. All of his major principles reflected the fact that he gave primacy to ideas, reason, and personal sincerity. Lincoln probably never read the Roman rhetorical theorist Quintilian, but his ideas on speaking spell out "a good man speaking well." Lincoln's guidelines provide sound advice for public speakers and, in fact, are consistent with the advice offered in most public speaking books today. The following propositions were major items in his overall counsel:[14]

Recognize the Value and Limitations
of Public Speaking

In notes for a law lecture, Lincoln wrote of the importance of public speaking: "Extemporaneous speaking should be practised and cultivated. It is the lawyer's avenue to the public. However able and faithful he may be in other respects, people are slow to bring him business if he cannot make a speech." But in these same notes he also warned against relying too much on good speaking and disregarding the importance of legal reasoning: "And yet there is not a more fatal error to young lawyers than relying too much on speechmaking. If any one, upon his rare powers of speaking, shall claim an exemption from the drudgery of the law, his case is a failure in advance."[15]

Speak for Practical Effect on Matters of Deep Conviction

Henry Clay was Lincoln's rhetorical and political hero. In his eulogy of Clay, the qualities Lincoln praised indicate what he valued in a public speaker:

Mr. Clay's eloquence did not consist . . . of antithesis, and elegant arrangements of words and sentences; but rather of that deeply earnest and impassioned tone, and manner, which can proceed only from great sincerity and a thorough conviction, in the speaker of the justice and importance of his cause. . . . All his efforts were made for practical effect. He never spoke merely to be heard.

Consistent with the thrust of this encomium, when Lincoln gave instructions to others about speaking, he usually focused on what their speech should do. For example, when he appointed Ulysses S. Grant to the commission of Lieutenant General of the Army, he met with Grant regarding the formal presentation. Lincoln gave Grant a copy of his remarks and instructed Grant not on what to say but on what he wanted Grant's answer to accomplish: "There are two points that I would like to have you make in your answer: First, to say something which shall prevent or obviate any jealousy of you from any of the other generals in the service; and second, something which shall put you on as good terms as possible with the Army of the Potomac." According to Herndon, in practice Lincoln usually won cases, no matter how difficult, when he believed the cause was right and just, and he usually lost cases, no matter how easy, when he did not believe in the cause he was advocating. All the evidence I have seen contributes to the conclusion that Lincoln thought speakers should first have significant content, then have reasoned form, and only afterward have language to give the ideas practical significance. Lincoln made a statement that succinctly epitomized this general stance: "I shall never be old enough to speak without embarrassment when I have nothing to talk about."[16]

Have the Listeners' Best Interests at Heart

Lincoln believed that persuasion occurred only when listeners felt that the speaker had their best interests at heart. He was probably not familiar with Aristotle's concept of *ethos*, but he certainly recognized the importance of speakers' showing their good will toward their listeners. In the *Ethics*, Aristotle explained that "good will" meant speakers showing their listeners that they are at least potentially friends. In his "Temperance Address" Lincoln argued that the temperance movement in 1842, the year of the speech, was far more successful than the movement of earlier times. The reasons, he said, were that preachers, lawyers, and hired agents were the early spokespeople for the movement, and the masses sometimes questioned whether these speakers had the best interests of ordinary people at heart. The new champions, however, were people who had been victims of intemperance and who now advocated sobriety. These new reformers were succeeding, Lincoln contended, because no one could question their sincerity. He eloquently summarized how friendliness relates to a speaker's credibility:

When the conduct of men is designed to be influenced, *persuasion*, kind, unassuming persuasion, should ever be adopted. It is an old and a true maxim, that a "drop of honey catches more flies than a gallon of gall." So with men. If you would win a man to your cause, *first* convince him that you are his sincere friend. Therein is a drop of honey that catches his heart, which, say what he will, is the great high road to his reason . . . such is man, and so *must* be understood by those who would lead him, even to his own best interest.

Keep Passion Under the Control of Reason, and Truth Will Prevail

In several speeches Lincoln contrasted hot passion with cool reason. He described passion as "wild" and "furious" and reason as "sober" and "calm." He called the human head "the natural guardian, director, and protector of the hands and mouth inseparately connected with it," and he argued that justice and progress could occur only if people consciously kept passion under the control of reason:

Passion has helped us; but can do so no more. It will in future be our enemy. Reason, cold, calculating, unimpassioned reason, must furnish all the materials for our future support and defence. ("Lyceum Address")

Happy day, when all appetites controlled, all passions subdued, all matters subjected, mind, all conquering *mind*, shall live and move the monarch of the world. Glorious consummation! Hail, fall of Fury! Reign of Reason, all hail! ("Temperance Address")

Lincoln argued that passion was fleeting and that acting hastily was dangerous. Near the end of his "First Inaugural Address" he told listeners, "Nothing valuable can be lost by taking time." He preferred to consider the long-range rather than the short-range consequences of actions, believing that if people kept passion under the control of reason, truth would prevail. For Lincoln, reason and truth were related synergistically. As Herndon explained, "Truth is the power of reason, and Lincoln loved truth for its own sake. It was to him reason's food."[17]

Choose Words Precisely

Not surprisingly, Lincoln's own way of studying and his belief in reason as the *summum bonum* of intellectual pursuits affected his ideas about word choice. He argued that speakers should choose their words carefully, directly, and precisely. In a discussion in the Illinois Legislature, he said that he "wanted to call things by their right names, no matter who was offended." In a message to a special session of Congress, held only a few months after the war began, he alluded to "rebellion thus sugar-coated." The government printer objected to the lack of dignity of the term "sugar-coated" and urged Lincoln to change it. Lincoln supposedly replied, "That word expresses precisely my idea, and I am not going to change it. The time will never come in this country when the people won't know exactly what *sugar-coated* means!" Significantly, Lincoln defended this particular figure of speech not because of its beauty but because of its usefulness in conveying his message precisely. This situation also illustrates the confidence Lincoln had in his own judgment.[18]

Use Stories and Analogies to Make Messages Clearer and More Persuasive

An observer described the young Lincoln as "figurative in his speeches." But the same observer went on to say, "He argued much from analogy and explained things . . . by stories, maxims, tales, and figures." The observer apparently recognized that it was for clarity, not ornamentation, that Lincoln used various forms of figuration. Lincoln, himself, seemed to understand the strategic power of figures. Explaining why analogy is a fundamental resource in argumentation, he said, "let me ask, how is it that we know any thing--that any event will occur, that any combination of circumstances will produce a certain result--except by the analogies of past experience? What has happened once, will invariably happen again, when the same circumstances which combined to produce it, shall again combine in the same way." He explained how analogies work when he continued, "We all feel that we know that a blast of wind would extinguish the flame of the candle that stands by me. How do we know it? We have never seen this flame thus extinguished. We know it, because we have seen through all our lives, that a blast of wind extinguishes the flame of a candle whenever it is thrown fully upon it."[19]

State Ideas Clearly and Concisely

No matter how accurately a word or story expresses a speaker's point, the message can still fail if the language remains unclear to the audience. In discussing slavery at the beginning of his "Peoria Address," Lincoln emphatically indicated the degree to which he was concerned about clarity: "I wish to MAKE and to KEEP the distinction between the EXISTING institution, and the EXTENSION of it, so broad, and so clear, that no honest man can misunderstand me, and no dishonest one, successfully misrepresent me" (Lincoln's emphasis). Testimony from numerous contemporaries supports Herndon's observation that Lincoln "wanted to be distinctly understood by the common people." Lincoln supposedly once told Herndon, "Billy, don't shoot too high--aim lower and the common people will understand you. They are the ones you want to reach--at least they are the ones you ought to reach. The educated and refined people will understand you any way. If you aim too high your ideas will go over the heads of the masses, and only hit those who need no hitting."[20]

Lincoln's ridicule of others often dealt with ideas about speaking, and the qualities he criticized reveal the qualities he valued. That conciseness and relevance were virtues Lincoln prized--both in principle and tactically--is illustrated by the following bits of ridicule:

Here he has introduced a resolution, embracing ninety-nine printed lines across common writing paper, and yet more than one-half of his opening speech has been made upon subjects about which there is not one word said in his resolution.

He can compress the most words in the fewest ideas of any man I ever met.

It's like the lazy preacher that used to write long sermons and the explanation was he got to writin' and was too lazy to stop.[21]

The qualities Lincoln valued in speaking (and writing) were all qualities that helped achieve accuracy, clarity, and precision. If a specific practice contributed pragmatically to these qualities, Lincoln endorsed it; if a practice did not so contribute, Lincoln opposed it. His beliefs about speech preparation and about when speech was and was not appropriate were natural outgrowths of the rhetorical qualities he sought.

Prepare Diligently

Lincoln realized that stating ideas accurately, clearly, and precisely required diligent preparation. In his notes for a law lecture, he wrote, "The leading rule for the lawyer, as for the man of every other calling, is diligence. Leave nothing for tomorrow which can be done to-day. . . . If a law point be involved, examine the books, and note the authority you rely on upon the declaration itself, where you are sure to find it when wanted." He explained the advantages of taking careful notes: "This course has a triple advantage; it avoids omissions and neglect, saves your labor when once done, performs the labor out of court when you have leisure, rather than in court when you have not." Lincoln believed that all speakers, not just lawyers, needed to prepare diligently and take notes carefully.[22]

Lincoln's belief in diligent, timely preparation corresponded with his preoccupation that communication be appropriate. This concern became especially apparent after he was elected president. Between election and inauguration, Lincoln maintained a policy of strategic silence, a policy I shall discuss in detail in a later chapter. As he put it, "I have been occupying a position since the Presidential election of silence, of avoiding public speaking, of avoiding public writing." He believed he should not make a long speech about slavery and secession until he had prepared diligently, analyzed the situation thoroughly, and weighed the options fairly; to do otherwise would be inappropriate. His reluctance to speak persisted throughout his presidential years. This cautious attitude seemed to stem from a belief that speakers are responsible for what they say, especially in volatile times. He stated his creed succinctly in a message to Congress: "In times like the present men should utter nothing for which they would not willingly be responsible through time and eternity."[23]

CONCLUSIONS

Lincoln's ideas about speaking form a coherent whole. They evolved from his predisposition to study carefully and value precision, from his legal training and practice, from his concern for reaching the "common man," and from his utter pragmatism about all uses of instrumentalities--including speech. His ideas about rhetoric and his interest in the art were there from the beginning of his self-education. They grew more refined and precise as experience taught him, but they did not change in fundamental ways. What seems unusual about Lincoln is the consistency and coherence of his rhetorical judgments and the utter pragmatism of his ideas. The next question becomes: Did Lincoln practice what he preached?

Lincoln speaking in one of seven debates against Stephen Douglas. The adjectives critics used to describe Lincoln's appearance—homely, kindly, serious, thoughtful, penetrating—were the same adjectives they used to describe his speaking. Photo courtesy of Leib Image Archives.

2

Did Lincoln Practice
What He Preached?
Characteristics and
Development of
Lincoln's Speeches

The inclination to exchange thoughts with one another is probably an original impulse of our nature.

Lincoln in his "Second Lecture on Discoveries and Inventions"

[Lincoln's] power as a public speaker was the foundation of his success . . . his elevation to the presidency would have been impossible without his oratory.

William Jennings Bryan

Lincoln has received abundant praise as a writer, but as an orator he has been considered second rate. For example, T. Harry Williams called Lincoln a writer who "stands in the front rank of those few masters of language who have stirred men's emotions" but a speaker who was "a second-rate figure," and Herbert Joseph Edwards and John Erskine Hankins wrote, "Decidedly, Lincoln was not an orator. He was something else--a literary artist--and he could work only with the tool of the literary artist, his pen." In this chapter I shall argue that Lincoln was an effective orator. I shall examine characteristics of his speaking that remained constant throughout his public career and qualities that changed as he moved from stump speaker and debater to president. To demonstrate that his speechmaking was generally effective and to help explain the comments that separate his oratorical and literary abilities, I shall examine his speechmaking from a rhetorical perspective, concerning myself with Lincoln the orator, a public man communicating with listeners. To paraphrase what Marie Hochmuth Nichols said of her study of Lincoln's "First Inaugural Address":

Unlike the historian, I am not concerned merely with Lincoln's speeches as a force in the shaping of American culture; nor am I concerned merely with their enduring worth as literature. Lincoln's speeches were speeches, meant to be heard and intended to exert an influence of some kind on those who heard it or those who read it at the time. I must, therefore, be concerned with evaluating his speeches as speeches. A speech is a medium distinct from other media, with methods peculiarly its own.[1]

From the age of twenty-three, when he became a candidate for representative in the Illinois State Legislature, Lincoln spoke publicly almost daily as a candidate, campaigner, legislator, lawyer, jester, debater, and/or president. His speeches included campaign appeals, legal arguments, eulogies, public debates, policy statements, public greetings, impromptu remarks, popular lectures, ceremonial speeches, and official proclamations. Throughout his life he spoke in precise language, used rhetoric to identify with the masses, and gained national prominence in the thrust and parry of debate. As Bryan declared, his rise to the presidency was achieved largely by oratory.

A myth about Lincoln as an orator is that his style developed out of the purity of his thought. Mark Van Doren explained, "The secret was simple, perhaps. Lincoln thought and felt every word he wrote . . . The depth of Lincoln's thought was one with the depth of his feeling; after which, no doubt, his style took care of itself." But as I demonstrated in the last chapter, Lincoln presented himself as someone who in various ways deliberately strove to increase his vocabulary, refine his logical abilities, and train himself in oral and written expression, not as someone who allowed his style to "take care of itself." His speaking style evolved over years of sustained and systematic reflection and practice.[2]

Just as Lincoln's general style emerged from deliberate study and practice, so his individual speeches were the results of serious thinking about the important issues of the day. He repeatedly rethought, refocused, rephrased, and revised ideas and wordings, and he continually tested his arguments on various audiences. In speech after speech he repeated and reworded ideas and entire passages.

Lincoln's routine recasting and reshaping of ideas resulted in rhetoric characterized by logical argument, detailed documentation, and factual accuracy. His "Cooper Union Address" was and still is hailed as a model of logical analysis. In minute detail he reported the individual votes of the thirty-nine framers of the Constitution on the issue of slavery to show that the Founding Fathers believed that jurisdiction over slavery in the territories resided in the federal government. His evidence even included reporting individuals who voted against his conclusion and reporting missing evidence.

Soundness of reasoning characterized Lincoln's speeches because reason functioned for him as the *summum bonum* of intellectual pursuits. As William Herndon explained:

He lived and acted from the standard of reason--that throne of logic, home of principle--the realm of Deity in man. . . . He reasoned from well-chosen principles with such clearness, force, and directness that the tallest intellects in the land bowed to him. He was the strongest man I ever saw, looking at him from the elevated standpoint of reason and logic. He came down from that height with irresistible and crashing force. His Cooper Institute and other printed speeches will prove this; but his speeches before the courts--especially the Supreme Court of Illinois--if they had been preserved, would demonstrate it still more plainly.

Contemporary reactions to Lincoln's speeches supported Herndon's point. Newspaper reporters and other "ear-witnesses" consistently described Lincoln's speaking using terms like the following: "Lucid logic," "accurate analysis," "thorough treatment," "convincing claims," and "unrefutable reasoning."[3]

Somewhat in contrast to the rigor, often elegance, of his logic, Lincoln portrayed himself as simple, humble, and unassuming. He projected himself as a poor man's son, an underdog, a humble person. Indeed, "humble" was a recurring term he used to describe himself, as when he called himself "the humblest of all individuals that have ever been elevated to the Presidency." Even more frequently he used phrases such as "in my humble way," "in my humble judgment," and "with all due humility." He also often referred to his humble origins as he did when he said in a speech in March 1860, "I am not ashamed to confess that twenty five years ago I was a hired laborer, mauling rails, at work on a flat-boat--just what might happen to any poor man's son!" Before his election to the presidency, Lincoln typically expressed humility by saying he was in no way "preferable to any other one of the twenty-five--perhaps hundred we have in the Republican ranks," whereas as president he typically expressed humility by calling himself a "humble instrument in the hands of the Almighty." So, while there were changes in Lincoln's humility appeal over time, the consistency of that appeal was more striking. Throughout his public life he tended in speeches to minimize and downplay his authority and *ethos*. "The first author of the Lincoln legend," wrote Richard Hofstadter, "was Lincoln himself."[4]

Portraying himself as an honest, ordinary person helped Lincoln identify with his audiences. Herndon explained, "The universal testimony, 'He is an honest man,' gave him a firm hold on the masses. . . . The trust and worship by the people of Lincoln were the result of his simple character. He held himself not aloof from the masses. He became one of them. They feared together, they struggled together, they hoped together . . . they became one in thought, one in will, one in action." In his most successful speech-making Lincoln practiced what rhetorical theorist Kenneth Burke called "identification." Burke contended that identification was achieved when "you can talk his [the listener's] language by speech,

gesture, tonality, order, image, attitude, idea, *identifying* your ways
with his." This Lincoln did. Throughout his life he adapted to
varying audiences: In his early speeches he used homely illustrations
with language natural to farming and frontier life. When he spoke
at Cooper Union to a sophisticated Eastern audience, he employed
more complex language and lines of reasoning. His adaptations
support Chauncey M. DePew's remark that Lincoln "knew the people
and how to reach them better than any man of his time."[5]

One way Lincoln identified with his listeners was by embracing
a myth already embedded in the culture of the time. His rhetoric
often concerned what Mircea Eliade called the "myth of the eternal
return." According to that myth, contemporary society had lost sight
of its untainted origins, making people yearn for a "return to [this]
mythical time of the beginning of things, to the 'Great Time.'"
According to Lincoln, America was founded on the ideals of the
Declaration of Independence. Consistent with the "myth of the
eternal return," Lincoln considered this document pure, calling it the
"immortal emblem of Humanity." He argued that the country had a
divine mission to prove to the world that a country founded on the
ideals articulated in the Declaration of Independence could endure.[6]

In giving voice to this myth, Lincoln adopted a cosmic perspective. He frequently spoke about time, which for him meant the entire
past, present, and future. He often oriented listeners in time. For
example, in his "Temperance Address" he said the practice of
drinking was "just as old as the world itself," and in his "Lyceum
Address" he said, "In the great journal of things happening under the
sun, we, the American People, find our account running, under date
of the nineteenth century of the Christian era." Just as the past
meant since the beginning of time, so the future encompassed
eternity, or, as Lincoln put it in his "Lyceum Address," "to the latest
generation that fate shall permit the world to know." Lincoln's
cosmic view extended to place; for him place encompassed the entire
earth. In his "Second Lecture of Discoveries and Inventions" he spoke
specifically about "all the Earth" and "the whole world."

The "Gettysburg Address" exemplified Lincoln's interpretation
of the "myth of the eternal return." The war would test "whether
that nation--or any nation, so conceived and so dedicated--can long
endure." Rhetorical theorist Richard Weaver declared, "The entire
opening sentence, with its sustained detachment, sounds like an
account of the action to be rendered at Judgment Day. It is not Abe
Lincoln who is speaking the utterance, but the voice of mankind, as
it were, to whom the American Civil War is but the passing vexation
of a generation."[7]

The more formal and official Lincoln's speaking became, the
more he adopted a cosmic perspective. As president he sometimes
projected a sense of isolation from himself, speaking as if he were

talking aloud to himself, revealing his innermost thoughts. He often referred to himself in the third person. For instance, in his "First Inaugural Address" he referred to himself as "him who now addresses you," the "Chief-Magistrate," the "Executive," one of the government's "public servants," and the "Administration." He wrote his 1860 campaign autobiography in the third person. He sometimes divorced himself from his message to such an extent that the resulting rhetoric sounded peculiar. For example, in one speech he called himself "my father's child." Weaver succinctly summarized this practice of self-effacement: "It was as if he projected a view in which history was the duration, the world the stage, and himself a transitory actor upon it. Of all his utterances the Second Inaugural is in this way the most objective and remote, its tone even seems that of an actor about to quit the stage."[8]

In this statement Weaver hinted at another characteristic of Lincoln's rhetoric--frequent usage of words usually associated with the theater (e.g., "stage," "scene," and "actor"). George B. Forgie has said, "In order to make his ideas available to the public and involve it in his own concerns, Lincoln dramatized the demons of his mind according to the dictates of popular culture. . . . The lines between drama and oratory were never clearly fixed in the nineteenth century." Thus, in discussing the threat of mob violence in his "Lyceum Address," Lincoln referred to the "horror-striking scene at St. Louis" and to gamblers being "annually swept, from the stage of existence." He mentioned the "interesting scenes of the revolution" five times during the speech. Employing dramatistic language further distanced him from his subjects; adhering to the dictates of his time further helped him to identify with his listeners.[9]

Frequent use of Biblical ideas, quotations, paraphrases, images, and cadences contributed still further toward projecting a cosmic, detached perspective. A quotation from the Bible sometimes furnished the theme for a speech as in the case of the "House Divided Speech," whose key statement, "A house divided against itself cannot stand," came from Mark 3:25: "And if a house be divided against itself, that house cannot stand." Particularly important phrases in some speeches had their roots in the Bible, such as the repeated words "our fathers" in the "Cooper Union Address." "Our fathers" occurs in the Bible over fifty times, most notably in the Lord's Prayer (Matthew 6: 9-13 and Luke 11: 2-4). As I shall argue in the next chapter, the Bible probably especially predisposed Lincoln to use stories and illustrations to make moral points and provided sources for those stories as well. Lincoln often referred to God in his speeches, usually directly saying "God" and occasionally "the Almighty" or "the Divine Being." Somewhat oddly, he never once mentioned "Jesus" or "Christ." When he rewrote the peroration that Seward suggested for his "First Inaugural Address," he made it clear that angels are in people, not in God. Seward had written, "The mystic chords which, proceeding from so many battlefields and so many patriotic graves, pass through all the hearts and all hearths in this broad continent of ours, will yet again harmonize in their ancient music when breathed upon by the guardian angel of the nation." Lincoln's editing of Seward's words produced: "The mystic chords of memory stretching from every battle-field and patriot grave to every living heart and hearthstone all over this broad land, will yet swell the chorus of the Union, when again touched, as surely they will be, by the better angels of our nature."[10]

The spiritual and prayer-like quality of many of Lincoln's speeches in some ways distanced him from listeners, but in other ways his frequent references to the Bible helped him identify with audiences because his listeners were well versed in the Scriptures. Before delivering his "House Divided" Speech Lincoln explained his use of the Biblical prophesy about a divided house: "I want to use some universally known figure expressed in simple language as universally well-known, that may strike home to the minds of men in order to raise them up to the peril of the times."[11]

Lincoln's broad perspective manifested itself also in his choice of various forms of figuration. He made wide use of figures of speech to bring abstract and complex ideas into the immediate ken of varying audiences. He learned to read by using the *Bible, Aesop's Fables*, and the works of Shakespeare. From these he acquired a facility for elegance and a knack for using figures of speech, especially metaphors, similes, and analogies, all of which express a likeness between otherwise unlike objects or concepts. Historian James M. McPherson has even claimed that "Lincoln Won the War with Metaphors."[12]

Generally Lincoln chose figures of speech that were broad, sweeping, timeless, and inclusive rather than narrow, folksy, or specific to particular situations or audiences. In his study of Lincoln's imagery, Theodore C. Blegen argued that "Lincoln recruited many of his metaphors and similes from experiences and areas universally familiar." Most of his figures were what rhetorical critic Michael M. Osborn has labeled "archetypal." These are associations that are timeless, cross-cultural, grounded in experiences common to all human beings, and a symbol of fundamental human motivations. Osborn's research has revealed that "the category of archetypes may include at least the following forms: disease/cure, family, structures, light/darkness, the sense of space (vertical and horizontal), water and the sea, and war/peace." Lincoln consistently favored images of the archetypal form, using each of the archetypal types identified by Osborn as standard and adding a few of his own. Instances of Lincoln's use of these images are numerous. Below is a discussion of the archetypal forms and a few representative examples.[13]

A year before assuming the presidency, Lincoln declared that efforts to settle the slavery issue had failed because "our best and greatest men have greatly underestimated the size of this question. They have constantly brought forward small cures for great sores-- plasters too small to cover the wound." Repeatedly Lincoln claimed that "slavery represents a wen on the neck of this country." Disease and cure metaphors are rhetorically potent because, as Osborn has explained, "Images of disease arouse strong feelings of fear; images of remedy focus that emotional energy towards the acceptance of some reassuring recommendation." The fears and remedies have a universal and timeless appeal because most people fear their own mortality.[14]

The metaphor of the family unit also crosses time and culture. As Forgie explained, "Americans did not invent these metaphors. Two propositions--that nations structurally resemble the family and that nations originated in families--are as old as political thought." At another point Forgie noted some specific ways that Americans in Lincoln's generation conceived of familial relations:

Familial language provided a way for Americans of the post-heroic generation to comprehend and express the transition from the founders' age to their own; one generation was passing to another, which now inherited the blessings of liberty--and the responsibility for preserving them so that they could be transmitted intact to posterity. Seeing the great men to their graves, the "whole family of Americans" united in bidding a sentimental farewell to the fathers and then set out to find their own role in history.

At the beginning of the "Lyceum Address," Lincoln expressed precisely the point Forgie articulated generations later:

We find ourselves in the peaceful possession, of the fairest portion of the earth. . . . We find ourselves under the government of a system of political institutions, conducing more essentially to the ends of civil and religious liberty, than any of which the history of former times tells us. We . . . found ourselves the legal inheritors of these fundamental blessings. We toiled not in the acquirement or establishment of them--they are a legacy bequeathed us. . . . Their's was the task . . . to uprear . . . a political edifice of liberty and equal rights; 'tis ours only, to transmit these, the former, unprofaned by the foot of an invader; the latter, undecayed by the lapse of time, and untorn by usurpation--to the latest generation that fate shall permit the world to know. This task of gratitude to our fathers, justice to ourselves, duty to posterity, and love for our species in general, all imperatively require us faithfully to perform.[15]

Besides using familial language to discuss the relationship of his generation to the Founding Fathers, Lincoln employed metaphors of family relationships to encourage unity. In his "First Inaugural Address" he argued, "A husband and wife may be divorced and go out

of the presence and beyond the reach of each other, but the different
parts of our country cannot do this. They cannot but remain face to
face, and intercourse, either amicable or hostile, must continue
between them. Is it possible, then, to make that intercourse more
advantageous or more satisfactory after separations than before?" In
a speech en route to Washington to assume the presidency, Lincoln
criticized the thinking of the secessionists by evoking images of
disease and images of family: "If sick, they would consider the little
pills of the homeopathist as already too large for them to swallow. In
their view, the Union, as a family relation, would not be anything like
a regular marriage at all, but only as a sort of free love arrangement,-
-[laughter,]--to be maintained on what that sect calls passionate
attraction. [Continued laughter.]"[16]

In addition to disease/cure and familial metaphors, Lincoln
often chose metaphors dealing with body parts and bodily sensations
and employed personification, attributing human qualities to
inanimate objects and concepts. In his "Lyceum Address" he claimed
that "towering genius . . . *scorns* to tread in the footsteps of any
predecessor" and "thirsts and burns for distinction," and in his
"Temperance Address" he declared, "Happy day, when, all appetites
controled" and "mind, all conquering *mind*, shall live and move the
monarch of the world." Throughout his "Second Lecture on Discoveries and Inventions," he talked about "Young America," the "most
current youth of the age," "the inventor and owner of the *present*, and
sole hope of the *future*." Like many of Lincoln's metaphors, the
metaphor of "Young America" advanced his case for a united America.
Forgie explained that the "Young America slogan speaks metaphorically of the nation as a single being." Like most of Lincoln's metaphors, this image was already popular when he used it. Using
images familiar to his listeners helped Lincoln identify with them.[17]

In his "House Divided" Speech Lincoln popularized the image
of the Union as a house, proclaiming that "A house divided against
itself cannot stand." In this context "house" was a family metaphor,
a personified image, and also a structural metaphor. In this speech
and elsewhere Lincoln claimed that the Democrats were involved in
a conspiracy to expand slavery; his argument was based on several
metaphors dealing with structures and one dealing with light and
darkness. Lincoln said,

It will throw additional light on the latter, to go back, and run the mind
over the string of historical facts already stated. Several things will now
appear less dark and mysterious than they did when they were transpiring . . . when we see a lot of framed timbers, different portions of which we
know have been gotten out at different times and places and by different
workmen--Stephen [Douglas], Franklin [Pierce], Roger [Taney], and James
[Buchanan], for instance--and when we see these timbers joined together,
and see they exactly make the frame of a house or a mill, all the tenons and

mortices exactly fitting, and all the lengths and proportions of the different pieces exactly adapted to their respective places, and not a piece too many or too few--not omitting even scaffolding--or, if a single piece be lacking, we see the place in the frame exactly fitted and prepared yet to bring such piece in--in such a case, we find it impossible not to believe that Stephen and Franklin and Roger and James all understood one another from the beginning, and all worked upon a common plan or draft drawn up before the first blow was struck.

As I said earlier in this chapter, Lincoln expressed a broad view of time and place. He often seemed preoccupied with these subjects, especially with the origins and histories of objects and ideas. In his "Second Lecture on Discoveries and Inventions" he even traced the process of invention to its origin--the invention of invention--and explained how Adam's "fig-leaf apron" was "the first of all inventions, of which we have any direct account." His "Farewell to Springfield Speech" was almost entirely a speech about time and place. He talked about the past as a pure and perfect time: "For more than a quarter of a century I have lived among you, and during all that time I have received nothing but kindness at your hands." He associated the place of Springfield with the earth, womb, and tomb: "Here the most sacred ties of earth were assumed; here all my children were born; and here one of them lies buried."

Lincoln frequently employed metaphors dealing with water and bodies of water. To discuss the progress of the Navy, he used images of family, personification and the human body, the sense of space, and water and bodies of water: "The signs look better. The Father of Waters again goes unvexed to the sea. . . . Nor must Uncle Sam's Web-feet be forgotten. At all the watery margins they have been present. Not only on the deep sea, the broad bay, and the rapid river, but also up the narrow muddy bayou, and wherever the ground was a little damp, they have been, and made their tracks."[18]

In Lincoln's time glorifying the past, especially the Revolutionary War, was common, and during the Civil War the price and rewards of war were forever on the minds of the citizenry. Therefore, it is no surprise that Lincoln often used metaphors dealing with war and peace. Again, examples abound. His "Temperance Address" contained several, including the following:

The cause [of temperance] itself seems suddenly transformed from a cold abstract theory, to a living, breathing, active, and powerful chieftain, going forth "conquering and to conquer." The citadels of his great adversary are daily being stormed and dismantled; his temples and his altars, where the rites of his idolatrous worship have long been performed, and where human sacrifices have long been wont to be made, are daily desecrated and deserted. The trump of the conqueror's fame is sounding from hill to hill, from sea to sea, and from land to land, and calling millions to his standard at a blast.

Later in this speech Lincoln spoke about the "inevitable price" of war. Of the Revolutionary War he said, "It breathed forth famine, swam in blood and rose on fire; and long, long after, the orphan's cry, and the widow's wail, continued to break the sad silence that ensued."

Two groups of images that Osborn did not mention but that certainly fit his definition of archetypal are images dealing with nature and images dealing with animals. Perhaps because he grew up close to the land, wild animals, and farmers whose livelihoods depended heavily on the weather, Lincoln's images often concerned nature--the land, the frontier, farming, trees, climate, the harvest, and so forth. The following example from his "Lyceum Address" is typical: "Thus went on this process of hanging . . . till, dead men were seen literally dangling from the boughs of trees upon every road side, and in numbers almost sufficient, to rival the native Spanish moss of the country, as a drapery of the forest." Perhaps emulating *Aesop's Fables*, Lincoln often used figures of speech dealing with animals. For instance, in his "Temperance Address" he discussed how to influence people, advising his listeners not to treat those they wanted to persuade as people "to be shunned and despised" because "tho' your cause be naked truth itself, transformed to the heaviest lance, harder than steel, and sharper than steel can be made, and tho' you throw it with more than Herculean force and precision, you shall no more be able to persuade [them], than to penetrate the hard shell of a tortoise with a rye straw."

In addition to using images expressing similarities, Lincoln frequently included rhetorical questions and repetitions in his speeches. Rhetorical questions are questions where the answers are implicit. By definition, they invite audience participation, encouraging listeners to think of their own answers and to see if their answers match the speaker's. Lincoln frequently asked several questions consecutively, and he sometimes provided answers. His questions usually served to remind listeners of the speech's theme; his answers usually served as transitions. The "Lyceum Address" contained several such instances including the following: "How, then, shall we perform it?--At what point shall we expect the approach of danger? By what means shall we fortify against it?--Shall we expect some transatlantic military giant, to step the Ocean, and crush us at a blow? Never!" By repeating significant words, phrases, and thoughts within individual speeches and over the course of several speeches, Lincoln emphasized points, provided transitions between points, and heightened the effect of his ridicule. For example, in his "Cooper Union Address" he frequently repeated the phrase "our fathers who framed the government under which we live," and throughout his formal debates with Stephen Douglas he repeated the statements he had made in his "House Divided Speech": "A house divided against itself cannot stand" and "I believe this government cannot endure permanently half slave and half free."

Lincoln's use of stylistic devices contributed to his persuasiveness in part because he often drew his images from more than one area of experience, as he did in the following example from his "Lyceum Address." About the Revolutionary War he said,

a *living history was* to be found in every family--a history bearing the indubitable testimonies of its own authenticity, in the limbs mangled, in the scars of wounds received, in the midst of the very scenes related--a history, too, that could be read and understood alike by all, the wise and the ignorant, the learned and the unlearned.--But *those histories are gone. They* can be read no more forever. They *were* a fortress of strength; but, what invading foemen could *never do*, the silent artillery of time *has done*; the levelling of its walls. They are gone.--They *were* a forest of giant oaks; but the all resistless hurricane has swept over them, and left only, here and there, a lonely trunk, despoiled of its verdure, shorn of its foliage; unshading and unshaded, to murmur in a few more gentle breezes, and to combat with its mutilated limbs, a few more ruder storms, then to sink, and be no more.

This passage included repetition and at least the following categories of archetypal forms: time, family, personification, the human body, disease, war, structures, place, nature, and water. Listeners who were unaffected by one type of image might have been affected by another type.

Throughout his life, especially before becoming president, Lincoln used more sensory than intellectual images. Sensory images refer to words and phrases that evoke images that listeners can see, hear, smell, taste, or feel; intellectual images refer to all images that are not sensory. According to rhetorical critic Carroll C. Arnold, "Sensory images tend to stimulate listeners to experience vicariously; to that extent the linguistic form invites them to become experientially, hence feelingly, involved in what is said."[19]

In general, forms of figuration are also difficult to refute because they appeal to the imagination. Lincoln's reliance on sensory images, forms of figuration that by definition encouraged listeners "to experience vicariously," made them even more difficult to refute. Like all imagery, Lincoln's imagery functioned operationally by setting up a series of inferences and inviting listeners to participate in reasoning through the inferences. To criticize the reasoning, opponents must criticize the listeners. Hence, Lincoln's figurative forms added to the persuasive force of his speeches.

Historians and rhetoricians consistently have commended Lincoln's style for being clear, simple, brief, and unadorned. To a degree this is true, for Lincoln usually did speak in straightforward sentences consisting primarily of short, simple words. And for his time he usually was brief. In an age of long-winded orators, he tended to say what he had to say and stop when he was through. His use of stories and illustrations helped him to be epigrammatic. But it was his concern with being precise more than a desire to be clear, simple, and unadorned that led to his conciseness. His penchant for precision had more to do with his style than any premise about style per se. His style was not derived from an aesthetic predilection; rather, his goal of precision frequently generated the qualities of style for which he has been commended.

Lincoln's desire to be precise sometimes led him to choose ambiguous or general words rather than concrete ones. There were practical reasons for this. Expressing his moderate positions sometimes required him to choose language that left "maneuvering room" for final, more specific choices. Moreover, exactness could divide or "turn off" audiences, whereas purposeful ambiguity often could help unite people around a general viewpoint. In her discussion of Lincoln's "First Inaugural Address," Hochmuth-Nichols gave the following explanation:

That Lincoln sought to control the behavior of his audience and the reader through the appropriately affective word is apparent throughout his address. There are times when even the level of specificity and concrete-ness, usually thought to be virtues of style, is altered in favor of the more general word or allusion. For instance, Lincoln had originally intended to say, "why may not South Carolina, a year or two hence, arbitrarily, secede from a new Southern Confederacy . . . ?" Finally, however, he avoided being specific, altering his remarks to read "why may not any portion of a new confederacy, a year or two hence, arbitrarily secede again . . . ?"

Most of Lincoln's "Second Inaugural Address" consisted of general, inclusive words that applied both to Northerners and Southerners. The judicious use of ambiguity here made Lincoln precise but not completely clear.[20]

Lincoln achieved precision also by putting his ideas into the form of stories. Herndon claimed it was Lincoln's almost obsessive need to express thoughts in the most precise way possible that accounted "for the frequent resort by him to the use of stories, maxims, and jokes in which to clothe his ideas, that they might be better comprehended." In the next chapter, I shall discuss Lincoln's storytelling in detail.[21]

Lincoln's style was not always clear, simple, brief, or un-adorned, despite what has often been said. For special effects and to make his thoughts more impressive and telling, he not infrequently reached beyond the simple and elemental. "Fourscore and seven" was certainly not a simple way to say eighty-seven. Some intellection and recognition of the spiritual undertone of the phrase was encouraged.

Logically, even people deeply immersed in Biblical lore would need to calculate twenty times four, then add seven, and then subtract eighty-seven from 1863 to realize Lincoln was referring to 1776, the year of the Declaration of Independence. It is not likely that many listeners did this sort of calculation. It is more likely that they simply affirmed the dignity and importance of the Founding Fathers' actions. As this and like moments show, it is incorrect to generalize that Lincoln sought simplicity of expression at all times. Frequently, especially as chief executive, he sought to arouse special attitudes by recourse to terms and phrases that were not in common use but whose tone would not be missed even though the language itself might be somewhat unfamiliar.

Neither is it safe to accept without qualification that Lincoln spoke briefly. Especially during his presidential years, he delivered short speeches, but before assuming the presidency, he often spoke for long periods of time. His "Peoria Address," for example, was estimated to have taken over four hours. Lincoln also did not always express thoughts in speeches economically. For instance, the following statements from the beginning of the "Lyceum Address" are, in my opinion, neither brief nor simple:

In the great journal of things happening under the sun, we, the American People, find our account running, under date of the nineteenth century of the Christian era.

Their's [our ancestors] was the task (and nobly they performed it) to possess themselves, and through themselves, us, of this goodly land; and to uprear upon its hills and its valleys, a political edifice of liberty and equal rights; 'tis ours only, to transmit these, the former, unprofaned by the lapse of time, and untorn by usurpation--to the latest generation that fate shall permit the world to know.

Finally, Lincoln's speeches were not plain and unadorned but made wide use of various forms of figuration. His figures of speech were piquant, pungent, pithy, primitive, and picturesque. They infused his speeches with life and gave precise meaning to abstract ideas. His images added vivacity to his ideas and made the ideas difficult for listeners to forget. Because the images were familiar, listeners could easily comprehend them. Use of various figures of speech helped Lincoln state his ideas precisely and identify with his listeners or, as Blegen succinctly put it, "Imagery bore the man to the people."[22]

LINCOLN'S DELIVERY

Lincoln's delivery reinforced other aspects of his speaking and contributed to his effectiveness as an extemporaneous speaker. He adopted an unassuming style, displaying unkempt hair and clothes that accentuated his homely appearance. He spoke slowly, averaging about one hundred words per minute (Henry Clay averaged about 145 words per minute). Lincoln enunciated words clearly and spoke in a deliberate, emphatic manner, apparently so he would not make factual errors and so everyone would hear his entire message. His voice was high-pitched, clear, and powerful; usually listeners who were physically far away could still hear him.

Throughout his life Lincoln experienced speech anxiety. Occasionally he spoke about his apprehension and about overcoming it by concentrating on his topic. In the first few minutes of a speech he usually appeared reticent, hesitant, and nervous; as he got "into" the subject he became comfortable and animated. He used his entire body to reinforce his message, contorting his facial expressions, sometimes grimacing, sometimes maintaining a poker face, and sometimes mimicking the expressions of others. He varied his vocal tone to fit what he was saying, shifting as needed from normal to a slow, deliberate drawl or to a falsetto shrillness.[23]

Lincoln was unsuccessful as a popular lecturer largely because in this context he lacked the animation and vocal variety that generally characterized his delivery. Mildred Freburg Berry explained:

The prairie audiences of the fifties saw Lincoln in his most vigorous and telling delivery on the stump. Unfortunately, he did not carry over this intensity in facial and bodily expression to occasions calling for . . . informative speeches. . . . [They] were delivered in a dry, unimpassioned manner. Possibly the inherent limitations of a manuscript conspired to defeat him, for he read most of these addresses. . . . In the field of persuasion, when the issues were sharp, the contest keen, Lincoln knew no peers in vigorous action on the platform; when the end of the speech was to inform or to impress, there was little in his manner to suggest the dynamic quality of his forensic style.[24]

THE DEVELOPMENT OF LINCOLN'S SPEAKING

When Lincoln assumed the presidency, his speaking changed in significant and noticeable ways. Before, he sought opportunities to speak; as president he seemed keenly aware of the enormous responsibilities and risks involved in the act of speaking and, hence, became a reluctant speaker. In a speech three weeks before taking office, he said that he felt "a becoming sense of the responsibility resting upon me." As president he seemed to think the premium was not just on being understood, but on not being misunderstood. Most of his presidential rhetoric consisted of brief utterances, often discussing why it was inappropriate for him to speak. Below, for example, is a speech from 1862 printed in its entirety:

In my present position it is hardly proper for me to make speeches. Every word is so closely noted that it will not do to make trivial ones, and I cannot be expected to be prepared to make a matured one just now. If I were as I have been most of my life, I might perhaps, talk amusingly to you for half an hour, and it wouldn't hurt anybody; but as it is, I can only return my sincere thanks for the compliment paid our cause and our common country.[25]

In Lincoln's brief presidential remarks, as in his early speeches, response to the give-and-take of oral discourse was apparent. For example, he responded to audience feedback when he addressed a crowd that serenaded him after the victory at Gettysburg: "In my position it is important that I should not say any foolish things. [A voice: 'If you can help it.'] It very often happens that the only way to help it is to say nothing."[26]

Lincoln's speaking also changed in other ways. Before becoming president, his speeches were generally spontaneous, long, and deliberative or forensic in nature. They often appealed to partisan concerns. Stylistically they were casual, colloquial, anecdotal, and full of sensory images. His pre-presidential speeches contained a generous amount of humor, including ridicule, and he generally presented these speeches extemporaneously. After becoming president, Lincoln's speeches were generally serious, short, and epideictic in nature. They appealed to national and universal concerns. The style was formal and employed primarily intellectual images. As President, Lincoln used ridicule and other types of humor sparingly in public speeches. He memorized most of his presidential speeches or read them from manuscript.

Two qualities of Lincoln's speaking that I discussed earlier in this chapter increased over time--his impersonal stance and his reliance on the Bible. Emotional detachment characterized his speeches in general, but the extent of this characteristic greatly increased as the war continued. In his "Gettysburg Address," for example, he never used a first person, singular pronoun ("I," "me," "my," "mine," "myself"); in his "Second Inaugural Address" he used only two ("myself" and "I"). Contrasting the opening statements of his two inaugural addresses reveals his increasingly impersonal stance:

In compliance with a custom as old as the Government itself, I appear before you to address you briefly, and to take in your presence the oath prescribed by the Constitution of the United States to be taken by the President before he enters on the execution of his office ("First Inaugural Address").

At this second appearing to take the oath of the Presidential office, there is less occasion for an extended address than there was at the first ("Second Inaugural Address").

Throughout the "Second Inaugural Address," Lincoln seemed deliberately to withdraw himself from the scene. In addition to referring to himself in the third person, he chose the passive voice and converted several verbs into nouns (e.g., appear/appearing, state/statement, declare/declaration, predict/prediction). The Bible found frequent expression in Lincoln's speeches throughout his public life, but his reliance on the Bible increased during his presidential years. The theme, language, tone, and rhythm of the "Gettysburg Address" echoed the Bible, and the "Second Inaugural Address" often has been referred to as "Lincoln's Sermon on the Mount." In discussing this speech, biographer Lord Charnwood wrote, "Probably no other speech of a modern statesman uses so unreservedly the language of intense religious feeling."[27]

As the war progressed, Lincoln referred more often to the New Testament. The "Second Inaugural Address," for example, relied heavily on the Bible in general and the New Testament in particular perhaps because the ideas of "laying aside malice" and being charitable are central themes of the New Testament. While the concepts of malice and charity are present in the Old Testament, the words themselves appear only in the New Testament. A form of the word "malice" is mentioned in the New Testament at least eight times (3 John 10, Romans 1:29, 1 Corinthians 5:8, Ephesians 4:31, Colossians 3:8, Titus 3:3, 1 Peter 2:1, and 1 Peter 2:16), and the word "charity" is mentioned in the New Testament at least twenty-seven times (1 Corinthians 8:1, 1 Corinthians 13:1, 1 Corinthians 13:2, 1 Corinthians 13:3, three times in 1 Corinthians 13:4, 1 Corinthians 13:8, two times in 1 Corinthians 13:13, 1 Corinthians 14:1, 1 Corinthians 16:14, Colossians 3:14, 1 Thessalonians 3:6, 2 Thessalonians 1:3, 1 Timothy 1:5, 1 Timothy 2:15, 1 Timothy 4:12, 2 Timothy 2:22, 2 Timothy 3:10, Titus 2:2, two times in 1 Peter 4:8, 1 Peter 5:14, 2 Peter 1:7, 3 John 6, and Revelation 2:19).

Lincoln's increased reliance on the Bible was consistent with his increased use of stylistic devices usually associated with literature such as grammatical parallelism, antithesis, and alliteration. Throughout his public life, he made extensive use of these figures of speech, but he used them much more extensively during his presidential years. These stylistic devices were especially prominent in the peroration of his "First Inaugural Address" and in his "Gettysburg Address" and "Second Inaugural Address." Basler has contended, "Repetition, grammatical parallelism, and antithesis may be considered the most obvious technical devices of Lincoln's general style. He uses these devices with such frequency and variety of effect that it seems to have been a consistent habit of his mind to seek repetitive sequences in both diction and sentence structure for the alignment of his thought." These observations are especially true of Lincoln's presidential speaking. He often combined parallelism (balancing ideas by putting them linguistically in a series) and antithesis (contrasting ideas by directly opposing them linguistically), creating in his speeches an overall tension between unity and division. The "Gettysburg Address," for instance, was full of parallel and antithetical structures. Lincoln stressed that deeds were more important than words when he contrasted saying and doing: "The world will very little note nor long remember what we say here; but it can never forget what they did here." The "Gettysburg Address" also included a linguistic form that combined repetition and parallelism, anaphora, meaning repetition of one or more words at the beginning of successive thoughts: "that from these honored dead we take increased devotion to that cause for which they *here* gave the last full measure of devotion; that we here highly resolve that these dead shall not have died in vain; that the nation shall, under God, have a new birth of freedom, and that government of the people, by the people, for the people, shall not perish from the earth." Lincoln's parallel constructions sometimes took the form of tricolons--series of three harmonious parts, sometimes of increasing power. Two tricolons in the "Gettysburg Address" were "we cannot dedicate, we cannot consecrate, we cannot hallow, this ground" and "government of the people, by the people, for the people." Lincoln was fond of threes, especially in his later speeches. The clause "of the people, by the people, for the people" contained three parallel phrases, each consisting of three words with the word "people" repeated three times. Sometimes Lincoln's parallelism was very subtle. For example, the beginning of the famous peroration of his "Second Inaugural Address" contained three parallel clauses, each consisting of six syllables: "With malice toward none, with charity for all, with firmness in the right."[28]

Alliteration, repeating the initial sound of two or more words in a thought, and assonance, repeating the same vowel sounds in two or more words, appeared with amazing frequency in Lincoln's speeches, especially his later ones. Usually they occurred as doublets (sets of two words) such as the following phrases from his "Second Inaugural Address:" "point and phase," "insurgent agents," "high hope," and "peculiar and powerful." He sometimes combined alliteration and assonance as when he said, "Woe unto the world," and he sometimes combined alliteration and parallelism such as when he said, "Fondly do we hope, fervently do we pray." Sometimes he used direct rhyme such as "dedicate" and "consecrate." Lincoln's extensive use of repetition, parallelism, antithesis, tricolon, anaphora, alliteration, assonance, and rhyme added to the rhythm and "ear-catching" appeal of his speeches, especially the "Gettysburg Address,"

"Second Inaugural Address," and peroration of the "First Inaugural Address."

LINCOLN'S FAMOUS SPEECHES: FROM AN ORATORICAL TO A LITERARY STYLE

Most scholars and lay people consider Lincoln's "Gettysburg Address," "Second Inaugural Address," and the peroration of the "First Inaugural Address" as among the best examples of oratorical excellence in recorded history. Significantly, all books and articles I have seen that discuss these speeches used words normally associated with literature such as "literary," "prose," "poetry," and "writer." Carl Sandburg called the "Gettysburg Address" the "Great American Poem," and Barzun and Edwards and Hankins used literary terms in their titles of books on Lincoln's speaking (*Lincoln the Literary Genius* and *Lincoln the Writer: The Development of His Literary Style*). I contend that these writers sensed that Lincoln's most famous speeches were composed more on literary than on oratorical principles. By saying that these speeches were "more than orations," the writers implied that oratory was on the bottom of a hierarchy of forms of discourse.

Several factors, I think, help to account for the evolution of Lincoln's style from oratorical to literary. As I have indicated, these famous speeches used the structures and rhetorical techniques generally associated with literature--repetition, parallelism, tricolon, antithesis, alliteration, anaphora, assonance, rhyme, and seeming simplicity and brevity. The pervasiveness of religious language and imagery, the intricate use of symbolism, the multiple levels of meaning, and the compelling rhythms helped forge the subtle yet poignant messages of these famous speeches. By transcending immediate, particular, urgent situations, Lincoln in these speeches addressed all people everywhere. He spoke to humanity, to "the better angels of our nature."

The study of Lincoln's speaking reveals a major paradox: The addresses deemed his finest by later generations were not considered great speeches by immediate audiences. Several factors help account for these mixed reactions. First, Lincoln's balanced sentence structures did not have the "building up" qualities of his narratives. His metaphors, analogies, and fables--used primarily in pre-presidential speeches--took the form of rhetorical narratives or stories with definite beginnings, middles, and endings. Lincoln's balanced structures did not have this "building up" step. Thus, listeners did not have time to orient themselves to particular ideas. Moreover, the words and phrases in Lincoln's "literary speeches" resonated and reverberated through multiple levels. Listeners did not have the time to contemplate complex meanings and savor subtle nuances.

The much admired, later passages and speeches were preceded by or embedded in less-than-gripping passages or events. Later generations of people read the peroration of Lincoln's "First Inaugural Address" without reading the entire speech and without having Northern or Southern biases. Similarly, scores of people read the "Gettysburg Address" without reading the oration by Edward Everett that preceded it and without mourning a loved one. The immediate audiences, of course, had to listen to the speeches as presented at those times, in those places, and under those circumstances.

The responsibilities of office and the harsh, political tensions of war led to an increase in the degree of emotional detachment conveyed in Lincoln's rhetoric. Immediate hearers were obviously affected by this distancing. To leisurely, reflective readers not engaged in the particular rhetorical situations, Lincoln's cosmic perspective could seem impressive. The fact that Lincoln read his later, most famed speeches further distanced him from immediate audiences, although this fact presented no problems for subsequent readers of the addresses. The fact that Lincoln appeared hesitant and nervous during the first few minutes of a speech until he got "into" the message also helps explain why most people who heard his "Gettysburg Address" were not impressed by his delivery of this less than three-minute message.

Lincoln's "Gettysburg Address," "Second Inaugural Address," and peroration of the "First Inaugural Address" were not calculated to grip listeners instantly but to render certain ideas and attitudes impressive. The deliberative elements of these speeches were not sharp, and the actions called for were not precise or immediately moving. Later readers were exonerated from <u>doing</u> anything and, hence, could contemplate and admire these addresses as epideictic texts.

Perhaps in his two inaugural addresses and in his "Gettysburg Address" Lincoln chose to speak to posterity. Joshua F. Speed, one of Lincoln's few close friends and confidants, related a conversation when Lincoln recalled a time in his life when he was deeply depressed because "he had 'done nothing to make any human being remember that he had lived,' and that to connect his name with the events transpiring in his day and generation, and so impress himself upon them as to link his name with something that would redound to the interest of his fellow man, was what he desired to live for."[29]

CONCLUSIONS

On the whole Lincoln was a very effective orator. His speaking brought him national prominence. Speeches like his "Lyceum

Address" that are considered "highly sophomoric" today were greatly successful in their day, whereas his most famous speeches today (his "Gettysburg Address," "Second Inaugural Address," and peroration of his "First Inaugural Address") were not considered great by most people at the times of delivery because, I contend, these speeches were composed on literary more than on oratorical criteria. I do not think I am exaggerating when I say that reactions to his pre-presidential speeches at the times of delivery were generally more favorable than to his presidential orations. For example, the "Lyceum Address" was more effective than the "Gettysburg Address" as a speech to an immediate audience. As addresses to posterity and as records of the historic meanings of historic moments, Lincoln's famed presidential addresses continue to stand as powerful, penetrating documents--a remarkable rhetorical achievement, but one not to be confused with discourse having qualities of immediacy that would seize the convictions and emotions of particular audiences in their unique rhetorical situations. Perhaps Lincoln found the best combination: successful speeches early in life that rocketed him to national power and more literary speeches later in life through which he continues to speak. As Basler wrote, "his prose may yet be recognized as his most permanent legacy to humanity."[30]

3

No Laughing Matter:
Lincoln's Use of Humor
as a Rhetorical Device

Two Quaker ladies were traveling on the railroad, and were heard discussing the probable termination of the war. "I think," said the first, "that Jefferson will succeed." "Why does thee think so?" asked the other. "Because Jefferson is a praying man." "And so is Abraham a praying man," objected the second. "Yes, but the Lord will think Abraham is joking," the first replied, conclusively.

Supposedly the best story Lincoln said he ever read about himself

Newton beheld the law of the universe in the fall of an apple. . . . Spencer saw evolution in the growth of a seed; and Shakespeare saw human nature in the laugh of a man. Nature was suggestive to all these men. Mr. Lincoln no less saw philosophy in a story and an object lesson in a joke.

Lincoln's law partner, William Herndon

"This reminds me of a little joke" were seven words heard often by friends and acquaintances of Abraham Lincoln. A study of Lincoln's rhetoric would be incomplete without consideration of his humor, for Lincoln was as much a humorist as he was an orator, statesman, politician, lawyer, and president. His comic sense was a distinguishing characteristic of his rhetoric, and a distinguishing characteristic of his humor was its rhetorical purpose.[1]

The word "humor" is misleading because humor can have a serious side. For Lincoln it did, regularly. Two distinguishing features of his humor were its rhetorical purpose and its being structured so the audience could participate in development of the story, incident, and/or phrasing. This chapter explores both these features by examining the roots, purposiveness, characteristics, and effects of Lincoln's humor.

Harper's Weekly, September 17, 1864.

THE ROOTS OF LINCOLN'S HUMOR

Lincoln's humor evolved, in varying degrees, from the influence of his father, from the privations of his frontier environment, and from the paradoxes of his personality. In the *Life* of Lincoln printed for his 1860 campaign for president, Lincoln made no changes in the description of his father's influence: "From his father came that knack of storytelling, which has made him so delightful among acquaintances, and so irresistible in his stump and forensic drolleries." Throughout his life, he often began a story or saying with some variation of the phrase, "My old Father used to have a saying that." What the father's detailed influence was cannot be determined from the records, but the allusions to him show that Lincoln did draw on his father's skills in narrative and commentary.[2]

The cruelty and crudity of frontier life in the early 1800s also had a formative influence on Lincoln's humor. In an environment of little entertainment, he became popular in part because of his ability to spin a yarn. His retentive memory allowed him to store a seemingly inexhaustible supply of stories. He once told newspaper reporter Noah Brooks, "I remember a good story when I hear it, but I never invented anything original. I am only a retail dealer." Even though Lincoln did not originate most of his stories, he was adept at adapting stories he had heard or read to particular audiences.[3]

Staples of frontier reading also supplied material and method for Lincoln's humor. His love of reading silently and aloud included the reading of joke books such as *Joe Miller's Jests* and James *Quin's Jests* as well as the *King James Bible* and *Aesop's Fables*. The last two books especially influenced Lincoln's humor; stories in the Biblical-parable tradition, like most of Lincoln's stories, sought to make points. He once told his cousin Dennis Hanks, "God tells truth in parables. They're easier fur common folks to understand an' ricollect."[4]

The paradoxical nature of Lincoln's personality further shaped his humor. Lincoln, fond of merriment, also experienced morbidly melancholy moods. His humor was tragicomic, a synthesis of pain and laughter. Carl Sandburg, perhaps the best known of Lincoln's many biographers, wrote, "Having swung far into laughter, did Lincoln at times need another swing back, into the borders of melancholy?" I think Sandburg's question also can be asked in reverse: "Having swung far into melancholy, did Lincoln at times need another swing back, into the borders of laughter?" Some of Lincoln's contemporaries recognized his mixing of humor with a melancholy view of life. For example, Judge David Davis remarked, "Lincoln's stories were merely devices to whistle down sadness." Even when he was weighted down with the pressures of the Civil

War, humor served Lincoln as a necessary salve. It was not simply wit and fondness for jokes that governed his humor but also his overall outlook on communicative strategies, the environment, and his view of life itself.[5]

THE RHETORICAL NATURE OF LINCOLN'S HUMOR

Historian James G. Randall wrote that "humor was no mere technique but a habit of [Lincoln's] mind." I contend that for Lincoln humor constituted both a habit of mind and a technique. Certainly not all of Lincoln's humor served a purpose, but a distinguishing feature of his humor was its purposive rhetorical quality. Through humor he illustrated, amplified, and proved points. Once he remarked that "it is not the story itself, but its purpose, or effect, that interests me."[6]

The story--narrative--is the oldest rhetorical form in recorded communication. The old myths, sagas, and poems make use of that structure. In prose we have examples with which Lincoln was especially familiar: Aesop's fables, the "historical narratives" of the Old Testament, and the parables of Jesus. These were simple stories--often very simple--told to illustrate moral principles in ways that others would understand and remember. Sandburg indicated that Lincoln followed in this tradition: He opened his chapter on "Lincoln's Laughter--and His Religion" with a quotation from Sir Thomas Browne, a famous English prose writer of the seventeenth century: "For unspeakable mysteries in the Scriptures are often delivered in a vulgar and illustrative way; and being written unto man, are delivered, not as they truly are, but as they may be understood." Lincoln explained his penchant for storytelling in a similar, pragmatic manner: "I have found in the course of a long experience that common people--common people--take them as they run, are more easily influenced and informed through the medium of a story than in any other way." The *New York Herald* reported that "Lincoln is called the American Aesop" and Colonel Alexander McClure remarked that Lincoln's stories "contain lessons that could be taught so well in no other way. Every one of them is a sermon. Lincoln, like the Man of Galilee, spoke to the people in parables."[7]

CHARACTERISTICS OF LINCOLN'S STORIES

Lincoln's pragmatic attitude toward life and speaking and his need to be understood--to reach the people--help explain the home-spun nature of his humor. Reflecting the Western frontier, his stories were colloquial, concrete, colorful, and occasionally off-color. They included commonplace details, vivid imagery, frontier vernacular, and short, straightforward sentences that sometimes deviated from the formal rules of grammar. The simplicity of his stories made them easier to digest. They usually employed analogical logic and sometimes used the techniques of exaggeration, distortion, and caricature often associated with the "tall tales" of the West. Few of his stories were uproariously funny; they sought to make listeners smile while understanding a serious point. In other words, he usually did not use humor simply to amuse or entertain; some rhetorical claim or claims almost invariably undergirded his resorts to humor. The following story, typical of Lincoln's humor, includes many of the features I have just mentioned. The story concerns a man who attacked another. To defend himself, the second man attacked the first. "To get even," the aggressor charged his victim/attacker with assault and battery. Lincoln defended the man charged, the second man:

[He] told the jury that his client was in the fix of a man, who, in going along the highway with a pitchfork on his shoulder, was attacked by a fierce dog that ran out at him from a farmer's dooryard. In parrying off the brute with the fork, its prongs stuck into the brute and killed him.
"What made you kill my dog?" said the farmer.
"What made him try to bite me?"
"But why did you not go at him with the other end of the pitchfork?"
"Why did he not come after me with his other end?"

Lincoln then used his arms to help the jury "see" this imaginary dog. "This was the defensive plea of 'son assault demesne'--loosely, that 'the other fellow brought on the fight,'--quickly told, and in a way the dullest mind would grasp and retain."[8]

Lincoln's pointed stories frequently were rendered more active by inclusion of dialogue. Many of the dialogues were distinguished by question-answer formats, which further enlivened them. Typically, Lincoln gave listeners clues about the interlocutors' personalities, but usually these character traits were important only because they uncovered deeper aspects of the arguments being espoused. The dialogue form invited Lincoln's listeners to participate in his stories. As the story/argument progressed, listeners could follow each twist and turn of logic. They could engage in imaginary verbal banters with the interlocutors, thinking of objections, for example, to the lines of reasoning presented. After participating in the interplay, listeners could see how the other person in the dialogue answered the questions. The effect was much like intently eavesdropping on a conversation.

It was easy for listeners to identify with Lincoln's humorous passages because the passages reflected popular roles, views, and stereotypes. People love to see parts of themselves reflected back upon themselves, and Lincoln appealed to this human desire to have ideas and values confirmed and amplified. For example, once in a

courtroom case, Lincoln opposed Stephen T. Logan, a serious lawyer
who came to court that day with his shirt on backwards. Lincoln took
advantage of this not uncommon human error: "After paying tribute
to Logan's usual effectiveness as an attorney, he went on to say, 'Still
he is sometimes wrong. Since the trial has begun, I have discovered
that with all his caution and fastidiousness, he hasn't the knowledge
enough to put his shirt on right!'" When listeners laughed at this
joke, they probably were really laughing at themselves.[9]

It is striking that Lincoln did not use great amounts of ethnic
humor, but when he did, the Irish were the group to whom he
referred. *Abe Lincoln Laughing* by Paul M. Zall, Professor Emeritus
of English and American Studies, contains thirteen stories dealing
with Irishmen. Lincoln singled out no other ethnic group. Why
might he have singled out the Irish? First, they constituted the
largest group of new immigrants in the United States in the mid-
nineteenth century. They clustered primarily in big cities and, hence,
were especially visible at the time. Further, most Civil War units in
the Union army came from specific locales, which made several Union
units heavily Irish. Finally, during Lincoln's time the Irish were the
butts and originators of many jokes. Telling jokes and stories
featuring Irish characters thus reflected popular views and used
conventional bases of humor.

What were the characteristics of Lincoln's ethnic references?
Of the thirteen stories in Zall's book, three featured Irish soldiers,
two mentioned Irish immigrants, five simply used popular Irish
names, eight were variations of stories found in jest books of the
period, and ten stories involved dialogue where the Irishmen spoke
in brogue. One of the stories came from the "Temperance Address."
To demonstrate the ludicrousness of promises or threats far in the
future, Lincoln mimicked an Irishman, "Better lay down that spade
you're stealing, Paddy,--if you don't you'll pay for it at the day of
judgment." "By the powers, if ye'll credit me so long, I'll take
another, jist." Lincoln's references to the Irish in this and the other
instances seldom denigrated them as a group or as individuals.
There were few "dumb Irishmen" in his accounts. More often than
not, Lincoln's Irish spokesmen displayed naive wit and sly insights
that often undercut more pretentious thoughts of other figures in
stories. Again, the moral bases of his wit may provide explanation.[10]

Whether ethnically based or not, Lincoln's humorous accounts
established identifications with listeners by portraying ordinary
people in ordinary situations. The characters in his stories included
young and old, rich and poor, intelligent and illiterate. This "Every-
man" feature of his characters also applied to the stories' themes.
Most of Lincoln's stories dealt with fundamental human emotions,
such as happiness, security, faith, and persistence. Even though most
of his humor exposed human foibles or poked fun at various aspects

of American life, his stories tried to leave listeners believing that good would triumph over evil. Consistent with his optimism and his belief in the power of truth, the hero in Lincoln's stories usually won, representing the might of right.

THE USES OF RIDICULE

Lincoln's reputation as a storyteller is well-known and has become part of the Lincoln legend. What is not well-known is that Lincoln was also a master of invective. Especially in his early speeches, he frequently employed raucous ridicule, stinging sarcasm, and rapid repartee. Whereas Lincoln used stories primarily to <u>make</u> his points, ridicule served him as a negative medium used primarily to <u>refute</u> the points of others by exposing spurious logic and unmasking vice and folly. Jules Feiffer, weekly cartoonist for the *Village Voice*, made a comment about cartoons that applies to ridicule: "I try to turn logic on its ear. I take the suppositions of the people I'm disagreeing with to their logical but ridiculous extremes, and try to show how these arguments fail. And through that I give the [listener] not just an opinion or an attitude, but a perception of what's really going on." It was by giving audiences "a perception of what's really going on" that Lincoln's ridicule functioned rhetorically. He seemed to understand the strategic and persuasive power of ridicule; he called "the power to hurt" a "weapon" and said its point "consists in the *truthfulness* of [its] application."[11]

Lincoln's ridicule had many of the same qualities that marked his storytelling. Like his constructive humor, Lincoln's destructive humor often employed logical reasoning, exaggeration, and frontier language. He typically refuted spurious logic with logic, taking an opponent's argument to its logical extreme to show the absurdity of the argument. Stephen Douglas was the major target of Lincoln's taunts. W. A. Dahlberg determined that "50 per cent of [Lincoln's] wit and sarcasm was at the expense of Judge Douglas, measured by actual count of humor and wit stimuli in all his significant political speeches and debates." The following example from the first Lincoln-Douglas debate is typical: "Judge Douglas," Lincoln exclaimed, "has read from my speech in Springfield, in which I say that 'a house divided against itself cannot stand.' Does the Judge say it *can* stand? [Laughter.] . . . If he does, then there is a question of veracity, not between him and me, but between the Judge and an authority of a somewhat higher character. [Laughter and applause.]." But Douglas was not the only target of Lincoln's "wit lash." In the "Cooper Union Address," for example, Lincoln exposed a fallacy in the thinking of Southern people, and he did so by taking their position to its logical conclusion:

But you will not abide the election of a Republican president. In that supposed event, you say, you will destroy the Union; and then you say, the great crime of having destroyed it will be upon us! That is cool. A highwayman holds a pistol to my ear, and mutters through his teeth, "Stand and deliver, or I shall kill you, and then you will be a murderer!"[12]

In attempting to lampoon victims with vitriolic thrusts, Lincoln frequently employed the techniques of exaggeration or overstatement and/or litotes or understatement. These techniques often took the form of analogies that, like his analogies in general, included commonplace details and the homespun language of the frontier. A typical example comes from a speech Lincoln delivered to members of Congress in an era when a successful military career helped political aspirants enormously. Lincoln ridiculed General Cass' reputation as a military hero; comparing his own military background to that of Cass, Lincoln humorously overstated his own military experiences and understated the military experiences of Cass:

By the way, Mr. Speaker, did you know I am a military hero? Yes sir; in the days of the Black Hawk War, I fought, bled, and came away. Speaking of Gen. Cass' career, reminds me of my own. I was not at Stillman's defeat, but I was about as near it, as Cass was to Hull's surrender.... If Gen. Cass went in advance of me in picking huckleberries, I guess I surpassed him in charges upon the wild onions. If he saw any live, fighting Indians, it was more than I did; but I had a good many bloody struggles with the musquetoes.[13]

Whereas Lincoln's storytelling often employed analogical reasoning that emphasized similarities, his ridicule tended to employ metaphors that emphasized differences. For example, in his "House Divided" Speech, he exclaimed that Douglas' supporters "remind us that he is a very great man, and that the largest of us are very small ones. Let this be granted. But 'a living dog is better than a dead lion.' Judge Douglas, if not a dead lion, for this work, is at least a caged and toothless one." By calling Douglas "dead," "caged," and "toothless," Lincoln suggested that Douglas lacked the vitality, independence, and strength that listeners wanted and expected their public leaders to possess.

As I demonstrated in Chapter 2, Lincoln's early speeches included numerous similes and metaphors involving animals and numerous sensory images. His ridicule, which was most prominent in pre-presidential speaking, also had these qualities. For example, Lincoln refuted Douglas' "do nothing" position of popular sovereignty by calling it "as thin as the homeopathic soup that was made by boiling the shadow of a pigeon that had starved to death," and he concluded an attack on Douglas' position of popular sovereignty by saying, "Judge Douglas is merely playing cuttlefish--a small species of fish that has no mode of defending himself when pursued except by throwing out a black fluid which makes the water so dark the enemy cannot see it, and thus escapes." Such animalistic images may be found frequently in Lincoln's early speeches.[14]

A series of questions was another rhetorical technique found frequently in Lincoln's ridicule. For example, to reveal the faulty logic of Douglas' position that popular sovereignty pertained to people in "an organized political community" with a minimum of 10,000 and a maximum of 20,000 people, Lincoln asked:

Now I would like to know what is to be done with the 9000? Are they all to be treated, until they are large enough to be organized into a political community, as wanderers upon the public land in violation of law? And if so treated and driven out at what point of time would there ever be ten thousand? [Great laughter.] If they were not driven out, but remained there as trespassers upon the public land in violation of the law, can they establish slavery there? No,--the Judge says Popular Sovereignty don't pertain to them then. Can they exclude it then? No, Popular Sovereignty don't pertain to them then. I would like to know . . . what condition the people of the Territory are in before they reach the number of ten thousand?

Like dialogue in his stories, the use of questions in his ridicule invited listeners to participate. By giving their own answers to the questions, listeners could become involved. If listeners gave the "correct" answers--the answers Lincoln wanted--they would reach the desired conclusion on their own.[15]

By asking a series of questions, Lincoln sometimes employed *tu quoque*, a retort charging an opponent with blameworthy actions similar to those charged by the opponent. For example, in the sixth Lincoln-Douglas debate, Lincoln responded to Douglas' charge that he was trying to undermine the authority of the Supreme Court by reminding listeners of Douglas' record of wielding political pressure to reverse Supreme Court decisions. After asking seven rhetorical questions consecutively, Lincoln concluded, "I know of no man in the State of Illinois who ought to know so well about *how much* villainy it takes to oppose a decision of the Supreme Court, as our honorable friend, Stephen A. Douglas. [Long continued applause.]"[16]

Lincoln poked fun not only at others but also at himself, and with purposeful self-deprecation. Lincoln--extremely tall, crooked-legged, stooped-shouldered, with especially long legs and big hands and feet--looked gawky and awkward. His tall body accentuated the points of his tall tales. Most of his self-effacing humor concerned his appearance. He frequently dwelled on his homeliness, perhaps as a way of identifying with ordinary citizens or as a way of appealing to Americans' love for the underdog. His appearance also sometimes served as a way to sidestep issues and to compliment his audience, as in the following example: "FRIENDS: I do not appear for the purpose of making a speech. I design to make no speech. I came merely to see you, and allow you to see me. [Cheers.] And I have to say to you, as I have said frequently to audiences on my journey, that, in the sight, I have the best of the bargain. [Tremendous cheers.]."[17]

Lincoln relied on his intuitive sense of when to interject a story. He sometimes worked a humorous story or joke into even the most serious of situations, as when he told a joke before reading the first draft of the Emancipation Proclamation to his Cabinet. He practiced the advice of the classical rhetorician, Aristotle: "You should kill your opponents' earnestness with jesting and their jesting with earnestness." Lincoln realized that a witty remark could dumbfound a serious opponent and a rational comment could silence a joking opponent. His sense of timing was impeccable; he seemed to "know" just how long to spend telling a particular story. He often built suspense, keeping secret the point of a story and its application until the end.[18]

THE EFFECTIVENESS OF LINCOLN'S HUMOR

Tom Corwin, himself a great orator and humorist, advised speakers, "Never make people laugh. If you would succeed in life, you must be solemn, solemn as an ass." Was Corwin's "Law" correct? Given that Lincoln was not a joker in the usual sense but a serious user of wit and ridicule for pragmatic, rhetorical purposes, did Corwin's "Law" apply? Humor almost always generates a response, from laughter to outrage. What response did Lincoln's humor generate? Did his use of humor help or hurt him rhetorically?

Certainly some people deemed Lincoln's levity during a time of war uncouth and unworthy of a national leader. Not surprisingly, his opponents tried to use his humor against him. In the 1864 presidential election, his humor became a campaign issue. Before his renomination, an editorial in the *New York Herald* tried to denigrate him by calling him "a joke incarnated, his election a very sorry joke, and the idea that such a man should be the President of such a country as this a very ridiculous joke."[19]

The *New York Herald*, however, also realized that humor was a formidable weapon for Lincoln. Another editorial commented, "With the caustic wit of Diogenes he combines the best qualities of all the other celebrated jokers of the world. He is more political than Horace, more spicy than Juvenal, more anecdotal than Aesop, more juicy than Boccacio [*sic*], more mellow than rollicking Rabelais, and more often quoted than the veteran Joe Miller." Douglas also understood the persuasive power of Lincoln's humor. He lamented that he never feared Lincoln's arguments, but "every one of his stories seems like a whack upon my back." Although in some ways Lincoln's reputation as the first humorist to reside in the White House hurt his reelection campaign, in other ways his reputation as a humorist helped him get reelected. By 1864, several Lincoln joke books circulated widely; Sandburg claimed that "as much, perhaps as his speeches and letters, the joke book played its part toward the end Lincoln wished--that people would say of the White House as the chess-player said of the automaton, 'There is a man in there!'" If nothing else, Lincoln's humor made him appear more human. During a particularly dark period in American history, his humor, for some people at least, also served to camouflage stinging truths and harsh realities. Lincoln seemed to disprove Corwin's "Law." Although his humor outraged some people, to the masses his humor "gave the impression of an intensely alive man in the White House, serious though quizzical, close to the plow, with kinship for the common man and 'the folks.'" His humor exerted a positive influence in part because it invited participation and was rarely without a moral or social point.[20]

CONCLUSIONS

For Lincoln, the use of humor was no laughing matter: Through the medium of humor, he sought to create a message that not only tickled the funny bone but made a point as well. The most oft-quoted Lincoln jokes were those that in a lighthearted manner made an eloquent statement, those that enabled listeners to smile as they followed the humorous and the serious sides of his stories and phrases.

Lincoln's humor is one more characteristic of his speaking that has contributed to the making of the Lincoln legend. Today's Lincoln lore includes numerous humorous stories. Although it is estimated that only one-sixth of the stories credited to Lincoln are authentic, many apocryphal stories are repeated so often that we accept them as Lincoln's and still find them moving. As Zall wrote, "At age 175, Lincoln still is living witness to the power of humor to hide the pain, heal the hurt, sustain the spirit."[21]

A political cartoon of Lincoln's "First Inaugural Address." Thomas Nast, the artist, wrote, "As the North received it" (the side depicting peace) and "As the South received it" (the side depicting war).

4

Lincoln's First Inaugural: Peace *and* Sword

No Message was ever received with greater favor. It is universally conceded to be alike clear, compact, and impressive--equally firm and conciliatory.

Albany Evening Journal, March 5, 1861

The Inaugural Address of Abraham Lincoln inaugurates civil war, as we predicted it would. . . . The sword is drawn and the scabbard thrown away.

Richmond Times Dispatch, March 5, 1861

Peace or sword? Which did Lincoln advocate in his "First Inaugural Address?" The above two quotations, published the day after the speech, typify the varying reactions to Lincoln's first message as president. Although a generalization with some notable exceptions, it is true to say that most Northerners interpreted the speech as conciliatory and most Southerners as a declaration of war. The Peoria *Daily Democratic Union* (March 7, 1861) commented on these divergent interpretations: "It is an interesting study to look over the various journals that have come to our table since the delivery of President Lincoln's Inaugural Address, and notice the different manner in which they speak of it. All these criticisms of the Address cannot be correct, for they clash materially."

Rhetorical and historical scholars seem to agree that "all these criticisms cannot be correct for they clash materially," and as history tends to side with the victor, rhetoricians and historians have tended to accept the conciliatory interpretation. In her oft-quoted analysis of Lincoln's "First Inaugural Address," Marie Hochmuth Nichols wrote, "Any fair-minded critic, removed from the passions of the times, must find himself much more in agreement with those

observers of the day who believed the Inaugural met the require-
ments of good rhetoric" and demonstrated a conciliatory attitude.[1]

I contend that all the criticisms can be correct even though
"they clash materially." To me the issue is not who interpreted the
speech "correctly" but how we can account for such divergent
reactions to the same words presented by the same speaker.
Obviously some Northerners and Southerners interpreted the speech
as both conciliatory and a declaration of war or as neither conciliatory
nor a declaration of war, but in this chapter I choose to look at the
extreme positions. My aim is not to suggest that Lincoln should have
given a different speech than the one he gave, but rather, to try to
understand why this speech as an experienced text was interpreted
so differently in the North and South of the country in March 1861.
The purposes of this chapter are to evaluate the conciliatory argument and to analyze systematically the "Inaugural Address" to help
explain why most Northerners viewed the speech as conciliatory and
most Southerners as a declaration of war. My understanding of the
mood of the country at the time of Lincoln's election and inauguration
and the reasons I give to account for the differing reactions to his
"First Inaugural Address" stem, in part, from reading the following
books: *Northern Editorials on Secession, Southern Editorials on
Secession,* and *Abraham Lincoln: A Press Portrait.*[2]

THE CONCILIATORY ARGUMENT

Scholars frequently make two arguments to "prove" the
Inaugural's conciliatory tone: (1) Lincoln originally planned to use
more inflammatory language, and (2) by March 4, 1861, the date of
Lincoln's Inaugural, the Civil War was inevitable.

In his book, *Lincoln's First Inaugural: Original Draft and Its
Final Form,* Judd Stewart detailed the forty-two changes Lincoln
made in the original draft of the Inaugural. The most famous change
occurs in the peroration. Lincoln originally intended to conclude by
saying, "With you, and not with me, is the solemn question of 'Shall
it be peace or a sword?'" William Seward, who was to become
Lincoln's Secretary of State, objected to the argumentative nature of
this conclusion. He said ending with a question was an ineffective
strategy because listeners might give the wrong answer. Instead, he
suggested that "something besides or in addition to argument is
needful--to meet and remove prejudice and passion in the South, and
despondency and fear in the East. Some words of affection--some of
calm and cheerful confidence." Seward submitted a draft for two
different perorations, one of which Lincoln accepted but put into his
own style. This peroration has become one of the most celebrated
perorations of any speech in history and is certainly more soothing in
tone than the conclusion Lincoln originally had planned. In fact, in

my opinion, thirty-three of the forty-two changes between the original and the final draft are more conciliatory, but <u>more</u> conciliatory is <u>not</u> necessarily conciliatory. Clearly many Southerners did not view the final draft of the speech as friendly.[3]

The second argument, that the Civil War was inevitable by March 4, 1861, is more difficult to confirm or deny. An entire generation of historians and rhetoricians have debated this point. I think, however, that even if we accept war as being inevitable by March 4, 1861, two important questions remain: (1) Why did Lincoln not see war as inevitable? and (2) Was war inevitable when Lincoln was elected president in November 1860?

Why Did Lincoln Not See War as Inevitable?

Most contemporary scholars agree that Lincoln was a realistic, shrewd, and practical politician. In an essay on his idea of colonizing Blacks, historian Gabor S. Boritt wrote that his essay confronts "an essential riddle that students have consistently sidestepped: Why did the pragmatic, down-to-earth President sincerely support a totally unrealistic design?" I think we can profit by asking Boritt's question of the Inaugural: "Why did the pragmatic, down-to-earth President seem to miss the inevitability of the Civil War and instead sincerely support a totally unrealistic design?"[4]

Certainly Lincoln might have seen war as inevitable, but if this were the case, it seems curious that little in his public or private discourse indicates this. In fact, in his "Inaugural Address" and afterward, he expressed an optimistic attitude that today seems naive and unrealistic. For example, in a "Special Message to Congress" four months after his inauguration, he explained the policy he had chosen to espouse in his "Inaugural Address": "The policy chosen looked to the exhaustion of all peaceful measures. . . . It was believed possible to keep the government on foot." Perhaps Lincoln did not want to say publicly, "We're going to have war," because he knew he was speaking to posterity, because people naturally want their public leaders to be optimistic, and/or because he wanted the South to fire the first shot. Perhaps he wrote little about war in his private letters because he normally shared little about his personal feelings in his private letters or perhaps because he knew his private letters would one day become matters of public record. Or maybe Lincoln really did not see war as inevitable. Perhaps his strong anti-war feelings helped blind him, as Boritt suggested in his essay, "Abraham Lincoln: War Opponent and War President." We may never know why Lincoln did not <u>seem</u> to see war as inevitable, but I think we need to question his seeming naivete and lack of realism on this issue.[5]

We need to remember also that in 1861, the choices were not limited to peace or a brutal four-year war. Other possibilities

included a partial war, a smaller war, a less violent war, or a war
against fewer states. In 1861, both sides seemed to see war as a
skirmish; at the time few people on either side foresaw the size or
length of the war.

Was War Inevitable When Lincoln
Was Elected President?

War's being inevitable when Lincoln was inaugurated in March
1861 does not mean that war was inevitable when he was elected
president in November 1860. Between election and inauguration,
Lincoln practiced what I call a rhetoric of silence, a policy of purposefully and strategically saying little. However, he did not keep his
policy of silence silent. Indeed, in speech after speech in his twelve-
day trip to Washington D.C. to assume the presidency, he spoke
about remaining silent. The following example is typical: "I have
been occupying a position, since the Presidential election, of silence,
of avoiding public speaking, of avoiding public writing."[6]
Why might Lincoln have chosen to adopt a policy of silence?
We can ascertain some reasons from his own words. First, he
believed it would be improper for him to speak before assuming the
presidency. He explained the impropriety of his speaking: "I have
not kept silent since the Presidential election from any party
wantonness or from any indifference to the anxiety that pervades the
minds of men about the aspect of political affairs of this country. I
have kept silent for the reason that I supposed it was peculiarly
proper that I should do so until the time came when, according to the
customs of the country, I should speak officially." Today politicians
often speak whenever they get the opportunity, but in 1861 remaining
silent during the campaign and before entering office was the norm.
In Chapter 1, I pointed out that Lincoln strongly believed
people should speak only after careful and thorough analyses of their
situations; to do otherwise would be improper. In the following
remarks, he justified his silence, indicating that he needed more time
to deliberate the current crisis fully:

I deem it just to you, to myself and to all that I should see everything, that
I should hear everything, that I should have every light that can be brought
within my reach, in order that when I do speak, I shall have enjoyed every
opportunity to take correct and true ground; and for this reason I don't
propose to speak at this time of the policy of the Government.

My intention is to give this subject all the consideration which I possibly
can before I speak fully and definitely in regard to it--so that, when I speak,
I may be as nearly right as possible.

Lincoln also had a keen awareness of how quickly political events were changing; thus, he thought speaking prematurely might commit him to foolish decisions. "It was peculiarly fitting," he said, for him to "see it all up to the last minute" before declaring his positions.[7]

Other reasons why Lincoln might have chosen a policy of silence include realizing the damage ill-chosen words could cause, knowing he was a minority president-elect trying to steer a middle course, mixed and contradictory opinions in the North about the best course of action, a volatile situation in the South, and the fact that the administration then in power under President James Buchanan was doing almost nothing about the ongoing crisis.

Was Lincoln's silence the best rhetorical strategy he could have chosen? I have examined reasons in favor of the policy. Let me now discuss why silence might not have been the best policy. First, Lincoln was an unknown candidate. Between election and inauguration, Southern editorials frequently included comments like the following: "You cite us to your [past] speeches as enunciating the principles upon which your official course will be based. . . . But we warn you that they will not satisfy fifteen States of the Union now, or in the future. They ask, and they have a right to ask, new pledges and new guarantees." Requests for new pledges and new guarantees do not seem unreasonable. Second, although silence was the custom in 1860-1861, this custom already showed signs of change. Custom proscribed active campaigning on one's own behalf, but Stephen Douglas had rejected the custom and campaigned actively for himself. Third, these were not ordinary times; crisis clearly permeated the events of the day. South Carolina seceded from the Union when Lincoln was elected president, and between election and inauguration six more states seceded. Finally, Lincoln's policy of strategic silence seemed to assume that the rhetorical situation would mature and then decay. This did not happen. Instead, the situation continued to grow and showed no signs of decaying.[8]

I am not arguing that Lincoln should have spoken during the interim between his election and his assumption of office or that historical events would have turned out differently had he chosen speech instead of silence; I am suggesting only that it is important to raise the question of whether silence was the best rhetorical policy.

ANALYSIS OF THE SPEECH

Whether Lincoln's policy of silence was rhetorically the best choice remains a question. There is no question, however, that this policy helped build suspense about what he would say in his "Inaugural Address." Many newspapers prefaced publication of the Address with statements like the following:

We publish the Inaugural in this day's issue, and are sure that we have never given to our readers an official document upon which the mingled hopes and fears of the people rested with deeper interest.

No message was ever looked for with more intense interest than the Inaugural Message of President Lincoln.[9]

No one questions the especially difficult rhetorical situation Lincoln faced. He was a minority president speaking in especially volatile times, and he needed to address several different audiences. At the very least, his audiences included strong Abolitionists, moderate Northerners, South Carolinians, citizens of the other six states that had already seceded, citizens of the Southern states that were considering secession, Southerners who were against seceding, and citizens of the border states.

My purpose in analyzing Lincoln's speech is not to prove that "any fair-minded critic" would view the speech as conciliatory (as Nichols claimed) nor to prove that any fair-minded critic would view the speech as a declaration of war. Neither is my purpose to suggest that Lincoln should have rendered the speech more conciliatory. I am interested only in exploring how the <u>same words</u> spoken by the <u>same person</u> could receive such divergent reactions. Several possible reasons may help explain <u>why</u> most Northerners interpreted the speech as conciliatory while most Southerners interpreted it as a declaration of war.

Selective Perception and Selective Listening

Selective listening, in effect, means that people hear what they expect and perhaps want to hear. All people listen selectively, hearing only part of any message. In the case of Lincoln's Inaugural, one could expect a great deal of selective listening because the situation was marked by a high degree of prejudice and because Lincoln had said little to counter these prejudiced views. Many of the editorials evaluating the "Inaugural Address" support the view that selective listening and selective perception help account for the divergent reactions to the speech. The statement from *The Richmond Times Dispatch* quoted at the beginning of this chapter, for example, demonstrates selective perception "in action": "The Inaugural Address of Abraham Lincoln inaugurates civil war, <u>as we have predicted it would from the beginning</u>" (emphasis added). Northern and Southern editorials tended to quote different portions of the speech: Northern editorials usually quoted the speech's conciliatory peroration, while Southern editorials usually quoted Lincoln's forceful statements about how he would treat the South.[10]

Even the same statements in the Address can be interpreted differently, depending upon what one expects to hear. Below are a

few such passages and indications of how Northerners and Southerners might have interpreted them:

Passage: "There is much controversy about the delivering up of fugitives
from service or labor. The clause I now read is as plainly written in the
Constitution as any other of its provisions:"
Possible Northern Interpretation: Lincoln is straightforward and calm. He
is speaking in plain language.
Possible Southern Interpretation: Lincoln is inferring that I cannot read!

Passage: "There is no alternative for continuing the Government but
acquiescence on the one side or the other. If a minority in such a case will
secede rather than acquiesce, they make a precedent which in turn will
divide and ruin them . . . why may not any portion of a new Confederacy
a year or two hence arbitrarily secede again, precisely as portions of the
present Union now claim to secede from it?"
Possible Northern Interpretation: Lincoln is explaining rationally why
secession will not work.
Possible Southern Interpretation: By saying, "There is no alternative,"
Lincoln has ruled out the possibility of compromise. He asserts that those
of us in the Southern states that have seceded have done so "arbitrarily"
and that we only "claim" to have seceded.

Passage: "All who cherish disunion sentiments are now being educated as
to the exact temper of doing this."
Possible Northern Interpretation: Lincoln is still calm and rational and
speaking in plain language.
Possible Southern Interpretation: Lincoln is being condescending. He is
telling us that we do not know what we are doing so he will "educate" us.
By using the word "plainly," he is saying that his point is obvious, implying
that we are stupid for not viewing the matter in the way he does.

Deductive Organization

Lincoln developed his speech deductively, beginning with
discussion of the current "apprehension among the people of the
Southern States" and with an explanation that "there has never been
any reasonable cause for such apprehension. Indeed, the most ample
evidence to the contrary has all the while existed, and been open to
their inspection." People expecting a conciliatory speech could easily
interpret his method of organization as straightforward, calm, and
reasonable. People expecting a declaration of war could as easily feel
offended by his sweeping beginning and his directness; his argument
implied that the Southern people had been unreasonable and unable
or unwilling to read the political evidence.

Conciliatory Peroration

As I have said, the peroration contained the most conciliatory and most poetic part of the speech. Terms of endearment like "friends" and "affection," the use of "we," an optimistic attitude and tone, and a mixture of religion and politics--features lacking in the rest of the speech--can be found in the peroration:

We are not enemies, but friends. We must not be enemies. Though passion may have strained, it must not break our bonds of affection. The mystic chords of memory stretching from every battle-field and patriot grave to every living heart and hearthstone all over this broad land, will yet swell the chorus of the Union, when again touched, as surely they will be, by the better angels of our nature.

The peroration contained almost one-third of all the terms of endearment and two-thirds of the terms with religious connotations used in the entire speech. This portion of the speech was conciliatory, but people who had already foreseen the speech as a declaration of war had excluded conciliatory possibilities long before Lincoln ever spoke these words.

Conservative Defense of the Status Quo

Lincoln's Inaugural Address was a conservative document that defended the status quo. For example, he explained, "All members of Congress swear their support to the whole Constitution; to this provision [the Fugitive Slave Clause] as well as to any other." At another point, he admitted that the status quo was not perfect but argued that it was as good as it could be. Near the end of the speech, he announced, "Such of you as are now dissatisfied still have the old Constitution unimpaired."

To a Northerner, Lincoln's defense of the status quo probably seemed rational and certainly not radical. Northerners were content with the status quo because they saw it as obstructing the spread of slavery and fostering the variety of economic developments emerging in their section of the country and in the West. Yet, in 1861 Southerners were by no means satisfied with the status quo. In one degree or another they had come to see the status quo as allowing and encouraging the North in its "aggressions" against Southern interests. Had they been satisfied with "the old Constitution unimpaired," Southern states would not have seceded or contemplated secession. In effect, Lincoln now told them that constitutional powers would not be changed and that the Fugitive Slave Clause would not become any better enforced than it already was. There is no doubt that most Southerners wanted any new president to outline a policy for changes--changes that would protect the institution of slavery, enforce the Fugitive Slave Clause, open territories at least to the possibility of instituting slavery, and support other "states' rights" positions that concerned them. Since Lincoln's speech did none of these things, it is not surprising that many Southerners interpreted it as a declaration of war--continued and/or incipient.

Downplaying His Ethos

Throughout his "Inaugural Address," Lincoln downplayed his ethos. He rarely used the pronoun "I," and he sometimes referred to himself in the third person (for example, "him who now addresses you"). In the speech he explained in detail that he possessed little power as president: "people have wisely given their public servants but little power . . . no administration, by any extreme wickedness or folly, can very seriously injure the Government in the short space of four years."

Again, Northerners could perceive Lincoln's seemingly deliberate attempt to downplay his ethos as a way of saying he would deal calmly with the current crisis and as a way of telling Southerners that he did not have the power to hurt them, even if he wanted to do so. Such an interpretation would make the speech seem conciliatory. Southerners, however, could view Lincoln's seemingly deliberate attempt to downplay his ethos as a way of avoiding personal responsibility for events that would follow and as an indication that he would be a weak leader who did not have the political power or leadership ability necessary to foster compromise. Perceiving the speech as a declaration of war follows given such an interpretation.

Portraying Southerners as the Aggressors

Throughout the "First Inaugural Address," Lincoln portrayed himself in a positive position and portrayed the South as the aggressor or potential aggressor. For example, he said, "There need be no bloodshed or violence, and there shall be none unless it is forced upon the national authority." Near the end of the speech he remarked, "In your hands, my dissatisfied fellow-countrymen, and not in mine, is the momentous issue of civil war. The Government will not assail you. You can have no conflict without being yourselves the aggressors. You have no oath registered in Heaven to destroy the Government, while I have the most solemn one to 'preserve, protect and defend' it." Throughout the speech Lincoln referred to Southerners as "you" rather than as part of "we," implying an attitude of "we versus you." For example, he said, "Suppose you go to-day, you cannot fight always, and when, after much loss on both sides and no gain on either, you cease fighting, the identical questions as to terms of intercourse are again upon you." This statement implied that the

South had all the problems. After fighting, the identical questions would be upon you, the South, not upon us.

Complex and Dull Language in Assuring Southerners

To assure Southerners that slavery would be protected, Lincoln quoted the resolution placed in the Republican platform and contended that those who nominated and elected him accepted this resolution as "law." Try to "listen" to the following words:

Resolved, That the maintenance inviolate of the rights of the States, and especially the right of each State to order and control its own domestic institutions according to its own judgment exclusively, is essential to that balance of power on which the perfection and endurance of our political fabric depend; and we denounce the lawless invasion by armed force of the soil of any State or Territory, no matter under what pretext, as among the gravest of crimes.

According to the Fog Index of readability for written discourse (emphasis mine), this passage is off the scale. According to the Index, this passage scores 21.75; a score of 13 or higher is above the "danger line" for readability. According to Rudolf Flesch's scale, another measure of reading ease, the passage ranks between the very difficult end of academic writing and close to scientific writing, the most difficult type of writing to read. According to Flesch's "human-interest" scale for writing, the passage offers absolutely no human interest! Certainly discourse that is extremely difficult and dull to read is extremely difficult and dull to hear. Thus, Southerners might not even have heard Lincoln's assurances.

Language of Reason

Throughout most of the "Inaugural Address," Lincoln did not use dry, legal language such as he used in his assurances, but he did use many words associated with reason such as "reason," "reasonable," "calm," "think," and "sensible." The use of such language could easily make the speech seem calm, rational, and conciliatory or could make Lincoln seem aloof and/or indifferent to the passionate concerns of some citizens--namely, Southerners.

The Contract Argument

Most Southerners in the states that had seceded and that were considering secession viewed secession as legal, and many thought the North would allow the Confederate states to go in peace. They argued that the government consisted of a contract between states. Two weeks before Lincoln's "Inaugural Address," Jefferson Davis delivered his "Inaugural Address" as president of the Confederacy. Davis explained the contract theory of government as follows: "governments rest upon the consent of the governed, and that it is the right of the people to alter or abolish governments whenever they become destructive of the ends for which they were established."

In his "Inaugural Address" Lincoln spent considerable time refuting this contract theory. He argued, "If the United States be not a government proper, but an association of States in the nature of a contract merely, can it as a contract be peaceably unmade by less than all parties who made it." By examining the history of the Union, he explained in detail why the government was not merely a contract between states.

The legality of secession and the contract theory of government were issues that had been in the public domain for a long time by March 4, 1861, but the "Inaugural Address" constituted the first time Lincoln responded to these important issues in detail. To some people his in-depth analysis might have seemed calm, rational, and thorough, while to others it might have seemed like a response given too late and mistakenly on such important issues.

Not Recognizing States That Seceded

In arguing that the government consisted not merely of a contract between states, Lincoln claimed "that no State, upon its own mere motion, can lawfully get out of the Union; that resolves and ordinances to that effect are legally void, and that acts of violence within any State or States against the authority of the United States are insurrectionary or revolutionary, according to circumstances." He continued, "I, therefore, consider that, in view of the Constitution and the laws, the Union is unbroken." Two of Lincoln's major themes in this address were that "the union of these States is perpetual" and that he would execute the laws of the Union in all states. In explaining and emphasizing these points, he ignored the fact that seven states had seceded already and that several other states were considering secession. Not punishing the states that had seceded could easily seem conciliatory. Not recognizing that secession had occurred also could easily seem offensive and accusatory. In effect, Lincoln told Southerners living in the states that had seceded that they were "unlawful," that their secession was "legally void," and that their acts against the authority of the United States were "insurrectory" or "revolutionary."

WHAT ELSE COULD LINCOLN HAVE SAID?

We can always speculate about what Lincoln might have said differently and about whether these differences would have altered the course of events that followed; but, of course, we can never really know. I discuss below some rhetorical strategies and techniques that he might have used. My purpose in exploring these choices is not to suggest that Lincoln should have adopted any of them; rather, I am arguing that considering some of the alternative choices that existed illustrates and clarifies how and why Lincoln's speech, as actually presented, was interpreted so very differently by Northerners and Southerners in March 1861.

Areas of Common Ground

A common rhetorical strategy used by speakers is to identify areas of common ground with their audience. In fact, most inaugural addresses discuss <u>shared</u> beliefs, a <u>common</u> heritage, past national leaders who are respected by <u>all</u> members of the audience, and traditional <u>family</u> values.   These subjects had already become standard *topoi* of inaugural addresses. Discussing shared heroes might have been particularly effective for Lincoln because most heroes before 1861 had come from the South. Most inaugural addresses talk about children, appealing to people's almost innate desire to make the world a better place for the next generation. It seems curious that Lincoln did not once mention children in his speech.

Lincoln could have established common ground while at the same time personalizing his message. He might have said something like the following: "I was born a Southerner. My wife's family are slaveholders. Having lived in the South and the West and having talked extensively with people from all regions of this country, I feel confident that I understand the beliefs and values we all share."

In several speeches before the "First Inaugural Address," Lincoln had made statements that, in my opinion, established common ground and personalized his message. Below are a few examples along with explanations of why each statement might have been rhetorically effective in the "First Inaugural":

Statement: I shall consider the whole people of [this country] my constituents, as well those that oppose, as those that support me.
Explanation: Appeals to all voters. Refers to people who did not vote for him as "those that oppose me," not as Southerners.

Statement: We mean to treat you [those who opposed him] as near as we possibly can, like Washington, Jefferson, and Madison treated you. We mean to leave you alone, and in no way to interfere with your institution; to abide by all and every compromise of the Constitution. . . . We mean to remember that you are as good as we; that there is no difference between us other than the difference of circumstances. We mean to recognise and

bear in mind that you have as good hearts in your bosoms as other people, or as we claim to have, and treat you accordingly.
Explanation: Addresses those who voted against him, assures them about not interfering with slavery, talks about "compromise," sees the opposition as people with good hearts.

Statement: I have often inquired of myself, what great principle or idea it was that kept this Confederacy so long together. It was not the mere matter of the separation of the colonies from the mother land; but something in that Declaration giving liberty, not alone to the people of this country, but hope to the world for all future time.
Explanation: Recalls a shared history, alludes to the theme of a Chosen People, appeals to people's desire to make the world a better place for future generations.

Statement: . . . I still have confidence that the Almighty, the Maker of the Universe will, through the instrumentality of this great and intelligent people, bring us through this as He has through all the other difficulties of our Country.
Explanation: Compliments the audience, is optimistic, refers to God, discusses a shared heritage, mentions the current "difficulties" without according blame.

Statement: Why shall we not be recognized and acknowledged as brethren again, living in peace and harmony one with another? I . . . [trust] that the good sense of the American people, on all sides of all rivers in America, under the Providence of God, who has never deserted us, that we shall again be brethren, forgetting all parties--ignoring all parties."
Explanation: Speaks to people in all states including people in the states that had seceded, refers to God, uses harmonizing language (such as "brethren," "peace," and "harmony"), ignores geographical and party barriers.[11]

A Plan of Action

In their inaugural addresses, presidents often outline their plans of action. Lincoln's silence between election and inauguration made listeners especially eager to know what his policy would be. How would he proceed once he was in office? What would he do to try to resolve the current crisis? Lincoln might have outlined a plan of action, such as meeting with members of Congress, suggesting a meeting with representatives of the states that had seceded and representatives from the border states, recommending possible compromises, and, in general, focusing on the future in concrete and conciliatory ways.

How Would the States that Had Seceded Return to the Union?

Instead of pretending that the seven states that had seceded had not done so, Lincoln might have made it easy for these states to reenter the Union. For example, he might have adopted a strategy similar to the one used by American Telephone and Telegraph (AT&T), which targets consumers who leave AT&T for other long-distance telephone services. Instead of ignoring that these people have left or chastising them for leaving, AT&T makes it easy for them to return, telling them that "there has never been a better time to come back" and that reinstallation is free. Instead of pretending that Southern states had not seceded or calling secession "unlawful," Lincoln could have made it easy for the states that had seceded to return to the Union without losing pride.

What all of these considerations suggest is that there existed other rhetorical options beyond those Lincoln chose for his speech. There were means of moderating "we versus them" formulations, enlivening and personalizing language in crucial places, elaborating common-ground arguments, outlining more attractive plans of future action, indicating how seceded states might find their way back into the Union, and, indeed, rendering the entire speech "conciliatory" in the manner of the peroration. I am not saying that Lincoln should have adopted any of these alternative strategies. My point is only that, as with all speeches, there were multiple, rhetorical ways for Lincoln to formulate his "First Inaugural Address."

CONCLUSIONS

Hindsight is supposed to be 20-20, but in the case of Lincoln's "First Inaugural Address" we can never know whether changes like the ones suggested above would have altered the course of events. Such choices might not have worked. For example, they might have offended strong abolitionists who were part of his constituency. Lincoln's Inaugural, like all inaugurals, had to appeal both to people who voted for him and to people who voted against him. At best, appealing to both these sides required a difficult balancing act. Further, in his Inaugural, as in all speeches, Lincoln had to be true to himself. He viewed secession as a mobocratic act, never justified because it contained the essence of anarchy, and on the principles of preventing the extension of slavery and preserving the Union, he was unwilling to make major concessions. Hence, in good conscience he probably could not have adopted a strategy like acknowledging that seven states had seceded from the Union. In addition to being constrained by the audience and situation, Lincoln, like all speakers, was constrained by his personal beliefs and values.

Although we can never know whether a different sort of inaugural address could have resulted in a different sort of war or in no war at all, my analysis has shown that with all we know about Lincoln, there are important historical and rhetorical questions related to this speech whose answers we do not know: Why did Lincoln not see war as inevitable at this point? Was his policy of campaign and post-election silence the "best" rhetorical strategy for the immediate situation? Could he have better guided perceptions of his "Inaugural Address" by speaking between election and inauguration? Could he have been loyal to his own principles and to his constituents and yet rendered the speech more conciliatory? Raising such questions reminds us that variable options exist in all rhetorical situations.

I am not suggesting that rhetorical choices different from those Lincoln actually chose would have yielded a better "Inaugural Address" on this particular occasion. Rather, I am arguing that considering Lincoln's speech, as actually presented, and some alternative choices helps to explain why, in March 1861, most Northerners interpreted the speech as conciliatory while most Southerners interpreted it as a declaration of war.

FIGURE 7: LINCOLN AND HIS CABINET.   READING OF THE EMANCIPATION PROCLAMATION.

Lincoln reading the Emancipation Proclamation in his Cabinet. His rhetoric on emancipation evolved over time. National Portrait Gallery, Smithsonian Institution.

5

Evolving Rhetorical Stances on Emancipation

[The issue of slavery] is the eternal struggle between these two principles--right and wrong--throughout the world.

Lincoln in the final Lincoln-Douglas debate

I will say then that I am not, nor ever have been in favor of bringing about in any way the social and political equality of the white and black races.

Lincoln in the fourth Lincoln-Douglas debate

How firmly and how consistently was Lincoln committed to emancipation? In this chapter I shall attempt to answer these questions. First I will examine what Lincoln said about slavery, next deal with what he said about Black people, then explore his conservatism as reflected in his rhetoric, and finally associate these considerations with the evolution of the Emancipation Proclamation.[1]

LINCOLN ON SLAVERY

Throughout his life Lincoln declared without qualification that slavery was morally and socially evil. On this point he was unwavering. I have seen no primary evidence that in any way contradicts what he said in 1864: "I am naturally anti-slavery. If slavery is not wrong, nothing is wrong. I can not remember when I did not so think and feel." In speech after speech he portrayed the evils of the institution. His rhetorical opposition to Stephen Douglas in the 1850s often focused on the question of whether slavery was inherently wrong. Lincoln often made comments like the following, from his last debate with Douglas: "The real issue in this controversy . . . is the sentiment on the part of one class that looks upon the institution of slavery *as a wrong*, and of another class that *does not* look upon it as a wrong." To Douglas' claims of not caring whether slavery "is voted up or voted down," Lincoln usually responded with a discussion of right and wrong. For example, in their last formal debate, he said, "Any man can say that who does not see anything wrong in slavery, but no man can logically say it who does see a wrong in it; because no man can logically say he don't care whether a wrong is voted up or voted down. He may say he don't care whether an indifferent thing is voted up or voted down, but he must logically have a choice between a right thing and a wrong thing."[2]

Lincoln maintained that slavery violated the meanings of liberty and equality, which he considered the bulwarks of democracy. The way he once defined democracy underscored its relationship to liberty and equality: "As I would not be a *slave*, so I would not be a *master*. This expresses my idea of democracy." In a now-famous "Fragment on Slavery," he elaborated on this definition:

If A. can prove, however conclusively, that he may, of right, enslave B.--why may not B. snatch the same argument, and prove equally, that he may enslave A.?--

You say A. is white, and B. is black. It is *color*, then; the lighter, having the right to enslave the darker? Take care. By this rule, you are to be slave to the first man you meet, with a fairer skin than your own.

You do not mean *color* exactly?--You mean the whites are *intellectually* the superiors of the blacks, and, therefore have the right to enslave them? Take care again. By this rule, you are to be slave to the first man you meet, with an intellect superior to your own.

But, say you, it is a question of *interest*; and, if you can make it your *interest*, you have the right to enslave another. Very well. And if he can make it his interest, he has the right to enslave you.

Lincoln frequently discussed the relationships among liberty, democracy, and slavery. The following example is typical: "In *giving* freedom to the *slave*, we *assure* freedom to the *free*--honorable alike in what we give, and what we preserve."[3]

On preventing the extension of slavery into new territories, Lincoln was unrelenting and uncompromising. While touring New England in the winter of 1860, he frequently used the metaphor of a venomous snake to illustrate the crawling menace of slavery. The following passage from a speech at New Haven, Connecticut, is typical:

But if there was a bed newly made up, to which the children were to be taken, and it was proposed to take a batch of young snakes and put them there with them, I take it no man would say there was any question how I ought to decide. . . . The new Territories are the newly made bed to which our children are to go, and it lies with the nation to say whether they shall have snakes mixed up with them or not.[4]

Lincoln argued unceasingly that slavery was wrong because it defiled the very nature of a democracy, but he fought to halt its spread--not to abolish it. For most of his political life he fought to protect slavery in the fifteen states where it then legally existed. To interfere with slavery in these states, he argued, would be morally, legally, and practically wrong. In his "First Inaugural Address," he reminded listeners of another speech in which he had said, "I have no purpose, directly or indirectly, to interfere with the institution of Slavery in the States where it exists. I believe I have no lawful right to do so, and I have no inclination to do so." Lincoln advocated gradual rather than sudden emancipation also because, he argued, eradicating slavery abruptly would result in even more evils than the evils caused by slavery itself. Comparing slavery to "an enormous wen" upon an old gentleman's neck, he said, "Everybody would say the wen was a great evil, and would cause the man's death after a while, but you couldn't cut it out for he'd bleed to death in a minute. The wen represents slavery on the neck of this country."[5]

Lincoln claimed that preventing the spread of slavery was a moral obligation based on the principle that slavery was wrong; not interfering with slavery in the states where it legally existed was a constitutional obligation based on the necessity of not producing greater wrongs. He presented himself as believing that time would make principle win; a policy of containment, he argued, would lead to the *ultimate* extinction of slavery. Note the word "permanently" in the famous declaration of his "House Divided" Speech: "A house divided against itself cannot stand.' I believe this government cannot endure permanently half slave and half free." Lincoln seemed to say that the Union then divided into free and slave states could not stay that way forever; slavery either would become ultimately extinguished or universally lawful. Douglas' doctrine of popular sovereignty, Lincoln argued, would perpetuate slavery, whereas his policy of halting the spread of slavery would lead to the institution's ultimate extinction. Consistent with the optimism that characterized his rhetoric, he predicted his position would win because he felt assured, as he put it, "of the inherent power of truth and of the ultimate and universal triumph of justice, humanity, and freedom."[6]

Lincoln's avowed position, then, was not to meddle with slavery where it existed but to prevent its extension and thereby inaugurate a policy that would treat slavery as an evil and lead to its ultimate disappearance. He defended this position by relating it to the intentions of the Founding Fathers and to the ideals of the Declaration of Independence. Our historical fathers, he said on several occasions, did not make this nation half slave and half free; rather, they found the nation half slave and half free, and they placed it in the course of ultimate extinction. As evidence for his interpretation, he cited the abolition of the African slave trade, the Northwest

Ordinance of 1787, which prohibited the spread of slavery into the Northwest Territory, and the absence of the word "slavery" in the Constitution. The Declaration of Independence, he maintained, also provided evidence that the Founding Fathers believed equality included Blacks as well as Whites. Surely the pronouncement that "all men are created equal" included Black people; in fact, he contended, until recently no one had ever suggested otherwise: "I believe the entire records of the world, from the date of the Declaration of Independence up to within three years ago [1855] may be searched in vain for one single affirmation, from one single man, that the negro was not included in the Declaration of Independence."[7]

Lincoln defined equality as equality of opportunity. In debate against Douglas at Ottawa and again at Quincey, he talked about the equality of Blacks "in the right to eat the bread without leave of anybody else which his own hand earns." Similarly, in a speech ten days before becoming president, he stated that the equality pronouncement of the Declaration of Independence "gave promise that in due time the weights should be lifted from the shoulders of all men, and that *all* should have an equal chance," and in a "Message to Congress in Special Session" four months after assuming the presidency, he spoke about a "government whose leading object is, to elevate the condition of men--to lift artificial weights from all shoulders--to clear the paths of laudable pursuit for all--to afford all, an unfettered start, and a fair chance, in the race of life." Equality of opportunity, the ability to enjoy the fruits of one's own labor, related to the ideal in the Declaration of Independence--the pursuit of happiness. Through an in-depth analysis of Lincoln's economic beliefs and policies, historian G. S. Boritt has concluded that Lincoln "extended" the meaning of equality to mean equality of opportunity or "the right to get ahead in life." Here, an historian's analysis of Lincoln's belief structure confirms my inferences drawn from his popular discourse.[8]

For Lincoln, freedom from any type of human bondage required equality of opportunity. The importance and generalized character of equal opportunity may be seen in an intriguing passage in his "Second Lecture on Discoveries and Inventions." In this lecture, presented on three different occasions in February 1859, Lincoln used the words "emancipate," "slavery," and "emancipation" metaphorically. While discussing the profound effects of the inventions of writing and printing and the discovery of America, he explained that improvements due to printing developed gradually because "the *capacity* to read, could not be multiplied as fast as the *means* of reading." He continued:

It is probable--almost certain--that the great mass of men, at that time, were utterly unconscious, that their *conditions*, or their *minds* were capable of improvement. They not only looked upon the educated few as superior beings; but they supposed themselves to be naturally incapable of rising to equality. To immancipate the mind from this false and under estimate of itself, is the great task which printing came into the world to perform. It is difficult for us, *now* and *here*, to conceive how strong this slavery of the mind was; and how long it did, of necessity, take, to break it's shackles, and to get a habit of freedom of thought, established. It is, in this connection, a curious fact that a new country is most favorable--almost necessary--to the immancipation of thought, and the consequent advancement of civilization and the arts.

"To emancipate the mind," "this slavery of the mind," and "the emancipation of thought" are indicators that Lincoln conceived of slavery in broader terms than just Black slavery. Further evidence comes from his "Temperance Address," where he mentioned a former "victim of intemperance" who "bursts the fetters that have bound him" and said that "the demon of intemperance . . . keeps our fathers, our brothers, our sons, and our friends, prostrate in the chains of moral death." With the success of the temperance revolution, he continued, "We shall find a stronger bondage broken, a viler slavery manumitted, a greater tyrant deposed" than in the political of revolution of 1776. To Lincoln, emancipation from slavery or limitations of any sort required equality of opportunity.

LINCOLN ON RACIAL EQUALITY

Lincoln's opposition to slavery and his emphasis on equal opportunity for all people did not make him a champion for complete racial equality. He spoke about slavery and slaves differently. In general, Lincoln and the Republicans were united on the question of slavery, but they were divided on the question of race. On the other hand, Douglas and the Democrats were united on the question of race but divided on the question of slavery.

Lincoln argued unequivocally that Black people were human beings, not animals, and that they deserved the inalienable rights enumerated in the Declaration of Independence: life, liberty, and the pursuit of happiness. However, he did not advocate complete equality. When discussing physical, social, or political equality, his ambivalent attitudes toward Black people surfaced, as in the following passage from the sixth debate with Douglas:

I have no purpose to introduce political and social equality between the white and black races. There is a physical difference between the two, which, in my judgment, will probably forever forbid their living together on the footing of perfect equality, and inasmuch as it becomes a necessity that there must be a difference, I as well as Judge Douglas am in favor of the race to which I belong having the superior position. [Cheers, "That's the doctrine."] I have never said anything to the contrary, but I hold that, notwithstanding all this, there is no reason in the world why the Negro is not entitled to all the rights enumerated in the Declaration of Independence--the right of life, liberty and the pursuit of happiness. I hold that he is as much entitled to these as the white man. I agree with Judge Douglas that he is not my equal in many respects, certainly not in color--perhaps not in intellectual and moral endowments; but in the right to eat the bread without leave of anybody else which his own hand earns, he is my equal and the equal of Judge Douglas, and the equal of every other man. [Loud cheers.][9]

In his debate with Douglas in Charleston, Lincoln articulated what today would be considered strongly racist sentiments; what he said, wrote Don Fehrenbacher, "is fast becoming the most quoted passage in all of Lincoln's writings, outstripping even the Gettysburg Address and the Second Inaugural." In trying to disarm Douglas' attempt to associate him with extreme abolitionists, Lincoln said:

I will say then that I am not, nor ever have been in favor of bringing about in any way the social and political equality of the white and black races, [applause]--that I am not nor ever have been in favor of making voters or jurors of negroes, nor of qualifying them to hold office, nor to intermarry with white people; and I will say in addition to this that there is a physical difference between the white and black races which I believe will for ever forbid the two races living together on terms of social and political equality. And inasmuch as they cannot so live, while they do remain together there must be the position of superior and inferior, and I as much as any other man am in favor of having the superior position assigned to the white race.[10]

Lincoln usually talked about slavery in the abstract and Blacks in the concrete. Whereas he used mostly positive arguments to denounce slavery, he often used humor, especially ridicule, to discuss racial equality. The examples below are typical:

I protest, now and forever, against that counterfeit logic which presumes that because I do not want a negro woman for a slave, I do necessarily want her for a wife. [Laughter and cheers.] My understanding is that I need not have her for either.

. . . anything that argues me into his [Douglas'] idea of perfect social and political equality with the negro is but a specious and fantastical arrangement of words by which a man can prove a horse-chestnut to be a chestnut horse.

Use of humor and of concrete, familiar images allowed Lincoln to deflect the subject while adapting to his audiences.[11]

Although Lincoln's attitudes toward Black people seem racist and anachronistic today, they were not so in his day. Note the cheers, applause, and laughter in the examples above. In the middle of the nineteenth century, Northerners and Southerners supported different positions on slavery, but their positions were relatively similar on race. Free Blacks at the time did not share equality with their White counterparts in law or in popular opinion. Even many abolitionists did not advocate social and political equality. Further, Lincoln's political survival depended on his adapting to his audiences and steering what in his day was a middle course.

Popular prejudices and opinions played a significant role in Lincoln's discussion of racial equality. After enumerating the inalienable rights of all men, the Declaration of Independence states, "That to secure these rights, governments are instituted among men, deriving their just powers from the consent of the governed." Lincoln recognized the importance of winning public consent. In his debate at Ottawa, he said, "public sentiment is everything. With public sentiment nothing can fail; without it nothing can succeed." Whether right or wrong, Lincoln said, racial prejudices existed that would prevent Blacks from ever achieving political and social equality with Whites. In his "Peoria Address," he asked and answered his own question about the future of Black people: "Free them, and make them politically and socially, our equals? My own feelings will not admit of this; and if mine would, we well know that those of the great mass of white people will not. Whether this feeling accords with justice and sound judgment, is not the sole question, if indeed, it is any part of it. A universal feeling, whether well or ill-founded, can not be safely disregarded." Perhaps Lincoln's concern that White people would never accept Black people as completely their equals was part of what led him before the Civil War to champion emancipation only if it were gradual, and to endorse separation of Blacks to a colony in Central America.[12]

LINCOLN'S CONSERVATISM

Lincoln, the architect and author of one of the most radical reforms in history, was not a radical reformer but a conventional, conservative, middle-of-the-road moderate. In an age of turmoil, he preached and practiced restraint. The content, method, and style of his rhetoric reflected a political posture that was essentially conservative.

Lincoln labeled himself a conservative. In his "Cooper Union Address" and a week later in a speech in New Haven, Connecticut, he criticized Southerners and Democrats, respectively, for considering themselves conservative, claiming Republicans were the true conservatives:

But you say you are conservative--eminently conservative--while we are revolutionary, destructive, or something of the sort. What is conservatism? Is it not adherence to the old and tried, against the new and untried? We stick to, contend for, the identical old policy on the point in controversy [slavery] which was adopted by our fathers who framed the Government under which we live; while you with one accord reject, and scout, and spit upon that old policy. . . . You have considerable variety of new propositions and plans, but you are unanimous in rejecting and denouncing the old policy of the fathers. . . . Not one of all your various plans can show a precedent or an advocate in the century within which our Government originated. Consider, then, whether your claim of conservatism for yourselves, and your charge of destructiveness against us, are based on the most clear and stable foundations.[13]

Lincoln defined conservatism as maintaining the status quo and adhering to policies that had historical precedent, especially to the beliefs of the Founding Fathers and the ideals of the Declaration of Independence. He devoted a great deal of discourse to defending existing laws and existing institutions and showing how his views on slavery were consistent with those of the Founding Fathers and with the ideals of the principal documents of the Fathers, especially the Declaration of Independence and the Constitution.

Arguments from definitions, first principles, axioms, maxims, and truths permeated Lincoln's speeches. Rhetorical theorist Richard Weaver claimed that Lincoln's preference for arguments from definition marked him as a true conservative. Arguments from definition, Weaver explained, consist of arguments from first principles, from that which is true in and of itself, from the nature of something. One of Weaver's examples was Lincoln's "First Inaugural Address," where Lincoln argued "from the nature of all government," declaring, "Perpetuity is implied, if not expressed, in the fundamental law of all national governments." Weaver claimed that "An index to a man's political philosophy is his characteristic way of thinking, inevitably expressed in the type of argument he prefers" and "Those who prefer the argument from definition, as Lincoln did, are conservatives in the legitimate sense of the word." Although I do not consider arguing from definition definitive proof that a speaker is conservative, I agree with Weaver that Lincoln did present himself as conservative and that his arguing frequently from definition is one proof for this conclusion.[14]

I disagree with Weaver's claim that Lincoln "was not a middle-of-the-roader." My disagreement stems from my belief that in addition to examining whether a speaker argued from first principles, it is important to consider what those principles were, how tenacious-ly the speaker adhered to them, and how consistently the speaker argued from them.

At least three principles spanned Lincoln's rhetoric: (1) that slavery must not be allowed to extend into new territories; (2) that each generation faced the task of striving toward the ideals embodied in the Declaration of Independence; and (3) that preserving the Union was of paramount importance. On all three issues Lincoln was uncompromising; he was willing to go to war rather than compromise even to the smallest degree any of these principles. In public speeches and private letters, he frequently defended his unyielding position on fundamental beliefs, arguing that "Important principles may, and must be inflexible."[15]

Lincoln's speeches and actions on all three principles showed remarkable consistency over more than a quarter of a century. In June 1860, *The Illinois State Journal* commented on the continuity of his record: "we think it difficult to find a political record running through twenty years, which has been so decided and yet so uniform and so consistent as that of Mr. Lincoln upon the great questions of the day. The same opinions which he held to and maintained when he was first elected to the Legislature, he has continued to hold to and defend up to the present time." The decisiveness and consistency of Lincoln's record make sense for a conservative speaker who argued from fundamental principles, which he held to resolutely.

Preventing the Extension of Slavery

In the mid-1850s and in the 1860 presidential election, preventing the extension of slavery was a moderate principle between the extremes of abolishing slavery and allowing slavery to spread. The chief adversary to this middle-ground principle was Douglas, whose concept of popular sovereignty would have allowed the people in each state and territory to decide for themselves whether to permit slavery within their borders. Lincoln argued that preventing the extension of slavery would lead to the ultimate extinction of the institution, but popular sovereignty would perpetuate slavery and allow the institution to grow. Further, he claimed that his moderate position provided a firm foundation for government because it was anchored in the principles of the Declaration of Independence and the Union, whereas Douglas' position lacked a secure foundation for government because it was void of any principle other than self-interest. In his "House Divided" Speech, Lincoln contrasted the Union as a stable structure with Douglas' position, which he professed was a structure built on sand: "Under the Dred Scott decision, 'squatter sovereignty' squatted out of existence, tumbled down like temporary scaffolding--like the mould at the foundry served through one blast and fell back into loose sand--helped to carry an election, and then was kicked to the winds." In his rhetorical analysis of this speech, Michael Leff compared this passage to a

section near the end of Jesus' "Sermon on the Mount," a speech
familiar to most listeners in the mid-nineteenth century. After
warning against false prophets, Jesus said:

Therefore whosoever heareth these sayings of mine, and doeth them, I liken
him unto a wise man, which built his house upon a rock:
And the rain descended, and the floods came, and the winds blew, and beat
upon that house; and it fell not: for it was founded upon a rock.
    And every one that heareth these sayings of mine, and doeth them
not, shall be likened unto a foolish man, which built his house upon the
sand:
    And the rain descended, and the floods came, and the winds blew,
and beat upon that house; and it fell: and great was the fall of it.

Leff applied Jesus' admonition to the charge Lincoln levied against
Douglas' position: "Where only a structure anchored in the rock of
principle can succeed, popular sovereignty rests on sand, wavering
and then falling against the winds of moral and political necessity.
It is an illusion, the expression of a vain hope for compromise where
no compromise is possible." At the end of his "Cooper Union
Address," Lincoln again argued, this time more directly, that no
middle ground existed on matters of right and wrong: "Let us be
diverted by none of those sophistical contrivances wherewith we are
so industriously plied and belabored--contrivances such as groping for
some middle ground between the right and the wrong, vain as the
search for a man who should be neither a living man nor a dead
man--such as a policy of 'don't care' on a question about which all
true men do care."[16]

Striving Toward the Ideals of the
Declaration of Independence

Lincoln dated the founding of the Union from the Declaration
of Independence and referred to it publicly more often than to any
other document, including the Constitution. In speech after speech
he talked about the ideals embodied in the Declaration, a document
he called "the immortal emblem of Humanity." In a speech at
Independence Hall in Philadelphia, he succinctly proclaimed the
relevance of the Declaration to his personal political philosophy: "I
have never had a feeling politically that did not spring from the
sentiments embodied in the Declaration of Independence . . . giving
liberty, not alone to the people of this country, but hope to the world
for all future time."[17]

    The ideals giving "hope to the world for all future time" were
frequent themes of Lincoln's discourse. Repeatedly he remarked that
this country had a divine mission to prove to the world that a
democratic nation founded on liberty and equality could endure and

that the fate of this country affected the fate of the world because the nation was, as he put it, "the last best hope of earth."[18]

According to historian Benjamin Thomas, Lincoln believed that each generation faced the task of fostering the mission and hope of this country:

A nearer realization of the American dream became the aim of Lincoln's life. Yet, he was no mere dreamer. He realized that the struggle of human freedom is eternal; he had no illusions of its ending in his lifetime or in ours. He understood that the antagonisms between man's better nature and his selfishness endure, and that it would be the fate of every generation of Americans to defend democracy from its enemies of greed, intolerance, and despotism.

Lincoln frequently spoke about how the Declaration of Independence provided the germ of liberty and equality and how each generation needed to help this germ grow for all people everywhere. He concluded his "Second Inaugural Address" with a plea for listeners "to do all which may achieve *and cherish* a just and lasting peace among ourselves and with all nations" (emphasis added). Achieving peace was not a conclusive state; rather, peace needed to be cherished, constantly and continually, for all people, everywhere on earth.[19]

In the next chapter I shall contend that in the "Gettysburg Address" Lincoln treated the Declaration of Independence's "self-evident truth" that "all men are created equal" as a proposition, a statement to be proved. In a speech at Springfield, Illinois, and again a year later in his final debate with Douglas, Lincoln explained that the authors of the Declaration of Independence "meant to set up a maxim for free society which should be familiar to all: constantly looked to, constantly labored for, and even though never perfectly attained, constantly approximated and thereby constantly spreading and deepening its influence and augmenting the happiness and value of life to all people, of all colors, everywhere." According to Weaver, "The true conservative is one who sees the universe as a paradigm of essences, of which the phenomenology of the world is a sort of continuing approximation." For Lincoln, the equality pronouncement of the Declaration of Independence was just this sort of "essence," toward which a "continuing approximation" would come only through each generation's accepting the task of moving slowly, steadily, and surely toward the ideals of the Declaration. Talking about the world in terms of continuous, gradual movement toward ideals provides further evidence of Lincoln's conservatism.[20]

Preserving the Union

For Lincoln, perpetuating the Union was a way to give meaning and force to the principles of preventing the extension of slavery and moving toward the ideals of the Declaration of Independence. He stated the principle of safeguarding the Union succinctly in a now-famous letter to *New York Tribune* editor Horace Greeley:

My paramount object in this struggle *is* to save the Union, and is *not* either to save or to destroy slavery. If I could save the Union without freeing *any* slave, I would do it, and if I could save the Union by freeing *all* the slaves I would do it; and if I could save it by freeing some and leaving others alone I would also do that. What I do about slavery, and the colored race, I do because I believe it helps to save the Union; and what I forbear, I forbear because I do *not* believe it would help save the Union.

Some historians have discounted these sentiments by pointing out that Lincoln wrote the letter after deciding to issue the Emancipation Proclamation; these historians have contended that Lincoln used the letter as a rhetorical strategy to prepare the public for emancipation. After deciding in favor of emancipation, all options could no longer be open, as the letter implied, but Lincoln's using the letter rhetorically does not necessarily negate the validity of his statement that his "paramount object" was "to save the Union." Lincoln clearly presented himself as an individual concerned with keeping the Union whole. Before the war he argued repeatedly for an undivided Union, and after the war he argued repeatedly for restoring the Union. His Preliminary Emancipation Proclamation began with an avowal that "hereafter, as heretofore, the war will be prosecuted for the object of practically restoring the constitutional relation between the United States and each of the states, and the people thereof." [21]

Historians have debated the question of whether Lincoln prized Union or liberty most, the former being a national idea, the latter a universal one. To me, Lincoln's rhetoric reveals the difficulty of choosing Union or liberty because for Lincoln Union and liberty were inexorably intertwined. On numerous occasions he argued that the best defense of liberty was equality, and the best defense of liberty and equality was an undivided Union. Repeatedly he maintained that preserving and restoring the Union were the only ways to protect and defend a democratic government founded on liberty and equality. [22]

Like preventing the extension of slavery, preserving the Union was a moderate principle between the extremes of secession and abolition. In discussing this middle-of-the-road position, Lincoln revealed how Union and liberty were inseparable. Secession obviously threatened the Union, but abolition also threatened the Union because Black people in the United States could not become free and equal if Southern states seceded. Hence, immediate or gradual emancipation required an undivided Union.

Other Indicators of Lincoln's Conservatism

In addition to arguing <u>from</u> definitions and principles, Lincoln frequently argued <u>about</u> definitions and principles. He frequently used the words "definition," "principle," and "in principle." His own copies of speeches and those made in shorthand by reporters often italicized these terms, suggesting that he emphasized the words while speaking. At times he seemed preoccupied with definitions, especially with those used by opponents. For example, in his "Message to Congress in Special Session," he said:

It might seem, at first thought, to be of little difference whether the present movement at the South be called "secession" or "revolution." The movers, however, well understand the difference. At the beginning, they knew they could never raise their treason to any respectable magnitude, by any name which implies *violation* of law. . . . Accordingly, they commenced by an insidious debauching of the public mind. They invented an ingenious sophism."[23]

In controversies Lincoln frequently identified fundamental principles that provided the clash. His process of reducing arguments to their "lowest terms" was apparently automatic. William Herndon explained that by nature Lincoln was causative, searching behind ideas to discover their origins and histories. As a lawyer, Herndon noted, Lincoln instinctively identified and scrutinized the root of an issue. In debate he focused on this root, conceding unessential points in order to carry the central ones. "Sometimes," Herndon observed, "he yielded nine points out of ten . . . but the tenth being a question of substance, he clung to with all his might. On the underlying principles of truth and justice his will was as firm as steel and as tenacious as iron." In his sixth debate with Douglas, Lincoln exemplified Herndon's point, explaining that the slavery issue "necessarily springs from the difference of opinion, and if we can learn exactly--can reduce to the lowest elements--what that difference of opinion is, we perhaps shall be better prepared for discussing the different systems of policy that we would propose in regard to that disturbing element. I suggest that the difference of opinion, reduced to its lowest terms. . . ."[24]

Even Lincoln's humor was based on locating the essence of a subject. In his analysis of Lincoln's humor, Charles E. Schutz claimed that "the analogical logic of storytelling is deeply conservative." Storytelling, Schutz explained, "proceeds from a concrete issue or problem, seeks its essence, and relates it to the tale of a similar problem that has been previously encountered, and from which an appropriate means for its resolution has been derived." Norman A. Graebner reached the same conclusion, although with different evidence: "Lincoln was innately conservative. Many of his stories illustrated the folly of attempting too much. 'Let men not promise what they ought not,' he once observed, 'lest they be called upon to perform what they cannot.'"[25]

Another indicator of Lincoln's conservative nature was the attitude toward change expressed in his rhetoric. He never presumed he would become the Great Emancipator, but he did suppose that slavery would end. Having "a patient confidence in the ultimate justice of the people" ("First Inaugural Address") and "faith that right makes might" ("Cooper Union Address"), he expressed the belief that the institution of slavery would die--slowly, somehow, someday, "in God's good time." His rhetoric revealed a man who saw a world that was not static but that was constantly changing, gradually. In his "Lyceum Address" he spoke of a *"living* history"; in his "Second Inaugural Address" he spoke of a *"living* God" (emphasis added). In his analysis of the Lincoln-Douglas Debates, rhetorical critic David Zarefsky noted that Douglas "took the past on its own terms . . . for him history was a source of documentary evidence" whereas Lincoln "viewed history as dynamic and projected forward into the future from motives uncovered through a reflective reading of the past. In this way, history has a narrative continuity; it is a source of stories rather than of documents."[26]

Several qualities of Lincoln's presidential speeches that I discussed in Chapter 2 contain earmarks of conservatism. For example, he frequently dealt with the history of a subject in connection with protecting, preserving, and perpetuating the past. He favored syllogistic reasoning with conclusions that followed naturally and automatically from premises. He usually organized his speeches according to time, tying past, present, and future together into a unified whole. Frequent Biblical references also connected listeners to enduring ideas. Balancing words, sounds, and structures gave a sense of balance, fairness, and moderation to what he said. His frequent use of passive voice expressed ideas precisely, absolutely, and with no qualification. This frequent use of the passive voice coupled with an almost complete lack of references to himself helped give his speeches perspective and transcendence. Weaver believed Lincoln's assuming this perspective and transcending the here and now were methods of definition that provided further evidence of Lincoln's conservatism.[27]

Finally, Lincoln presented himself as mild-mannered and cautious. He expressed an aversion to hasty action, recommending instead that people think calmly and deliberately. Examples of his advocating caution and patience are numerous. In his "Cooper Union Address" he counseled, "Let us do nothing through passion and ill temper," and in his "First Inaugural Address" he stated, "Nothing valuable can be lost by taking time." He urged that reforms be gradual and not move too far ahead of popular opinion. His proposals on how to deal with slavery illustrated his belief in gradual change:

His plan to colonize the Black people was a proposal to do so gradually, as was his plan for emancipation with compensation. When he spoke about these ideas, he emphasized that "I do not speak of emancipation *at once*, but of a *decision* at once to emancipate *gradually*" and "The change it contemplates would come gently as the dews of heaven, not rending or wrecking anything." Throughout most of his political life, Lincoln supported gradual, not immediate, emancipation; in his "Message to Congress" only six months before announcing his Preliminary Emancipation Proclamation, he explained that in his "judgment, gradual, and not sudden emancipation, is better for all." Even the Emancipation Proclamation, a military edict that freed slaves only in those states that had seceded from the Union, can be viewed as a cautious, conservative, and moderate measure.[28]

THE EMANCIPATION PROCLAMATIONS

Lincoln really issued two emancipation proclamations--a preliminary one on September 22, 1862, and the official one on January 1, 1863. In the preliminary proclamation, he endorsed emancipation with compensation to slave owners, gradual emancipation, and colonization. The hundred-day interval between the two documents gave people the opportunity to rejoin the Union and keep their slaves or to free them voluntarily while being financially compensated for their losses. Lincoln explained his deliberate timing: "After the commencement of hostilities I struggled nearly a year and a half to get along without touching the 'institution'; and when finally I conditionally determined to touch it, I gave a hundred days fair notice of my purpose, to all the States and people, within which time they could have turned it wholly aside, by simply becoming good citizens of the United States."[29]

Neither Emancipation Proclamation denounced slavery as a moral wrong or commended equality as a moral right. Both documents stressed emancipation as a military necessity whose practical objective was to suppress the war and restore the Union. As Lincoln explained, "the moment came when I felt that slavery must die that the nation might live!" He continued with an illustrative metaphor "of a man with a diseased limb, and his surgeon. So long as there is a chance of the patient's restoration, the surgeon is solemnly bound to try and save both life *and* limb; but when the crisis comes, and the limb must be sacrificed as the only chance of saving the life, no honest man will hesitate." At another point, in a letter to Albert G. Hodges, editor of the Frankfort, Kentucky *Commonwealth*, Lincoln recounted the events as follows:

I could not feel that, to the best of my ability, I had even tried to preserve the constitution, if, to save slavery, or any minor matter, I should permit the wreck of government, country, and Constitution all together. When, early in the war, Gen. Fremont attempted military emancipation, I forbade it, because I did not then think it an indispensable necessity. When a little later, Gen. Cameron, then Secretary of War, suggested the arming of the blacks, I objected, because I did not yet think it an indispensable necessity. When, still later, Gen. Hunter attempted military emancipation, I again forbade it, because I did not yet think the indispensable necessity had come. When, in March and May, and July 1862 I made earnest, and successive appeals to the border states to favor compensated emancipation, I believed the indispensable necessity for military emancipation, and arming the blacks would come, unless averted by that measure. They declined the proposition; and I was, in my best judgment, driven to the alternative of either surrendering the Union, and with it, the Constitution, or of laying strong hand upon the colored element. I chose the latter.

Declaring that he was "driven" to emancipating the slaves does not sound like the thought of a person who felt in full control of the situation. And, Lincoln did not profess to have orchestrated events. He continued, "In telling this tale I attempt no compliment to my own sagacity. I claim not to have controlled events, but confess plainly that events have controlled me." Lincoln concluded this letter, dated April 4, 1864, with a discussion that anticipated the thesis of his "Second Inaugural Address" a year later:

Now, at the end of three years struggle the nation's condition is not what either party, or any man devised, or expected. God alone can claim it. Whither it is tending seems plain. If God now wills the removal of a great wrong, and wills also that we of the North as well as you of the South, shall pay fairly for our complicity in that wrong, impartial history will find therein new cause to attest and revere the justice and goodness of God.[30]

THE "SECOND INAUGURAL ADDRESS"

Lincoln's apparent purpose in his "Second Inaugural Address" was to reunite the Union. This required justifying the conflict to a war-weary audience in a way that would make them not seek retribution. In the speech Lincoln argued that slavery "was somehow the cause of the war," but rather than blame Southerners for slavery, he contended that slavery was a national sin. The war was God's punishment to both North and South for the sin of slavery, and the war provided a way for both parties to become cleansed and purified in order to become whole again. Lincoln expressed similar sentiments in a "Proclamation Appointing a National Fast Day," March 30, 1863: "And, insomuch as we know that, by His divine law, nations like individuals are subjected to punishments and chastisements in this world, may we not justly fear that the awful calamity of civil war, which now desolates the land, may be but a punishment, inflicted upon us, for our presumptuous sins, to the needful end of our national reformation as a whole People?" He continued with the hope that "a day of national humiliation, fasting, and prayer" would be "answered with blessings, no less than the pardon of our national sins, and the restoration of our now divided and suffering Country, to its former happy condition of unity and peace."[31]

In the "Second Inaugural Address" Lincoln spoke about the war as a punishment for the national sin of slavery, but he absolved himself from having personal responsibility for slavery or the war. He frequently chose passive-voice verb forms and used a first-person singular pronoun only twice in the entire speech ("I" and "myself"). He went so far to avoid the active voice and personal constructions that his thoughts sometimes sounded awkward. Try, for example, to listen to the following:

At this second appearing to take the oath of the Presidential office

Now at the expiration of four years . . . little that is new could be presented.

With high hope for the future, no prediction in regard to it is ventured.

In addition to being awkward, avoidance of the active voice and of references to himself implied that Lincoln was a passive president being acted upon rather than being an active participant in the events of the past four years. He more directly fostered this impression by identifying himself with the party "devoted altogether to *saving* the Union without war." The religious connotation of "devoted" coupled with the absolute nature of "altogether" furthered the impression that he was a man with the best of intentions. He continued that "one party would *make* war rather than let the nation survive, and the other would *accept* war rather than let it perish." In his rendition Lincoln did not make war; he only accepted it, a clearly passive position. His only other choice would have been to let the nation die. He completed this passage by saying, "and the war came," suggesting that the war had a force of its own and came of its own volition. In her analysis of the "Second Inaugural Address," Amy Slagell made the following observation:

"And the war came" is reminiscent of the biblical account of creation in *Genesis* 1, where 29 of the 31 verses begin with "And." For an audience steeped in biblical thought this phrase may have implied that the war was as much a creation of God as were the heavens and the earth. In this way, the phrase foreshadows the rest of the speech, in which we discover that the war came as an instrument of God's judgment and as a tool for redemption.[32]

In addition to downplaying his ethos, Lincoln downplayed factionalism, presumably also to prepare listeners to accept God or destiny as responsible for the war. Whereas in his "First Inaugural Address" he frequently referred to Southerners as "Southerners," "you," and "they," in his "Second Inaugural Address" he conspicuously avoided mentioning Southerners directly or speaking about them in an accusatory way. Only twice in the address did he refer directly to the South: Early in the speech he said that slaves were "not distributed over the Union, but localized in the Southern part of it," referring to the South here in terms of place rather than in terms of its people or moral values; and later in the speech he claimed that God "gives to both North and South this terrible war," here uniting North and South. This last statement was also Lincoln's only mention in the speech of the North or Northerners. Instead of using language likely to divide Northerners and Southerners, Lincoln spent most of the speech uniting the two sides. In several statements the words "all," "both," "neither," "parties," and "each" included both Northerners and Southerners. Frequent use of parallel structures indirectly argued that both North and South possessed parallel problems. In addition to specific word choices and structures, Lincoln stressed the similarities of each side, especially the shared attitudes toward war and shared religious values:

All dreaded it; all sought to avoid it.

Both parties deprecated. . . .

Neither party expected for the war the magnitude or the duration, which it has already attained.

Neither anticipated that the *cause* of the conflict might cease with or even before the conflict itself should cease.

Each looked for an easier triumph and a result less fundamental and astounding.

Both read the same Bible and pray to the same God, and each invokes His aid against the other.

The prayers of both could not be answered--that of neither has been answered fully.

These statements totaled 101 words and constituted over 14 percent of the entire message. They clearly fostered the impression that neither side was responsible for the war; rather, the conflict had a life of its own, independent of the actions and wishes of the human beings involved.

Lincoln further united North and South by saying, "Let us judge not that we be not judged." His admonition came from Matthew 7:1, which advised: "Judge not, that ye be not judged." Adding "let us" and changing "ye" to the inclusive "we" were further indicators that Lincoln's counsel applied to both North and South. Slagell has offered two interpretations of this scriptural verse. First, she wrote that "the verse teaches that it is not right to judge another because each of us is guilty of sin. Matthew 7:4 expands this point figuratively: 'How wilt thou say to thy brother, Let me pull out the mote out of thine eye; and behold, a beam is in thine own eye?'" She continued, "Second, the injunction of Matthew 7:1 is often used in scripture to direct the reader's attention to the one true judge. In Romans 14:10, for example, Paul writes: 'But why dost thou judge thy brother? . . . for we shall all stand before the judgment seat of Christ?'" Both interpretations apply to Lincoln's "Second Inaugural Address." The first deals with what he was saying at that moment; the second anticipated his claim that the war was God's judgment for the offense of slavery.[33]

Indicators that God was the Ultimate Controller of events include fourteen direct references to God and several Biblical quotations and paraphrases, especially from the New Testament, which focuses on charity and forgiveness. In one, referring to Matthew 18:7, Lincoln directly assigned to God responsibility for the "offense" of slavery and for the war:

If we shall suppose that American Slavery is one of these offenses, which in the providence of God must needs come, but which having continued through His appointed time He now wills to remove, and that He gives to both North and South this terrible war as the woe due to those by whom the offense came, shall we discern therein any departure from those Divine attributes which the believers in a living God always ascribe to Him?

God was portrayed as the Supreme Controller: American slavery came "in the providence of God," it "continued through His appointed time," "He now wills to remove" slavery, and "He gives to both North and South this terrible war" as punishment for the sin of slavery.

If the war was a punishment for the national sin of slavery, listeners probably would wonder why "the cause of the conflict [slavery] might cease . . . before the conflict itself should cease." Lincoln anticipated this probable question. He claimed that "the Almighty has His own purposes," that God alone would decide for how much longer the war continued, and that "the judgments of the Lord are true and righteous altogether." Most of Lincoln's listeners, indoctrinated in Protestant theology and familiar with the Bible, could accept Lincoln's reasoning, especially his last statement, taken from Psalms 19:9, that "the judgments of the Lord are true and righteous altogether."

In his typical way, Lincoln had covered the past and present; his peroration concerned the future. Whereas he used primarily the passive voice to discuss the past and present, he used the active voice to discuss the future: "With malice toward none, with charity for all, with firmness in the right, as God gives us to see the right, let us strive on to finish the work we are in, to bind up the nation's wounds, to care for him who shall have borne the battle, and for his widow and his orphans; to do all which may achieve and cherish a just and lasting peace among ourselves and with all nations." His plea for reunion based on charity followed from his assigning responsibility for slavery and the war to God. The peroration set the tone for a policy of reconstruction that without malice would restore the Union, "bind up the nation's wounds," and "achieve and cherish a just and lasting peace."

CONCLUSIONS

Lincoln did not spend his political life planning and preparing to become the Great Emancipator. In antebellum America, racial equality was not even a major public issue. As Fehrenbacher has explained, "Only widespread emancipation could make it so, and until the outbreak of the Civil War, that contingency seemed extremely remote." Examining one of the "roads not taken" reveals how utterly unforeseeable emancipation was. In his "First Inaugural Address" (and elsewhere), Lincoln endorsed a proposed amendment to the Constitution that without the outbreak of war would have legalized slavery where it already existed. The amendment that "No amendment shall be made to the Constitution which will authorize or give to Congress the power to abolish or interfere within any state with the domestic institutions thereof, including that of persons held to labor or service by the laws of said state," had been passed by the Senate and House of Representatives and signed by President James Buchanan just before he left office. Had Southern states not seceded and war not ensued, this amendment would have become the thirteenth amendment, and slavery would have been preserved and protected where it already existed.

Although Lincoln did not portray himself as intending to become the Great Emancipator, and although he endorsed and even advocated plans other than immediate emancipation, he ultimately expressed pride over issuing the Emancipation Proclamation. He claimed that emancipation represented a moral victory for himself, the nation, and the world, a claim that was consistent with his personal abhorrence of slavery and with his concern that this country serve as a model for the world. He also recognized the importance of being the architect of this historical document, declaring, "If my name ever goes down into history, it will be for this act."[34]

Although he understood the historic significance of the Emancipation Proclamation, Lincoln denied controlling the events that led up to it. To claim responsibility for emancipation would have required him also to claim responsibility for a brutal, bloody, four-year war. I have seen no evidence in Lincoln's rhetoric showing that he felt responsible for the war or for emancipation. Instead, he presented himself as a passive president who accepted the war rather than let the Union die and who issued the Emancipation Proclamation to help the Union reunite. In numerous ways his rhetoric revealed a conservative politician who believed that change should, and would, come gradually.

Lincoln's moderation and middle-of-the-road principles helped him get elected to the presidency, where he was in an admirable position to sway public opinion and author a major reform. Whether major reforms are due more to the work of moderates or radicals, and whether slavery would have ended had someone else been president are perennial questions. It seems no question, however, that Lincoln's commitment to immediate emancipation evolved from supporting gradual emancipation to establishing universal freedom as a national principle.

The Lincoln Address Memorial is supposedly the only monument in this country memorializing a speech rather than a person.

6

Lincoln's Gettysburg Address: Immediate Failure and Lasting Success

The world will very little note nor long remember what we say here.

Lincoln in his "Gettysburg Address"

The Great American Poem.

Carl Sandburg's description of the "Gettysburg Address"

Almost all rhetorical and historical scholars today consider Lincoln's "Gettysburg Address" one of the greatest speeches in American history. Yet, most people who heard the address reacted to it with criticism or indifference. Press reaction to the speech varied greatly. Ronald F. Reid's examination of the responses of 260 newspapers revealed that a few praised Lincoln's remarks, several were critical, and still others made no comment. The newspapers devoted more space to Edward Everett's speech, the day's main oration, than to Lincoln's address. Reid's study showed that the political views of the newspaper editors were consistent with their evaluations of Lincoln's speech. In 1863, then, the "Gettysburg Address" was not considered a great speech by most people. Thus, we are faced with a speech that is hailed today as one of the greatest but that most people did not consider a great speech at the time of delivery.[1]

Neither rhetorical nor historical critics have offered in-depth analyses of the "Gettysburg Address" as a speech or thorough explanations for the speech's lack of immediate success. In his review of developments in American public address, Stephen Lucas wrote, "Indeed, our persistent neglect of major texts in the history of American oratory is nothing short of astonishing. How can it be that we are in our seventh decade as an academic discipline and have yet to produce a body of rich critical literature providing authoritative textual studies of such acknowledged masterpieces as . . . Abraham Lincoln's Gettysburg Address?"[2]

I think rhetorical and historical critics have failed to explain why the "Gettysburg Address" did not impress the audience in 1863 because they have evaluated the address by literary rather than by oratorical standards. In his book, *Lincoln at Gettysburg*, historian William Barton discussed this issue:

It is as literature, not oratory, that the Gettysburg Address is to be judged. The first critical judgments published concerning it were not from the pens of those who heard it, but from those whose knowledge was limited to its appearance in print. From the beginning, its judgments have been based on literary, not oratorical criteria. And it is as literature the world must continue to judge of it, for whatever impression it made on human ears that heard it at Gettysburg is now lost to us save as it reaches us through faint and not wholly consistent tradition.

I disagree with Barton's final point. Since the address was intended as a speech, it would be valuable to analyze it as a speech and compare this analysis to a literary analysis of the piece. Evaluating the "Gettysburg Address" by both oratorical and literary standards helps to reconcile the mediocre to negative evaluations of the speech in 1863 with the consistent praise of the speech today. Many of the factors that hurt the "Gettysburg Address" in the oral arena are precisely the factors that make the message a literary masterpiece.[3]

For an oratorical judgment of the "Gettysburg Address," we need to recreate the situation of which it was a part. The Battle of Gettysburg, which took place on July 1, 2, and 3 of 1863, seems an obvious place to begin. Many historians consider that battle the turning point of the Civil War. Here the Northern army defeated Lee's supposedly invincible force. Afterward, the Southern army was never again able to invade the North. In addition to being a significant military victory, the Battle of Gettysburg resulted in a more humane treatment of the dead. Soldiers who died in the Revolutionary War, the War of 1812, the Mexican War, and the first two years of the Civil War were buried where they fell. Now, in 1863, the national cemetery at Gettysburg would replace the shallow and soon forgotten graves of past wars.

Under the direction of lawyer David Wills, several state governors planned a ceremony for the dedication and consecration of the cemetery. They asked Edward Everett, perhaps the most prominent speaker of the day, to deliver the main address. Wills' letter of invitation to Lincoln indicates what the people in charge expected from Lincoln's "Gettysburg Address":

I am authorized by the Governors of the different States to invite you to be present, and participate in these ceremonies, which will doubtless be very imposing and solemnly impressive. It is the desire that, after the Oration, You as Chief Executive of the Nation formally set apart these grounds to their Sacred use by a few appropriate remarks.

It will be a source of great gratification to the many widows and orphans that have been made almost friendless by the Great Battle here, to have you here personally and it will kindle anew in the breasts of the Comrades of these brave dead, who are now in the tented field or nobly meeting the foe in the front, a confidence that they who sleep in death on the Battle Field are not forgotten by those in highest authority: and they will feel that, should their fate be the same their remains will not be uncared for.

We hope you will be able to be present to perform this solemn act to the Soldier dead on this Battle Field.

The letter seems to ask Lincoln to console the widows and orphans by stamping the dedication ceremony with his office. The formal presidential <u>act</u> of speaking would constitute a small but important part of the ceremonial observance. The letter did not ask for a piece of persuasion but for a *pro forma* utterance to add the prestige of the office of the presidency to the dedication ceremony.[4]

In addition to the people who planned the ceremony, who judged whether Lincoln's address fulfilled expectations? In 1863 Lincoln spoke to at least three audiences at Gettysburg--people at the dedication ceremony who heard his words, people in the country at large who read his short message in the few newspapers that carried it, and people who had someone read the newspaper account to them. Unlike Everett, Lincoln did not send a copy of his message to the press before speaking at Gettysburg. Thus, even the newspaper accounts of the speech were influenced by the reporters' aural perceptions of it. In the Introduction we saw that newspaper readers usually do not read a piece over and over again and that the illiteracy rate was relatively high in the 1860s. Thus, in 1863 there were many people who read the speech only once and many people who could not read the speech at all. Those who had someone read the newspaper copy of the speech to them were, like the people at Gettysburg, a <u>listening</u> audience.[5]

The immediate audience at the dedication ceremony constituted the largest crowd ever assembled in Gettysburg. Distinguished guests included eight governors, seven generals, the secretary of state, and, of course, Everett and Lincoln. The crowd was composed primarily of people who had traveled some distance. Most listeners had lost close relatives and/or friends in the Battle of Gettysburg or in other battles of the Civil War. By memorializing the dead, they hoped to ease their own anxieties. It was, therefore, a mournful crowd. One reporter described the audience in the following way:

Most of them were fathers, mothers, brothers and sisters, who had come from distant parts to look at and weep over the remains of their fallen kindred, or to gather up the honored relics and bear them back to the burial grounds of their native homes--in relating what they had suffered and endured, and what part their loved ones had borne in the memorable days of July.

The people probably came to Gettysburg, then, expecting to hear Everett and their president pay tribute to their loved ones.[6]

SAVORING THE MULTIPLE MEANINGS AND SUBTLE NUANCES OF THE "GETTYSBURG ADDRESS"

Applying the critical tools of both literature and rhetoric allows us to appreciate the "Gettysburg Address" more fully and to understand more clearly why so little attention was paid to the speech until it appeared in print. I begin with a literary analysis, examining Lincoln's words phrase-by-phrase to reveal their multiple meanings and subtle nuances.

Fourscore and seven years ago,

In the "Gettysburg Address" Lincoln never directly mentioned the Bible, but the speech was full of Biblical allusions. The first example was his choosing to begin the speech with "Fourscore and seven years ago" rather than the more common eighty-seven years ago. Abram was "fourscore and six years old" when his first son was born, and Joshua said, "Lo, I *am* this day fourscore and five years old." Anna was said to be "a widow of about fourscore and four years," and the ninetieth psalm reads, "The days of our years *are* threescore years and ten; and if by reason of strength *they be* fourscore years." By noting that the nation was already over the Biblical age of fourscore years, Lincoln thus emphasized the importance of continuity and of the struggle for freedom. The indirect reference to the Bible implied also that God had watched over the nation and that there was a holy duty to preserve something that had been divinely fostered for so many years.[7]

our fathers

The phrase "our fathers" was one of the few attempts Lincoln made in the "Gettysburg Address" to identify with his immediate audience. By linking the Founding Fathers with the audience, Lincoln tried to make the tradition of freedom seem like a family tradition. Just as a son needed to preserve his family's honor, so citizens needed to preserve their country's honor. Daniel Webster, an orator whom Lincoln greatly admired, had popularized the phrase "our fathers" in a series of epideictic speeches. The phrase, therefore, was well-known in 1863. "Our fathers" is also used repeatedly in the Bible. Lincoln may have chosen these words as a way to link the audience's historical forefathers with their Biblical ones. One Biblical father with whom God had a covenant was Abraham, Lincoln's own name, and in 1863 Lincoln was already being portrayed by some as Father Abraham.

brought forth upon this continent

Lincoln continued to allude to the Bible. In English, the Bible frequently uses the words "brought forth." These words are used also in other religious contexts such as in the story of Passover, a story about the Israelites being "brought forth" from human bondage and their exodus to freedom.

The phrase, "brought forth upon this continent," could also imply that freedom dwelt in the land waiting for people to bring it forth. Robert Frost's poem, "The Gift Outright," presented almost 100 years later at John F. Kennedy's inauguration, embodies this idea. The poem begins, "The land was ours before we were the land's." That freedom was not an alien quality brought over from Europe but was inherent in the American continent is a theme that was often expounded even in the nineteenth century.

a new nation

The word "new" in this phrase had at least two connotations. First, "new" meant brand new, connoting that the nation was not a product of the Old World but was rather an original concept. "New" also had a chronological meaning. At the time of the "Gettysburg Address," the nation was still young. Both senses of "new" underscored the importance of the nation.

conceived in liberty

With the word "conceived," Lincoln began a birth-death theme that he carried throughout the speech, and he again used a word found frequently in the Bible. With his first mention of "liberty," he capped his idea that freedom was not a quality brought over from Europe but was indigenous to this country. So interpreted, the sacrifices that soldiers made for their country could be seen as part of growth and devotion to an ideal.

and dedicated to the proposition

In its context this phrase also referred indirectly to the Bible and had birth-growth connotations. The Bible repeatedly tells of people dedicating a child to the service of God as a token of appreciation for the child's birth. Consider the following Biblical passage from 1 Samuel 1:27-28 concerning the birth of Samuel: "For this child I prayed; and the LORD hath granted me my petition which I asked of him: Therefore also I have lent him to the LORD; as long as he liveth he shall be lent to the LORD." In return for God's giving Hannah a son, she dedicated the son to the Lord's service. In return for God letting "our fathers" have a child (i.e., the nation), they dedicated the nation to the ideals of freedom and equality. Throughout this first sentence, Lincoln raised the task of preserving freedom to a holy mission.

The use of the geometric term "proposition" has puzzled many historians. The Declaration of Independence called the principle that "all men are created equal" a "self-evident truth." A self-evident truth is necessarily true; a "proposition" is a statement to be debated, a statement requiring proof. Roy Basler explained:

Thus democracy, as an active, living thing, meant to Lincoln the verification or the proving of the proposition to which its very existence was in the beginning dedicated. Eighty-seven years had gone into the proving, the Civil War had come at a critical stage in the argument, the Union armies at Gettysburg had won an immediate victory, and the affirmation that 'all men are created equal' was still a live rather than a dead issue.[8]

that all men are created equal

The inclusion of the Jeffersonian ideal of the equality of men was the culmination of freedom's being born and dedicated. By inserting this phrase, Lincoln indicated that the historic and divine mission of the nation was to create and preserve equality for all men, an issue that had become critical in the Civil War. With this phrase, Lincoln rendered the issue of equality the reason for the nation's very existence. He encouraged recall of the words of the Declaration of Independence and suggested that these words were the covenant that the Union was fighting the war to preserve and that was now being memorialized at Gettysburg.

The above twenty-nine words comprised the first section of Lincoln's address. The thoughts were not new ones for Lincoln. Compare the beginning of the "Gettysburg Address" to part of an impromptu speech that Lincoln gave on July 7 to a group who came to the White House to congratulate him on the victories of Gettysburg and Vicksburg: "How long ago is it?--eighty odd years--since on the Fourth of July for the first time in the history of the world a nation by its representatives, assembled and declared as a self-evident truth that all men are created equal." In the "Gettysburg Address," Lincoln apparently sought to give special dignity to the rhetorical question and answer of his July 7 speech. "How long ago is it?--eighty odd years" became "fourscore and seven years ago." He changed "a nation by its representatives" to the simpler "our fathers." "Assembled and declared" became "conceived in liberty and dedicated." He replaced "a self-evident truth" with the word "proposition," strongly suggesting that he deliberately chose the geometric term. Both speeches included the equality pronouncement, "that all men are created equal," indicating that Lincoln viewed the preservation of equality as the mission of the nation and the war.[9]

Now we are engaged in a great civil war,

Lincoln moved forward in time from "fourscore and seven years ago" to "now." He shifted his focus from the Revolution, where everyone fought on the same side, to the Civil War, where half of the people were trying to break the covenant to preserve freedom and equality. Lincoln subtly contrasted the ideals of the Founding Fathers with issues of the current war. The effect was to make Southerners appear unchristian and alien because they were breaking their covenant with God and with history.

testing whether that nation--or any nation,

According to Lincoln, the war had implications that reached beyond this continent. It was a test to see whether the divinely inspired principles of freedom and equality could survive on a corrupted earth. The term "testing" also suggested references in the Bible to people's faith being tested, including the faith of Abraham.

so conceived and so dedicated--

This phrase referred back to the first paragraph of the Address, but it did so with great economy. "So conceived and so dedicated" stood for "conceived in liberty and dedicated to the proposition that all men are created equal." With the terms "conceived" and "dedicated," Lincoln reiterated his themes of divinely inspired birth and growth.

can long endure.

"Endure" is another Biblical term; "continue" would not have given the same spiritual quality to Lincoln's point. Even the word order--putting "can long" before "endure"--sustained a Biblical tone, since this word order is frequently found in familiar English translations of the Bible. Consider how spiritually diminished Lincoln's point would have been had he said, "whether that nation--or any nation . . . can last very long." With the phrase, "can long endure," Lincoln alluded to the threats now facing the country's original values.

We are met on a great battle-field of that war.

This was a simple factual statement. Lincoln repeated the word "great," having used it first in "great civil war." The repetition emphasized the magnitude of the struggle for freedom and equality.

We are met to dedicate a portion of it

This was the third time in the speech that Lincoln used the Biblical term "dedicate." The people were gathered at Gettysburg "to dedicate a portion of" the battlefield, presumably placing the fallen in God's hands in the hope that He would have mercy on the souls that came before Him.

as a final resting-place

Lincoln chose the dignified and dignifying euphemism "final resting-place" rather than the harsher and more common "cemetery" or "graveyard." The term "resting place" also appears in the Bible.

of those who have given their lives

With these words Lincoln established that those who died had sacrificed. The phrase implied martyrdom because they died defending God's plan of freedom and equality.

that that nation might live.

Lincoln renewed the birth-death motif. He suggested that the nation would perish if not all free. Lincoln here reiterated the point he had made in his "House Divided Speech" in 1858: "I believe this government cannot endure permanently half slave and half free." In the context of the "Gettysburg Address," the words suggested that America was not <u>ordained</u> to be part slave.

It is altogether fitting and proper that we should do this.

"This," of course, referred to dedicating the cemetery. With "fitting" and "proper" Lincoln was endorsing his own position by asking his listeners to respond affirmatively to all he had just said, and he was preparing the audience for what was to come. "Fitting" and "proper" are formal terms, implying that dedicating the cemetery was a formal act of duty and responsibility.

But, in a larger sense,

Lincoln began the third and final section of his speech by trying to focus attention on what he was about to say. "In a larger sense" suggested that what Lincoln had said so far was peripheral. What he was about to say would be more important.

we cannot dedicate, we cannot consecrate,
we cannot hallow, this ground.

In the next few sentences, Lincoln developed the futility of anything "we" could do at the cemetery when compared with what the soldiers had already done. Lincoln explained his point in the next sentence.

The brave men, living and dead, who struggled here,
have consecrated it, far above our power
to add or to detract.

According to Lincoln, the listeners at Gettysburg could not truly dedicate the ground because the soldiers had already dedicated it. Lincoln felt it would be presumptuous for them to believe their words could be a higher form of dedication than the soldiers' actions. By including both "living and dead" when referring to "brave men," Lincoln made it clear that dying was not a prerequisite for bravery.

The world will very little note nor long remember
what we say here; but it can never forget
what they did here.

With these words, Lincoln reiterated that the important point was not the present ceremony at Gettysburg but what happened on the battlefield. From this sentence, we gain an insight into Lincoln's view of his "Gettysburg Address." He did not consider his speech of major importance. The humility he stressed throughout makes sense in light of his insistence on minimizing what "we" can do. From Lincoln's point of view, a flowery or bombastic speech would have been a desecration of the divine, historic ideals for which "the living and dead" fought. If one reads this speech without remembering Everett's oration--as most of us do--Lincoln's perspective on the occasion seems especially noble.

It is for us, the living, rather,

to be dedicated, here,

Lincoln unexpectedly shifted the focus from the dead to the living, from eulogizing to exhorting. The clue to this shift in emphasis is the word "rather." Rather than dedicating the ground as a cemetery, which he had already suggested was futile, Lincoln asked that "we" dedicate "ourselves."

to the unfinished work that they have
thus far so nobly carried on.

With "unfinished work" Lincoln referred to finishing the war. In November 1863 the war was far from over. Lincoln urged the audience not to rest on past laurels. There was still much to do, and Lincoln took the opportunity to urge all citizens to recommit themselves to those tasks. The dead had shown the living the way. The living now needed to follow this path.

It is rather for us to be here dedicated
to the great task remaining before us;

Through repetition, Lincoln reiterated the responsibility of the living. He had described dedicating the cemetery as "fitting" and "proper," but he now implied this was true only in a limited sense. The dedication of the living was more important. It was a responsibility, an obligation, a "task." Lincoln was telling his listeners that they owed it to history, ideals, God, and the "living and dead" soldiers to complete the "tasks" to which their national history committed them.

that from these honored dead we take
increased devotion to that cause for which
they here gave the last full measure of devotion;

This phrase appears to be Lincoln's description of the "task" awaiting the listeners. He returned to a religious tone by speaking of "devotion," a word implying commitment and often associated with faith and religion.

that we here highly resolve that these dead
shall not have died in vain;

Lincoln gave the crowd the responsibility for redeeming the sacrifices that the dead had made. He continued to emphasize the responsibility of the living; they had to prevent the dead from dying in vain. Lincoln's thought and wording here may have been influenced by Mason L. Weems' book on George Washington. Concerning the graves of soldiers of the Revolutionary War, Washington had said, "perhaps some good angel has whispered, that their fall was not in vain."[10]

that the nation shall, under God,

None of the drafts of the Gettysburg Address in Lincoln's handwriting included the phrase "under God." We will never know, of course, what prompted Lincoln to include this phrase while speaking. Perhaps it was something in the solemnity of the occasion. Perhaps it was because Everett had mentioned God several times in his speech. Perhaps it was because William Seward, his secretary of state, had suggested he include it. Whatever the cause, by asserting that God was concerned with what was happening at Gettysburg, Lincoln implied that preserving freedom and equality had ramifications beyond the earthly, mortal level.

have a new birth of freedom,

Reports indicate that it was at this point that Lincoln reached his climax. He returned to the birth-death theme with "new birth" referring to resurrection and to the triumph of life over death. The implication was that as the resurrection of Christ gave people a second chance, so the resurrection or "new birth" of the nation would give America a second chance for a more perfect freedom. So viewed, the listeners' dedication could be thought of as a purification ritual.

and that government of the people,
by the people, for the people,

Ask elementary school children what a democracy is and probably they will answer, "A government of the people, by the people, and for the people." For many years historians have tried to discover Lincoln's source for this phrase. Two sources in particular were speeches that Lincoln was known to admire. Daniel Webster's reply to Robert Hayne on January 26, 1830, defined the American government as "the people's government, made for the people, made by the people, and answerable to the people." Closer to Lincoln's definition was that of Theodore Parker, an abolitionist preacher. In three different speeches (May 29, 1850; May 31, 1854; and July 4, 1858), Parker had defined democracy as a "government over all the people, by all the people, for all the people.[11]

Another question that has interested historians is whether Lincoln emphasized the prepositions or the word "people." It seems more likely to me that Lincoln emphasized "people" because "people" compliments the birth-death theme he had developed. Throughout the speech Lincoln had stressed the similarities between the inception and struggle in a person's life and the inception and struggle in the life of this country. Emphasizing the word "people" also would underscore the equality of the people in and under our government. Lincoln probably wanted to close his address with this kind of emphasis because it was the people who would win the war, not the government.[12]

shall not perish from the earth.

Lincoln concluded his speech with another Biblical term; the word "perish" appears frequently in the Bible. For example, Proverbs 29:18 reads, "Where *there is* no vision, the people perish," and the Book of Job (18:17) talks about the extinction of one where even "his remembrance shall perish from the earth." "Perish" is also a dying term; with its use Lincoln established a sense of urgency, suggesting that doom would occur if a united government did not survive. Lincoln saw the nation as an experiment. If she failed, then the destiny of democracy failed. Many people shared this belief in the middle of the nineteenth century. Lincoln's use of "not" in "shall not perish" was consistent with his usual optimistic tone and with his frequent way of ending his speeches by looking toward the future.

ANALYZING THE "GETTYSBURG ADDRESS" WITHOUT CAREFUL READING

If the "Gettysburg Address" is analyzed as rhetoric in a particular situation, it is obvious that listeners could not possibly have perceived all of the nuances and implications revealed by a literary criticism. This is especially true because of the brevity of the speech. Lincoln's address was estimated to have taken less than three minutes. When he sat down, many thought he had just begun. The photographer was still adjusting his tripod. Many listeners were probably still orienting themselves as well.

The brevity of the speech resulted in at least four problems. First, if listeners coughed, yawned, or were otherwise distracted, they missed a large portion of the speech. Most people in the audience were seeing the president in person for the first time and, thus, were probably just looking at him rather than listening to him as the speech began. Lincoln finished before many could absorb the substance of what he said.

Second, today we consider brevity in speaking a virtue, but a three-minute, formal, public speech was all but unheard of in 1863. Although Lincoln was asked to deliver only "a few appropriate remarks," the definition of "few" in 1863 differed from the definition of "few" today. Even the benediction given at the end of the dedication ceremony lasted longer than Lincoln's speech. Some listeners may have felt insulted by this gross deviation from the norm of public oratory.

Third, Lincoln's composition placed a heavy burden on each word. In literature, it is a virtue for an author to create subtle nuances of meaning, but to do this in a speech creates a risk of people not understanding. In the first paragraph, for example, Lincoln made his only concrete mention of what the people were to dedicate themselves to--"dedicated to the proposition that all men are created equal." Never in the Address did he directly connect this clause to the Civil War or to the "task" he wanted the living to carry on. In the second paragraph, it was up to the audience to tie the phrase, "so conceived and so dedicated," to the earlier statement of the nation's ideals.

Fourth, the burden each word had to carry was especially problematic in a speech where many phrases carried multiple meanings and some were unusual. Most listeners, for example, would not immediately know that "fourscore and seven years ago" meant eighty-seven years ago, and if they stopped to do the calculation, they would miss a large part of the speech. Even listeners steeped in the Bible, who were familiar with the terminology, probably had to multiply and add.

Considering that the audience had less than three minutes to orient themselves to speaker, speech, and situation and that virtually every phrase was freighted with multiple meanings, it becomes easy to understand why so many listeners did not even hear the whole speech, let alone grasp more than a few of its many subtleties. Even those who read Lincoln's speech in 1863 probably read it quickly and only once. Hence, they, too, probably did not grasp the multiple meanings and subtle nuances of all the phrases. Leisurely readers can savor the beauty of Lincoln's conceptions and phrasings because, as they read the text, they can pause and review whenever they want to think out meanings, nuances, and inter-connections. Lincoln's listeners had no such leisure, and it is unlikely that those who read the speech at the time read it leisurely. The brevity of the speech, I contend, is one of the major reasons why in 1863 most people did not consider the "Gettysburg Address" a great speech.

What interpretation did the listeners at Gettysburg probably apply to Lincoln's brief address? At best they might have summed up his meaning as follows: A great sacrifice was made at Gettysburg; an even greater task remains to be done by us. Given the complex nature and unusual brevity of the speech, it is by no means clear that even this simplistic interpretation was worked out by a majority of those present.

Were the people at Gettysburg who understood Lincoln's message willing to accept the new responsibility that Lincoln gave them? One way to determine an audience's probable response is to examine their expectations. People's expectations are determined by the norms of particular situations. What was the norm in the Gettysburg situation? The dedication ceremony called for epideictic or ceremonial speech, a eulogy praising the people in whose honor the ceremony was being held.

In his analysis of the "Gettysburg Address," Harold Zyskind maintained that the speech was deliberative rather than epideictic in nature. I agree with Zyskind's conclusion. In only three statements in the "Gettysburg Address" did Lincoln directly praise the dead, and even in these statements he spoke also of the living:

The brave men, living and dead, who struggled here, have consecrated it, far above our power to add or to detract.

that from these honored dead we take increased devotion; to that cause for which they here gave the last full measure of devotion;

that we here highly resolve that these dead shall not have died in vain. (emphasis added)

Lincoln, then, created a role for the living; he gave the crowd a responsibility, a "task." The entire burden of redeeming the sacrifices of the dead was placed into their hands.[13]

Certainly an appeal to carry on in the spirit and honor of the departed is standard in a eulogistic setting; this sort of appeal is one of the commonplaces of epideictic speaking. What is not common, however, is to spend almost no time directly praising the dead before making the appeal to carry on. Listeners who came to Gettysburg to mourn the loss of their loved ones probably wanted their president to spend a lot of time telling them how their relatives and friends had died as heroes. Although Zyskind considered the deliberative nature of the "Gettysburg Address" a positive quality, I maintain that Lincoln's failure to spend more time praising the dead and his request that listeners act to accomplish a "task" may have been perceived as inappropriate by the mournful crowd at Gettysburg and may offer another explanation for why most people did not consider the speech a great speech in 1863.

Lincoln was certainly capable of praising the dead in eloquent language. Interestingly, his famous "Letter to Mrs. Bixby" did just that:

Madam,--I have been shown in the files of the War Department a statement of the Adjutant General of Massachusetts, that you are the mother of five sons who have died gloriously on the field of battle.

I feel how weak and fruitless must be any words of mine which should attempt to beguile you from the grief of a loss so overwhelming. But I cannot refrain from tendering to you the consolation that may be found in the thanks of the Republic they died to save.

I pray that our Heavenly Father may assuage the anguish of your bereavement, and leave you only the cherished memory of the loved and lost, and the solemn pride that must be yours, to have laid so costly a sacrifice upon the altar of Freedom. Yours, very sincerely and respectfully. A. Lincoln.[14]

Another problem with Lincoln's focus on the living was that his call for action was ambiguous. He failed to specify what the action should be. He told listeners to dedicate themselves but not how to dedicate themselves or to what. Here, we see once again how oral excellence differs from literary excellence. Readers today can pause to reflect on the many possible kinds of dedication: sustaining the war effort, supporting the goals of freedom and equality, honoring the union as an institution, believing in and fighting for the historic national experiment. The listeners at Gettysburg had no time for even so limited a review of possibilities. If they perceived Lincoln to be calling for continued support of the war, most of those present were already doing that. For the most part, the audience was already patriotic and doing what they could to save the Union. What new action was Lincoln calling for from them? There were surely few Confederates, draft dodgers, or war profiteers in the audience. Who, then, was to change and in what ways? If Lincoln wanted more than reaffirmation of existing goals and efforts, he failed to provide the audience with the necessary specifications and motivations. As readers today, we can admire the lofty tone of Lincoln's charge to people other than ourselves. The listeners at Gettysburg, however, heard themselves charged with an ambiguous "task."

Lincoln's abstractness as to the course of action forced listeners to get themselves emotionally involved in the speech. Compare the end of the "Gettysburg Address" with the end of Pericles' Funeral Oration, also given to honor those who had died in war:

those of you who are of the right age must bear up and take comfort in the thought of having more children. In your own homes these new children will prevent you from brooding over those who are no more. . . . As for those of you who are now too old to have children. . . . As for those of you here who are sons or brothers of the dead. . . . Perhaps I should say a word or two on the duties of women to those among you who are widowed.

By specifically telling "those of the right age," "the old," "the sons and brothers of the dead," and "the widows" what to do, Pericles established a personal bond with all sectors of his audience. In its entirety, this section of Pericles' speech included several sensory images. Thus, when listeners finished hearing the "Funeral Speech," they knew exactly what to do, and they could picture their home lives. When listeners finished hearing the "Gettysburg Address," they did not know exactly what to do, and Lincoln did little to help them see their lives. His speech called for action, but the action was unspecified. The audience needed to fill in the details and get themselves emotionally involved.[15]

One could argue that although the occasion did not debar Lincoln from directly involving his audience in specific action-oriented thoughts, as Pericles had done, Lincoln's assignment was not to give a complete eulogy. That was Everett's job. Perhaps Lincoln purposefully viewed his speech as a peroration to the day's ceremonies. In Chapter 2 we saw that Lincoln usually concluded his speeches with an abstract call for action. On November 19, Lincoln knew he would follow Everett, and, as he might have predicted, Everett had described the Battle of Gettysburg as the greatest battle ever fought and had compared the dead to the greatest heroes in history. In some ways, the "Gettysburg Address" was a fitting peroration to Everett's speech. As a speech of its own, however, it was incomplete for many listeners at Gettysburg. Although they had just heard their loved ones praised by a well-known speaker and statesman, they probably wanted to hear additional praise from their president, and they probably wanted their president's speech to be intimate and involving rather than abstract and contemplative.

In his speech Lincoln seemed to make an almost deliberate attempt to detach himself from the audience. He avoided even the most commonplace means of encouraging personal identification. He never used the pronoun "I." In fact, at no point did he refer directly to himself or even to the office he represented. Throughout his short message, he used the editorial "we" rather than a term suggesting active collaboration.

It is true that Lincoln was personal with the audience to a small degree. As a citizen, he, like his listeners, shared inherited ideals and duties. This was clearly implied by his use of "we" and "us" as he discussed dedication. But the linking of speaker and listener was institutional and historic rather than a personalized sharing; all were members of a generalized citizenry. Such features may explain why Gerald P. Mohrmann and August W. Staub wrote that in the "Gettysburg Address" *ethos* "is gained for the product rather than for the maker." Lincoln asserted God's sanctification of the causes of freedom, equality, and union, but he did little in the Address to build directly his own ethical appeal either as citizen or as president. If identification occurred in this rhetorical situation, it had to occur by listeners identifying themselves with Lincoln; Lincoln attempted to identify himself with them only in indirect ways.[16]

Lincoln's style also forced listeners to work hard. When only the words are considered, his style appears simple and clear. Of the 265 words in the address, 194 have only one syllable, 50 have two syllables, and only 21 have three or more syllables. Over four-fifths of the words are of Anglo-Saxon derivation. When Lincoln put the simple words together, however, his style became more difficult. The average length of his thought units was 18.9 words. Half of the thought units were especially long, having 29, 24, 25, 21, 22, 24, and 23 words, respectively. Only one of the fourteen thought units was simple; the others were compound or complex--another potential cause of difficulty. The speech contained eight unclear referents. Readers can reread a sentence to clarify a referent, but listeners have only one chance to understand a message. According to Robert Gunning's Fog Index of readability for written discourse, the "Gettysburg Address" crossed the "danger line." No popular magazine is as difficult. According to Rudolf Flesch's scale, another yardstick of "reading ease" (emphasis mine), the "Gettysburg Address" was fairly easy when one considers the number of syllables per 100 words but fairly difficult when one considers the average number of words per sentence. Similarly, Flesch's "human-interest" scale for writing shows the "Gettysburg Address" to be interesting when one considers the percent of personal words but dull when one considers the percent of personal sentences. Certainly discourse that is in some ways difficult and dull to read is even more difficult and dull to hear. Lincoln used few sensory images in the "Gettysburg Address," further lessening the speech's interest. Intellectual or non-sensory images and abstract concepts dominated, making it difficult for listeners to become emotionally involved. In short, listeners at Gettysburg received an ideological defense of freedom. Lincoln did not talk with his listeners; rather, he spoke to them in a meditative and prayer-like manner.[17]

The "Gettysburg Address" had a prayer-like quality also because, as I have said, it was full of Biblical language. Lincoln never directly mentioned the Bible, but so many of the words he used in the speech are used so often in the Bible that listeners likely sensed a Biblical tone. The following list indicates the number of times some of the words in the "Gettysburg Address" appear in the Bible: "fourscore" (35 times), "seven" (285), "fathers" (520), "nation" (488), "conceived" (40), "dedicated" (24), "created" (45), "equal" (20), "great" (863), "war" (237), "endure" (43), "portion" (89), "consecrate" (14), "hallow" (16), "ground" (169), "power" (284), "world" (271), "remember" (123), "in vain" (39), "God" (4,210), "people" (2,030), "perish" (100), and "earth" (831). The religious tone of the "Gettysburg Address" was hardly to be missed, but that fact further depersonalized the speech.[18]

Several features in the "Gettysburg Address" consisted of arrangements of three, suggesting the religious symbolism of three. As we have seen, one of the central themes of the speech was birth, death, and rebirth, which corresponded to another set of three images--nation, battlefield, and earth. These formulations also corresponded to the past, present, and future structure of the speech. Our forefathers brought forth this nation (birth, nation, past). Their sons died on the battlefield that this nation might live (death, battlefield, present). The living needed to dedicate themselves to make sure this government did not perish from the earth (rebirth, earth, future). The "Gettysburg Address" also contained two major tricolons (series consisting of three parts): "of the people, by the people, for the people" and "we cannot dedicate, we cannot consecrate, we cannot hallow."

In addition to grammatical parallelisms, the "Gettysburg Address" frequently used antithesis. One interesting example occurred in the middle of the speech (I use "+" to denote the importance of the dead's dedication and "-" to denote the unimportance of our dedication):

- But, in a larger sense, we cannot dedicate, we cannot consecrate, we cannot hallow, this ground.

+ The brave men, living and dead, who struggled here, have consecrated it, far above our power to add or to detract.

- The world will very little note nor long remember what we say here;

+ but it can never forget what they did here.

In this last sentence, Lincoln also juxtaposed "little" and "long," "note" and "remember," "remember" and "forget," "we" and "they," and "say" and "did."

The balanced sentence structures of the "Gettysburg Address" gave it an almost compelling rhythm. The cadence of the short speech was remarkably similar to that of the Lord's Prayer and other parts of the King James Version of the Bible. From this fact, listeners were likely to have sensed a prayer-like quality in the speech, although probably they were unaware of the pervasiveness of Biblical terminology, arrangements of three, balanced sentence structures, and religious cadences. Still, even sensing the religious tone of the speech could have made it unclear to the listening audience whether they had just heard a eulogy, a prayer, or a sermon.

Lincoln was reported to have read his speech, maintaining little eye contact with the audience. He was said to have spoken in a high-pitched voice with a Kentucky accent, and to have used few hand gestures. If these reports are true, Lincoln's delivery represented another reason why the "Gettysburg Address" received an unenthusiastic reception at the time it was given.

CONCLUSION

Lincoln's "Gettysburg Address" was not a great <u>speech</u>. The situation called for memorializing the dead and sanctifying a battlefield as a national cemetery. Lincoln chose, instead, to devote most of his speech to giving an ambiguous responsibility to the living. In building the context for this responsibility, he densely packed his words and phrases with historic and Biblical allusions and implications. Listeners had less than three minutes to make sense of the complex nuances and economical phrasings; Lincoln tried to say too much, too deeply, in the short time his immediate audience had to think with him. His content and style placed conceptual burdens on listeners and newspaper readers that they could not fully bear at that time and in their situations. Apparently the "Gettysburg Address" could achieve admiration and fame only after it could be seen by the eye, to be pondered and savored. Where nuances are complex and phrasings are economical, listeners and newspaper readers are burdened, but leisurely readers are not. People who read the "Gettysburg Address" today also do not have expectations associated with mourning the loss of loved ones nor are they living through a Civil War.

Paradoxically, had Lincoln made the types of changes that might have made the "Gettysburg Address" a great speech in its occasion, he probably would not have composed a great piece of literature. Many of the factors that make the "Gettysburg Address" a lasting success are precisely the factors that made it an immediate failure. The depth and density of thoughts, the precision in choice of words, the seeming simplicity touched by archaic usages, and the brevity all combine to form a unified piece of English composition. The power of each word, which was harmful in the oral arena, is advantageous when the "Gettysburg Address" is examined as a piece of literature.

The "Gettysburg Address" is a lasting success also because much of the situation that led to the dedication ceremony at Gettysburg still exists. We are no longer involved in a Civil War, but we still have civil rights problems. We are still emancipating the Blacks, and we are still "testing whether any nation, so conceived and so dedicated--can long endure." Today, the situation no longer calls for memorializing the dead, and the audience includes everyone, not just the mournful crowd at the dedication ceremony or the people who read (or were read) the Address at the time. Unfortunately, the changes that might have made the "Gettysburg Address" a successful speech would probably have made it unsuccessful literature.

Conclusion: The Making of a Legend

Let him have the marble monument, along with the well-assured and more enduring one in the hearts of those who love liberty, unselfishly, for all men.

Lincoln about a monument in memory of Representative Owen Lovejoy

Cast forth thy act, thy word, into the ever-living, ever-working universe; it is a reed-grain that cannot die; unnoticed to-day, it will be found flourishing as a banyan grove, perhaps, alas, as a hemlock forest, after a thousand years.

Thomas Carlyle, Scottish essayist, historian, and sage

When Lincoln died, a process began transforming him as an orator from a public man speaking to listeners at particular times to a God-like man addressing humankind for all time to come. Collectively, the critical chapters of this book help to explain this making of the Lincoln legend: Lincoln became immortalized as a speaker, in part, because of his ideas on speaking, the characteristics of his speeches, his use of humor, his "First Inaugural Address," his coming to be considered the Great Emancipator, and his "Gettysburg Address." His rhetoric has endured also because he identified with the "common man," adapted skillfully to varying audiences, spoke about timeless topics, and transformed the nation's suffering and guilt from the Civil War to an act of purification and a doctrine of forgiveness.[1]

I wish to close this section of the book by paraphrasing what Richard M. Ohmann said in the beginning of his study of George Bernard Shaw: Of course not everything in Lincoln's rhetoric is admirable, and in the course of these critical chapters I have said some ungracious things about his style and his development of ideas.

The Lincoln Memorial, with the "Gettysburg Address" and the "Second Inaugural Address" engraved on the sides, epitomized the legendary man and his speaking.

I think it nevertheless is evident how highly I regard him, but let me preclude any doubt by saying here that in my estimation Lincoln is one of the greatest American orators and an exceedingly inspirational speaker to study. "Listen" to Lincoln's speeches yourself and form your own opinions.[2]

II

LINCOLN SPEAKS OUT: TEXTS OF SELECTED SPEECHES

"Lyceum Address"

Springfield, Illinois, January 27, 1838

As a subject for the remarks of the evening, *the perpetuation of our political institutions*, is selected.

In the great journal of things happening under the sun, we, the American People, find our account running, under date of the nineteenth century of the Christian era.--We find ourselves in the peaceful possession, of the fairest portion of the earth, as regards extent of territory, fertility of soil, and salubrity of climate. We find ourselves under the government of a system of political institutions, conducing more essentially to the ends of civil and religious liberty, than any of which the history of former times tells us. We, when mounting the stage of existence, found ourselves the legal inheritors of these fundamental blessings. We toiled not in the acquirement or establishment of them--they are a legacy bequeathed us, by a *once* hardy, brave, and patriotic, but *now* lamented and departed race of ancestors. Their's was the task (and nobly they performed it) to possess themselves, and through themselves, us, of this goodly land; and to uprear upon its hills and its valleys, a political edifice of liberty and equal rights; 'tis ours only, to transmit these, the former, unprofaned by the foot of an invader; the latter, undecayed by the lapse of time, and untorn by usurpation--to the latest generation that fate shall permit the world to know. This task of gratitude to our fathers, justice to ourselves, duty to posterity, and love for our species in general, all imperatively require us faithfully to perform.

How, then, shall we perform it?--At what point shall we expect the approach of danger? By what means shall we fortify against it?--Shall we expect some transatlantic military giant, to step the Ocean, and crush us at a blow? Never!--All the armies of Europe,

Asia and Africa combined, with all the treasure of the earth (our own excepted) in their military chest; with a Buonaparte for a commander, could not by force, take a drink from the Ohio, or make a track on the Blue Ridge, in a trial of a thousand years.

At what point then is the approach of danger to be expected? I answer, if it ever reach us, it must spring up amongst us. It cannot come from abroad. If destruction be our lot, we must ourselves be its author and finisher. As a nation of freemen, we must live through all time, or die by suicide.

I hope I am over wary; but if I am not, there is, even now, something of ill-omen amongst us. I mean the increasing disregard for law which pervades the country; the growing disposition to substitute the wild and furious passions, in lieu of the sober judgement of Courts; and the worse than savage mobs, for the executive ministers of justice. This disposition is awfully fearful in any community; and that it now exists in ours, though grating to our feelings to admit, it would be a violation of truth, and an insult to our intelligence, to deny. Accounts of outrages committed by mobs, form the every-day news of the times. They have pervaded the country, from New England to Louisiana;--they are neither peculiar to the eternal snows of the former, nor the burning suns of the latter;--they are not the creature of climate--neither are they confined to the slave-holding, or the non-slave-holding States. Alike, they spring up among the pleasure hunting masters of Southern slaves, and the order loving citizens of the land of steady habits.--Whatever, then, their cause may be, it is common to the whole country.

It would be tedious, as well as useless, to recount the horrors of all of them. Those happening in the State of Mississippi, and at St. Louis, are, perhaps, the most dangerous in example, and revolting to humanity. In the Mississippi case, they first commenced by hanging the regular gamblers; a set of men, certainly not following for a livelihood, a very useful, or very honest occupation; but one which, so far from being forbidden by the laws, was actually licensed by an act of the Legislature, passed but a single year before. Next, negroes, suspected of conspiring to raise an insurrection, were caught up and hanged in all parts of the State: then, white men, supposed to be leagued with the negroes; and finally, strangers, from neighboring States, going thither on business, were, in many instances, subjected to the same fate. Thus went on this process of hanging, from gamblers to negroes, from negroes to white citizens, and from these to strangers; till, dead men were seen literally dangling from the boughs of trees upon every road side; and in numbers almost sufficient, to rival the native Spanish moss of the country, as a drapery of the forest.

Turn, then, to that horror-striking scene at St. Louis. A single victim was only sacrificed there. His story is very short; and is, perhaps, the most highly tragic, of any thing of its length, that has ever been witnessed in real life. A mulatto man, by the name of McIntosh, was seized in the street, dragged to the suburbs of the city, chained to a tree, and actually burned to death; and all within a single hour from the time he had been a freeman, attending to his own business, and at peace with the world.

Such are the effects of mob law; and such are the scenes, becoming more and more frequent in this land so lately famed for love of law and order; and the stories of which, have even now grown too familiar, to attract any thing more, than an idle remark.

But you are, perhaps, ready to ask, "What has this to do with the perpetuation of our political institutions?" I answer, it has much to do with it. Its direct consequences are, comparatively speaking, but a small evil; and much of its danger consists, in the proneness of our minds, to regard its direct, as its only consequences. Abstractly considered, the hanging of the gamblers at Vicksburg, was of but little consequence. They constitute a portion of population, that is worse than useless in any community; and their death, if no pernicious example be set by it, is never matter of reasonable regret with any one. If they were annually swept, from the stage of existence, by the plague or small pox, honest men would, perhaps, be much profited, by the operation.--Similar too, is the correct reasoning, in regard to the burning of the negro at St. Louis. He had forfeited his life, by the perpetration of an outrageous murder, upon one of the most worthy and respectable citizens of the city; and had he not died as he did, he must have died by the sentence of the law, in a very short time afterwards. As to him alone, it was as well the way it was, as it could otherwise have been.--But the example in either case, was fearful.--When men take it in their heads to day, to hang gamblers, or burn murderers, they should recollect, that, in the confusion usually attending such transactions, they will be as likely to hang or burn some one, who is neither a gambler nor a murderer as one who is; and that, acting upon the example they set, the mob of to-morrow, may, and probably will, hang or burn some of them, by the very same mistake. And not only so; the innocent, those who have ever set their faces against violations of law in every shape, alike with the guilty, fall victims to the ravages of mob law; and thus it goes on, step by step, till all the walls erected for the defence of the persons and property of individuals, are trodden down, and disregarded. But all this even, is not the full extent of the evil.--By such examples, by instances of the perpetrators of such acts going unpunished, the lawless in spirit, are encouraged to become lawless in practice; and having been used to no restraint, but dread of punishment, they thus become, absolutely unrestrained.--Having ever regarded Government as their deadliest bane, they make a jubilee of the suspension of its operations; and pray for nothing so much, as its total annihilation. While, on the other hand, good men, men who love tranquility, who desire to abide by the laws, and enjoy their benefits, who would gladly spill their blood in the defence of their country; seeing their property destroyed; their families insulted, and their lives endangered; their persons injured; and seeing nothing in prospect that forebodes a change for the better; become tired of, and disgusted with, a Government that offers them no protection; and are not much averse to a change in which they imagine they have nothing to lose. Thus, then, by the operation of this mobocratic spirit, which all must admit, is now abroad in the land, the strongest balwark of any Government, and particularly of those constituted like ours, may effectually be broken down and destroyed--I mean the *attachment* of the People. Whenever this effect shall be produced among us; whenever the vicious portion of population shall be permitted to gather in bands of hundreds and thousands, and burn churches, ravage and rob provision stores, throw printing presses into rivers, shoot editors, and hang and burn obnoxious persons at pleasure, and with impunity; depend on it, this Government cannot last. By such things, the feelings of the best citizens will become more or less alienated from it; and thus it will be left without friends, or with too few, and those few too weak, to make their friendship effectual. At such a time and under such circumstances, men of sufficient talent and ambition will not be wanting to seize the opportunity, strike the blow, and overturn that fair fabric, which for the last half century, has been the fondest hope, of the lovers of freedom, throughout the world.

I know the American People are *much* attached to their Government;--I know they would suffer *much* for its sake;--I know they would endure evils long and patiently, before they would ever think of exchanging it for another. Yet, notwithstanding all this, if the laws be continually despised and disregarded, if their rights to be secure in their persons and property, are held by no better tenure than the caprice of a mob, the alienation of their affections from the Government is the natural consequence; and to that, sooner or later, it must come.

Here then, is one point at which danger may be expected.

The question recurs "how shall we fortify against it?" The answer is simple. Let every American, every lover of liberty, every well wisher to his posterity, swear by the blood of the Revolution, never to violate in the least particular, the laws of the country; and never to tolerate their violation by others. As the patriots of seventy-six did to the support of the Declaration of Independence, so to the support of the Constitution and Laws, let every American pledge his life, his property, and his sacred honor;--let every man remember that to violate the law, is to trample on the blood of his father, and to tear the character of his own, and his children's liberty.

Let reverence for the laws, be breathed by every American mother, to the lisping babe, that prattles on her lap--let it be taught in schools, in seminaries, and in colleges;--let it be written in Primmers, spelling books, and in Almanacs;--let it be preached from the pulpit, proclaimed in legislative halls, and enforced in courts of justice. And, in short, let it become the *political religion* of the nation; and let the old and the young, the rich and the poor, the grave and the gay, of all sexes and tongues, and colors and conditions, sacrifice unceasingly upon its altars.

While ever a state of feeling, such as this, shall universally, or even, very generally prevail throughout the nation, vain will be every effort, and fruitless every attempt, to subvert our national freedom.

When I so pressingly urge a strict observance of all the laws, let me not be understood as saying there are no bad laws, nor that grievances may not arise, for the redress of which, no legal provisions have been made.--I mean to say no such thing. But I do mean to say, that, although bad laws, if they exist, should be repealed as soon as possible, still while they continue in force, for the sake of example, they should be religiously observed. So also in unprovided cases. If such arise, let proper legal provisions be made for them with the least possible delay; but, till then, let them if not too intolerable, be borne with.

There is no grievance that is a fit object of redress by mob law. In any case that arises, as for instance, the promulgation of abolitionism, one of two positions is necessarily true; that is, the thing is right within itself, and therefore deserves the protection of all law and all good citizens; or, it is wrong, and therefore proper to be prohibited by legal enactments; and in neither case, is the interposition of mob law, either necessary, justifiable, or excusable.

But, it may be asked, why suppose danger to our political institutions? Have we not preserved them for more than fifty years? And why may we not for fifty times as long?

We hope there is *no sufficient* reason. We hope all dangers may be overcome; but to conclude that no danger may ever arise, would itself be extremely dangerous. There are now, and will hereafter be, many causes, dangerous in their tendency, which have not existed heretofore; and which are not too insignificant to merit attention. That our government should have been maintained in its original form from its establishment until now, is not much to be wondered at. It had many props to support it through that period, which now are decayed, and crumbled away. Through that period, it was felt by all, to be an undecided experiment; now, it is understood to be a successful one. Then, all that sought celebrity and fame, and distinction, expected to find them in the success of that experiment. Their *all* was staked upon it:--their destiny was *inseparably* linked with it. Their ambition aspired to display before an admiring world, a practical demonstration of the truth of a proposition, which had hitherto been considered, at best no better, than problematical; namely, *the capability of a people to govern themselves.* If they succeeded, they were to be immortalized: their names were to be transferred to counties and cities, and rivers and mountains; and to be revered and sung, and toasted through all time. If they failed, they were to be called knaves and fools, and fanatics for a fleeting hour; then to sink and be forgotten. They succeeded. The experiment is successful; and thousands have won their deathless names in making it so. But the game is caught; and I believe it is true, that with the catching, end the pleasures of the chase. This field of glory is harvested, and the crop is already appropriated. But new reapers will arise, and *they*, too, will seek a field. It is to deny, what the history of the world tells us is true, to suppose that men of ambition and talents will not continue to spring up amongst us. And, when they do, they will as naturally seek the gratification of their ruling passion, as others have so done before them. The question then, is, can that gratification be found in supporting and maintaining an edifice that has been erected by others? Most certainly it cannot. Many great and good men sufficiently qualified for any task they should undertake, may ever be found, whose ambition would aspire to nothing beyond a seat in Congress, a gubernatorial or a presidential chair; *but such belong not to the family of the lion, or the tribe of the eagle.* What! think you these places would satisfy an Alexander, a Caesar, or a Napoleon?--Never! Towering genius disdains a beaten path. It seeks regions hitherto unexplored.--It sees *no distinction* in adding story to story, upon the monuments of fame, erected to the memory of others. It *denies* that it is glory enough to serve under any chief. It *scorns* to tread in the footsteps of *any* predecessor, however illustrious. It thirsts and burns for distinction; and, if possible, it will have it, whether at the expense of emancipating slaves, or enslaving freemen. Is it unreasonable then to expect, that some man possessed of the loftiest genius, coupled with ambition sufficient to push it to its utmost stretch, will at some time, spring up among us? And when such a one does, it will require the people to be united with each other, attached to the government and laws, and generally intelligent, to successfully frustrate his designs.

Distinction will be his paramount object; and although he would as willingly, perhaps more so, acquire it by doing good as harm; yet, that opportunity being past, and nothing left to be done in the way of building up, he would set boldly to the task of pulling down.

Here then, is a probable case, highly dangerous, and such a one as could not have well existed heretofore.

Another reason which *once was*; but which, to the same extent, is *now no more*, has done much in maintaining our institutions thus far. I mean the powerful influence which the interesting scenes of the revolution had upon the *passions* of the people as distinguished from their judgment. By this influence, the jealousy, envy, and avarice, incident to our nature, and so common to a state of peace, prosperity, and conscious strength, were, for the time, in a great measure smothered and rendered inactive; while the deep rooted principles of *hate*, and the powerful motive of *revenge*, instead of being turned against each other, were directed exclusively against the British nation. And thus, from the force of circumstances, the basest principles of our nature, were either made to lie dormant, or to become the active agents in the advancement of the noblest of cause--that of establishing and maintaining civil and religious liberty.

But this state of feeling *must fade, is fading, has faded*, with the circumstances that produced it.

I do not mean to say, that the scenes of the revolution *are now* or *ever will be* entirely forgotten; but that like every thing else, they must fade upon the memory of the world, and grow more and more dim by the lapse of time. In history, we hope, they will be read of, and recounted, so long as the bible shall be read;--but even granting that they will, their influence *cannot be* what it heretofore has been. Even then, they *cannot be* so universally known, nor so vividly felt, as they were by the generation just gone to rest. At the close of that struggle, nearly every adult male had been a participator in some of its scenes. The consequence was, that of those scenes, in the form of a husband, a father, a son or a brother, a *living history was* to be found in every family--a history bearing the indubitable testimonies of its own authenticity, in the limbs mangled, in the scars of wounds received, in the midst of the very scenes related--a history, too, that could be read and understood alike by all, the wise and the ignorant, the learned and the unlearned.--But *those* histories are gone. They *can* be read no more forever. They *were* a fortress of strength; but, what invading foemen could *never do*, the silent artillery of time *has done*; the levelling of its walls. They are gone.--They *were* a forest of giant oaks; but the all resistless hurricane has swept over them, and left only, here and there, a lonely trunk, despoiled of its verdure, shorn of its foliage; unshading and unshaded, to murmur in a few more gentle breezes, and to combat with its mutilated limbs, a few more ruder storms, then to sink, and be no more.

They *were* the pillars of the temple of liberty; and now, that they have crumbled away, that temple must fall, unless we, their descendants, supply their places with other pillars, hewn from the solid quarry of sober reason. Passion has helped us; but can do so no more. It will in future be our enemy. Reason, cold, calculating, unimpassioned reason, must furnish all the materials for our future support and defence.--Let those materials be moulded into *general intelligence, sound morality* and, in particular, *a reverence for the constitution and laws*; and, that we improved to the last; that we remained free to the last; that we revered his name to the last; that, during his long sleep, we permitted no hostile foot to pass over or desecrate his resting place; shall be that which to learn the last trump shall awaken our Washington.

Upon these let the proud fabric of freedom rest, as the rock of its basis; and as truly as has been said of the only greater institution, *"the gates of hell shall not prevail against it."*

"Address Before the Washington Temperance Society"

Springfield, Illinois, February 22, 1842

Although the Temperance cause has been in progress for near twenty years, it is apparent to all, that it is, *just now*, being crowned with a degree of success, hitherto unparalleled.

The list of its friends is daily swelled by the additions of fifties, of hundreds, and of thousands. The cause itself seems suddenly transformed from a cold abstract theory, to a living, breathing, active, and powerful chieftain, going forth "conquering and to conquer." The citadels of his great adversary are daily being stormed and dismantled; his temples and his altars, where the rites of his idolatrous worship have long been performed, and where human sacrifices have long been wont to be made, are daily desecrated and deserted. The trump of the conqueror's fame is sounding from hill to hill, from sea to sea, and from land to land, and calling millions to his standard at a blast.

For this new and splendid success, we heartily rejoice. That that success is so much greater *now* than *heretofore*, is doubtless owing to rational causes; and if we would have it to continue, we shall do well to enquire what those causes are. The warfare heretofore waged against the demon of Intemperance, has, some how or other, been erroneous. Either the champions engaged, or the tactics they adopted, have not been the most proper. These champions for the most part, have been Preachers, Lawyers, and hired agents.--Between these and the mass of mankind, there is a want of *approachability*, if the term be admissible, partially at least, fatal to their success. They are supposed to have no sympathy of feeling or interest, with those very persons whom it is their object to convince and persuade.

And again, it is so easy and so common to ascribe motives to men of these classes, other than those they profess to act upon. The *preacher*, it is said, advocates temperance because he is a fanatic, and desires a union of Church and State; the *lawyer*, from his pride and vanity of hearing himself speak; and the *hired* agent, for his salary. But when one, who has long been known as a victim of intemperance, bursts the fetters that have bound him, and appears before his neighbors "clothed, and in his right mind," a redeemed specimen of long last humanity, and stands up with tears of joy trembling in eyes, to tell of the miseries *once* endured, *now* to be endured no more forever; of his once naked and starving children, now clad and fed comfortably; of a wife, long weighed down with woe, weeping, and a broken heart, now restored to health, happiness, and renewed affection; and how easily it all is done, once it is resolved to be done; however simple his language, there is a logic, and an eloquence in it, that few, with human feelings, can resist. They cannot say that *he* desires a union of church and state, for he is not a church member; they can not say *he* is vain of hearing himself speak, for his whole demeanor shows, he would gladly avoid speaking at all; they cannot say *he* speaks for pay for he receives none, and asks for none. Nor can his sincerity in any way be doubted; or his sympathy for those he would persuade to immitate his example, be denied.

In my judgment, it is to the battles of this new class of champions that our late success is greatly, perhaps chiefly, owing.-- But, had the old school champions themselves, been of the most wise selecting, was their *system* of tactics, the most judicious? It seems to me, it was not. Too much denunciation against dram sellers and dram-drinkers was indulged in. This, I think, was both impolitic and unjust. It was *impolitic*, because, it is not much in the nature of man to be driven to any thing; still less to be driven about that which is exclusively his own business; and least of all, where such driving is to be submitted to, at the expense of pecuniary interest, or burning appetite. When the dram-seller and drinker, were incessantly told, not in the accents of entreaty and persuasion, diffidently addressed by erring man to an erring brother; but in the thundering tones of anathema and denunciation, with which the lordly Judge often groups together all the crimes of the felon's life, and thrusts them in his face just ere he passes sentence of death upon him, that *they* were the authors of all the vice and misery and crime in the land; that *they* were the manufacturers and material of all the thieves and robbers and murderers that infested the earth; that *their* houses were the workshops of the devil; and that *their* persons should be shunned by all the good and virtuous, as moral pestilences--I say, when they were told all this, and in this way, it is not wonderful that they were slow, *very slow*, to acknowledge the truth of such denunciations, and to join the ranks of their denouncers, in a hue and cry against themselves.

To have expected them to do otherwise than as they did--to have expected them not to meet denunciation with denunciation, crimination with crimination, and anathema with anathema, was to expect a reversal of human nature, which is God's decree, and never can be reversed. When the conduct of men is designed to be influenced, *pesuasion*, kind, unassuming persuasion, should ever be adopted. It is an old and a true maxim, that "a drop of honey catches more flies than a gallon of gall." --So with men. If you would win a man to your cause, *first* convince him that you are his sincere friend. Therein is a drop of honey that catches his heart, which, say what he will, is the great high road to his reason, and which, when once gained, you will find but little trouble in convincing his judgment of the justice of your cause, if indeed that cause really be a just one. On the contrary, assume to dictate to his judgment, or to command his action, or to mark him as one to be shunned and despised, and he will retreat within himself, close all the avenues to his head and his heart; and tho' your cause be naked truth itself, transformed to the heaviest lance, harder than steel, and sharper than steel can be made, and tho' you throw it with more than Herculean force and precision, you shall no more be able to pierce him, than to penetrate the hard shell of a tortoise with a rye straw.

Such is man, and so *must* he be understood by those who would lead him, even to his own best interest.

On this point, the Washingtonians greatly excel the temperance advocates of former times. Those whom *they* desire to convince and persuade, are their old friends and companions. They know they are not demons, nor even the worst of men. *They* know that generally, they are kind, generous and charitable, even beyond the example of their more staid and sober neighbors. *They* are practical philanthropists; and *they* glow with a generous and brotherly zeal, that mere theorizers are incapable of feeling.--Benevolence and charity possess *their* hearts entirely; and out of the abundance of their hearts, their tongues give utterance. "Love through all their actions run, and all their words are mild." In this spirit they speak and act, and in the same, they are heard and regarded. And when such is the temper of the advocate, and such of the audience, no good cause can be unsuccessful.

But I have said that denunciations against dram-sellers and dram-drinkers, are *unjust* as well as impolitic. Let us see.

I have not enquired at what period of time the use of intoxicating drinks commenced; nor is it important to know. It is sufficient that to all of us who now inhabit the world, the practice of drinking them, is just as old as the world itself,--that is, we have seen the one, just as long as we have seen the other. When all such of us, as have now reached the years of maturity, first opened our eyes upon the stage of existence, we found intoxicating liquor, recognized by every body, used by every body, and repudiated by nobody. It commonly entered into the first draught of the infant, and the last draught of the dying man. From the side-board of the parson, down to the ragged pocket of the houseless loafer, it was constantly found. Physicians prescribed it in this, that, and the other disease. Government provided it for its soldiers and sailors; and to have a rolling or raising, a husking or hoe-down, any where without it, was *positively insufferable.*

So too, it was every where a respectable article of manufacture and of merchandize. The making of it was regarded as an honorable livelihood; and he who could make most, was the most enterprising and respectable. Large and small manufactories of it were every where erected, in which all the earthly goods of their owners were invested. Wagons drew it from town to town--boats bore it from clime to clime, and the winds wafted it from nation to nation; and merchants bought and sold it, by wholesale and by retail, with precisely the same feelings, on the part of seller, buyer, and by-stander, as are felt at the selling and buying of flour, beef, bacon, or any other of the real necessaries of life. Universal public opinion not only tolerated, but recognized and adopted its use.

It is true, that even *then*, it was known and acknowledged, that many were greatly injured by it; but none seemed to think the injury arose from the *use* of a *bad thing*, but from the *abuse* of a *very good thing*.--The victims to it were pitied, and compassionated, just as now are, the heirs of consumptions, and other hereditary diseases. Their failing was treated as a *misfortune*, and not as a *crime*, or even as a *disgrace.*

If, then, what I have been saying be true, is it wonderful, that *some* should think and act *now*, as *all* thought and acted *twenty years* ago? And is it *just* to assail, contemn, or despise them, for doing so! The universal *sense* of mankind, on any subject, is an argument, or at least an *influence* not easily overcome. The success of the argument in favor of the existence of an over-ruling Providence, mainly depends upon that sense; and men ought not, in justice, to be denounced for yielding to it, in any case, or for giving it up slowly, *especially*, where they are backed by interest, fixed habits, or burning appetites.

Another error, as it seems to me, into which the old reformers fell, was, the position that all habitual drunkards were utterly incorrigible, and therefore, must be turned adrift, and damned without remedy, in order that the grace of temperance might abound to the temperate *then*, and to all mankind some hundred years *thereafter*.--There is in this something so repugnant to humanity, so uncharitable, so cold-blooded and feelingless, that it never did, not ever can enlist the enthusiasm of a popular cause. We could not love the man who taught it--we could not hear him with patience. The heart could not throw open its portals to it. The generous man could not adopt it. It could not mix with his blood. It looked so fiendishly selfish, so like throwing fathers and brothers overboard, to lighten the boat for our security--that the noble minded shrank from the manifest meanness of the thing.

And besides this, the benefits of a reformation to be effected by such a system, were too remote in point of time, to warmly engage many in its behalf. Few can be induced to labor exclusively for posterity; and none will do it enthusiastically. Posterity has done nothing for us; and theorise on it as we may, practically we shall do very little for it, unless we are made to think, we are, at the same time, doing something for ourselves. What an ignorance of human nature does it exhibit, to ask or expect a whole community to rise up and labor for the *temporal* happiness of *others* after *themselves* shall be consigned to the dust, a majority of which community take no pains whatever to secure their own eternal welfare, at a no greater distant day? Great distance, in either time or space, has wonderful power to lull and render quiescent the human mind. Pleasures to be enjoyed, or pains to be endured, *after* we shall be dead and gone, are but little regarded, even in our *own* cases, and much less in the cases of others.

Still, in addition to this, there is something so ludicrous in *promises* of good, or *threats* of evil, a great way off, as to render the whole subject with which they are connected, easily turned into ridicule. "Better lay down that spade you're stealing, Paddy,--if you don't you'll pay for it at the day of judgment." "By the powers, if ye'll credit me so long, I'll take another, jist."

By the Washingtonians, this system of consigning the habitual drunkard to hopeless ruin, is repudiated. *They* adopt a more enlarged philanthrophy. *They* go for present as well as future good. *They* labor for all *now* living, as well as all *hereafter* to live.--*They* teach *hope* to all--*despair* to none. As applying to *their* cause, *they* deny the doctrine of unpardonable sin. As in Christianity it is taught, so in this *they* teach, that

"While the lamp holds out to burn,
The vilest sinner may return."

And, what is matter of the most profound gratulation, they, by experiment upon experiment, and example upon example, prove the maxim to be no less true in the one case than in the other. On every hand we behold those, who but yesterday, were the chief of sinners, now the chief apostles of the cause. Drunken devils are cast out by ones, by sevens, and by legions; and their unfortunate victims, like the poor possessed, who was redeemed from his long and lonely wanderings in the tombs, are publishing to the ends of the earth, how great things have been done for them.

To these *new champions*, and this *new* system of tactics, our late success is mainly owing; and to *them* we must chiefly look for the final consummation. The ball is now rolling gloriously on, and none are so able as *they* to increase its speed, and its bulk--to add to its momentum, and its magnitude.-- Even though unlearned in letters, for this task, none others are so well educated. To fit them for this work, they have been taught in the true school. *They* have been in *that* gulf, from which they would teach others the means of escape. *They* have passed that prison wall, which others have long declared impassable; and who that has not, shall dare to weigh opinions with *them*, as to the mode of passing.

But if it be true, as I have insisted, that those who have suffered by intemperance *personally*, and have reformed, are the most powerful and efficient instruments to push the reformation to ultimate success, it does not follow, that those who have not suffered, have no part left them to perform. Whether or not the world would be vastly benefitted by a total and final banishment from it of all intoxicating drinks, seems to me not *now* to be an open question. Three-fourths of mankind confess the affirmative with their *tongues*, and, I believe, all the rest acknowledge it in their *hearts*.

Ought *any*, then, to refuse their aid in doing what the good of the *whole* demands?--Shall he, who cannot do *much*, be, for that reason, excused if he do *nothing*? "But," says one, "what good can I do by signing the pledge? I never drink even without signing." This question has already been asked and answered more than millions of times. Let it be answered once more. For the man to suddenly, or in any other way, to break off from the use of drams, who has indulged in them for a long course of years, and until his appetite for them has become ten or a hundred fold stronger, and more craving, than any natural appetite can be, requires a most powerful moral effort. In such an undertaking, he needs every moral support and influence, that can possibly be brought to his aid, and thrown around him. And not only so; but every moral prop, should be taken *from* whatever argument might rise in his mind to lure him to his backsliding. When he casts his eyes around him, he should be able to see, all that he respects, all that he admires, and all that he loves, kindly and anxiously pointing him onward; and none beckoning him back, to his former miserable "wallowing in the mire."

But it is said by some, that men will *think* and *act* for themselves; that none will disuse spirits or any thing else, merely because his neighbors do; and that *moral influence* is not that powerful engine contended for. Let us examine this. Let me ask the man who would maintain this position most stiffly, what compensation he will accept to go to church some Sunday and sit during the sermon with his wife's bonnet upon his head? Not a trifle, I'll venture. And why not? There would be nothing irreligious in it: nothing immoral, nothing uncomfortable.--Then why not? Is it not because there would be something egregiously unfashionable in it? Then it is the influence of *fashion*; and what is the influence of fashion, but the influence that *other* people's actions have on our own actions, the strong inclination each of us feels to do as we see all our neighbors do? Nor is the influence of fashion confined to any particular thing or class of things. It is just as strong on one subject as another. Let us make it as unfashionable to withhold our names from the temperance pledge as for husbands to wear their wives bonnets to church, and instances will be just as rare in the one case as the other.

"But," say some, "we are no drunkards; and we shall not acknowledge ourselves such by joining a reformed drunkard's society, whatever our influence might be." Surely no Christian will adhere to this objection.--If they believe, as they profess, that Omnipotence condescended to take on himself the form of sinful man, and, as such, to die an ignominious death for their sakes, surely they will not refuse submission to the infintely lesser condescension, for the temporal, and perhaps eternal salvation, of a large, erring, and unfortunate class of their own fellow creatures. Nor is the condescension very great.

In my judgment, such of us as have never fallen victims, have been spared more from the absence of appetite, than from any mental or moral superiority over those who have. Indeed, I believe, if we take habitual drunkards as a class, their heads and their hearts will bear an advantageous comparison with those of any other class. There seems ever to have been a proneness in the brilliant, and the warm-blooded, to fall into this vice.--The demon of intemperance ever seems to have delighted in sucking the blood of genius and of generosity. What one of us but can call to mind some dear relative, more promising in youth than all his fellows, who has fallen a sacrifice to his rapacity? He ever seems to have gone forth, like the Egyptian angel of death, commissioned to slay if not the first, the fairest born of every family. Shall he now be arrested in his desolating career? In that arrest, all can give aid that will; and who shall be excused that *can*, and will not? Far around as human breath has ever blown, he keeps our fathers, our brothers, our sons, and our friends, prostrate in the chains of moral death. To all the living every where, we cry, "come sound the moral resurrection trump, that these may rise and stand up, an exceeding great army"--"Come from the four winds, O breath! and breathe upon these slain, that they may live."

If the relative grandeur of revolutions shall be estimated by the great amount of human misery they alleviate, and the small amount they inflict, then, indeed, will this be the grandest the world shall ever have seen.--Of our political revolution of '76, we all are justly proud. It has given us a degree of political freedom, far exceeding that of any other of the nations of the earth. In it the world has found a solution of that long mooted problem, as to the capability of man to govern himself. In it was the germ which has vegetated, and still is to grow and expand into the universal liberty of mankind.

But with all these glorious results, past, present, and to come, it had its evils too.--It breathed forth famine, swam in blood and rose on fire; and long, long after, the orphan's cry, and the widow's wail, continued to break the sad silence that ensued. These were the price, the inevitable price, paid for the blessings it bought.

Turn now, to the temperance revolution. In *it*, we shall find a stronger bondage broken; a viler slavery, manumitted; a greater tyrant deposed. In *it*, more of want supplied, more disease healed, more sorrow assauged. By *it* no orphans starving, no widows weeping. By *it*, none wounded in feeling, none injured in interest. Even the dram-maker, and dram seller, will have glided into other occupations *so* gradually, as never to have felt the shock of change; and will stand ready to join all others in the universal song of gladness.

And what a noble ally this, to the cause of political freedom. With such an aid, its march cannot fail to be on and on, till every son of earth shall drink in rich fruition, the sorrow quenching draughts of perfect liberty. Happy day, when, all appetites controled, all passions subdued, all matters subjected, *mind*, all conquering *mind*, shall live and move the monarch of the world. Glorious consummation! Hail fall of Fury! Reign of Reason, all hail!

And when the victory shall be complete--when there shall be neither a slave nor a drunkard on the earth--how proud the title of that *Land*, which may truly claim to be the birth-place and the cradle of both those revolutions, that shall have ended in that victory. How nobly distinguished that People, who shall have planted, and nurtured to maturity, both the political and moral freedom of their species.

This is the one hundred and tenth anniversary of the birth-day of Washington.--We are met to celebrate this day. Washington is the mightiest name of earth--*long since* mightiest in the cause of civil liberty; *still* mightiest in moral reformation. On that name, an eulogy is expected. It cannot be. To add brightness to the sun, or glory to the name of Washington, is alike impossible. Let none attempt it. In solemn awe pronounce the name, and in its naked deathless splendor, leave it shining on.

"House Divided" Speech

Springfield, Illinois, June 16, 1858

Mr. President and Gentlemen of the Convention. If we could first know where we are, and whither we are tending, we could better judge what to do, and how to do it. We are now far into the fifth year, since a policy was initiated with the avowed object, and confident promise, of putting an end to slavery agitation. Under the operation of that policy, that agitation has not only, not ceased, but has constantly augmented. In my opinion, it will not cease, until a crisis shall have been reached and passed. "A house divided against itself cannot stand." I believe this government cannot endure permanently half salve and half free. I do not expect the Union to be dissolved--I do not expect the house to fall--but I do expect it will cease to be divided. It will become all one thing, or all the other. Either the opponents of slavery, will arrest the further spread of it, and place it where the public mind shall rest in the belief that it is in the course of ultimate extinction; or its advocates will push it forward, till it shall become alike lawful in all the States, old as well as new--North as well as South.

Have we no tendency to the latter condition?

Let any one who doubts, carefully contemplate that now almost complete legal combination--piece of machinery so to speak--compounded of the Nebraska doctrine, and the Dred Scott decision. Let him consider not only what work the machinery is adapted to do, and how well adapted; but also, let him study the history of its construction, and trace, if he can, or rather fail, if he can, to trace the evidences of design, and concert of action, among its chief architects, from the beginning.

The new year of 1854 found slavery exuluded from more than half the States by States Constitutions, and from most of the national territory by Congressional prohibition. Four days later, commenced the struggle, which ended in repealing that Congressional prohibition. This opened all the national territory to slavery; and was the first point gained.

But, so far, Congress only, had acted; and an indorsement by the people, real or apparent, was indispensable, to save the point already gained, and give chance for more.

This necessity had not been overlooked; but had been provided for, as well as might be, in the notable argument of "squatter sovereignty," otherwise called "sacred right of self government," which latter phrase, though expressive of the only rightful basis of any government, was so perverted in this attempted use of it as to amount to just this: That if any *one* man, choose to enslave *another*, no *third* man shall be allowed to object. That argument was incorporated into the Nebraska bill itself, in the language which follows: "It being the true intent and meaning of this act not to legislate slavery into any Territory or State, nor to exclude it therefrom; but to leave the people thereof perfectly free to form and regulate their domestic institutions in their own way, subject only to the Constitution of the United States." Then opened the roar of loose declamation in favor of "Squatter Sovereignty," and "Sacred right of self-government." "But," said opposition members, "let us amend the bill so as to expressly declare that the people of the Territory may exclude slavery." "Not we," said the friends of the measure; and down they voted the amendment.

While the Nebraska bill was passing through Congress, a *law case* involving the question of a negro's freedom, by reason of his owner having voluntarily taken him first into a free State and then into a Territory covered by the congressional prohibition, and held him as a slave, for a long time in each, was passing through the U.S. Circuit Court for the District of Missouri; and both Nebraska bill and law suit were brought to a decision in the same month of May 1854. The negro's name was "Dred Scott," which name now designates the decision finally made in the case. Before the then next presidential election, the law case came to, and was argued in, the Supreme Court of the United States; but the decision of it was deferred until after the election. Still before the election, Senator Trumbull, on the floor of the Senate, requests the leading advocate of the Nebraska bill to state *his opinion* whether the people of a Territory can constitutionally exclude slavery from their limits; and the latter answers, "That is a question for the Supreme Court."

The election came. Mr. Buchanan was elected, and the indorsement, such as it was, secured. That was the second point gained. The indorsement, however, fell short of a clear popular majority by nearly four hundred thousand votes, and so, perhaps, was not overwhelmingly reliable and satisfactory. The outgoing President, in his last annual message, as impressively as possible echoed back upon the people the weight and authority of the indorsement. The Supreme Court met again; did not announce their decision, but ordered a reargument. The Presidential inauguration came, and still no decision of the court; but the incoming President in his inaugural address, fervently exhorted the people to abide by the forthcoming decision, whatever it might be. Then, in a few days, came the decision. The reputed author of the Nebraska bill finds an early occasion to make a speech at this capital indorsing the Dred Scott decision, and vehemently denouncing all opposition to it. The new President, too, seizes the early occasion of the Silliman letter to indorse and strongly construe that decision, and to express his astonishment that any different view had ever been entertained!

At length a squabble springs up between the President and the author of the Nebraska bill, on the mere question of *fact*, whether the Lecompton Constitution was or was not, in any just sense, made by the people of Kansas; and in that quarrel the latter declares that all he wants is a fair vote for the people, and that he cares not whether slavery be voted *down* or voted *up*. I do not understand his declaration that he cares not whether slavery be voted down or voted up, to be intended by him other than as an apt definition of the policy he would impress upon the public mind--the principle for which he declares he has suffered so much, and is ready to suffer to the end. And well may he cling to that principle. If he has any parental feeling, well may he cling to it. That principle is the only shred left of his original Nebraska doctrine. Under the Dred Scott decision, "squatter sovereignty" squatted out of existence, tumbled down like temporary scaffolding--like the mould at the foundry served through one blast and fell back into loose sand--helped to carry an election, and then was kicked to the winds. His late joint struggle with the Republicans, against the Lecompton Constitution, involves nothing of the original Nebraska doctrine. That struggle was made on a point, the right of a people to make their own constitution, upon which he and the Republicans have never differed.

The several points of the Dred Scott decision, in connection with Senator Douglas' "care not" policy, constitute the piece of machinery, in its present state of advancement. The working points of that machinery are:--

First, That no negro slave, imported as such from Africa, and no descendant of such slave, can ever be a citizen of any State, in the sense of that term as used in the Constitution of the United States. This point is made in order to deprive the negro, in every possible event, of the benefit of that provision of the United States Constitution, which declares that: "The citizens of each State shall be entitled to all privileges and immunities of citizens in the several States."

Secondly, That "subject to the Constitution of the United States," neither Congress nor a Territorial Legislature can exclude slavery from any United States Territory. This point is made in order that individual men may fill up the Territories with slaves, without danger of losing them as property, and thus to enhance the chances of permanency to the institution through all the future.

Thirdly, That whether the holding a negro in actual slavery in a free State, makes him free, as against the holder, the United States courts will not decide, but will leave to be decided by the courts of any slave State the negro may be forced into by the master. This point is made, not to be pressed immediately; but, if acquiesced in for a while, and apparently indorsed by the people at an election, then to sustain the logical conclusion that what Dred Scott's master might lawfully do with Dred Scott, in the free State of Illinois, every other master may lawfully do with any other one, or one thousand slaves, in Illinois, or in any other free State.

Auxiliary to all this, and working hand in hand with it, the Nebraska doctrine, or what is left of it, is to educate and mould public opinion, at least Northern public opinion, not to care whether slavery is voted down or voted up. This shows exactly where we now are; and partially, also, whither we are tending.

It will throw additional light on the latter, to go back, and run the mind over the string of historical facts already stated. Several things will now appear less dark and mysterious than they did when they were transpiring. The people were to be left "perfectly free," "subject only to the Constitution." What the Constitution had to do with it, outsiders could not then see. Plainly enough now, it was an exactly fitted niche, for the Dred Scott decision to afterwards come in, and declare the perfect freedom of the people, to be just no freedom at all. Why was the amendment, expressly declaring the right of the people, voted down? Plainly enough now: the adoption of it would have spoiled the niche for the Dred Scott decision. Why was the court decision held up? Why even a Senator's individual opinion withheld, till after the Presidential election? Plainly enough now: the speaking out then would have damaged the perfectly free argument upon which the election was to be carried. Why the outgoing President's felicitation on the endorsement? Why the delay of a re-argument? Why the incoming President's advance exhortation in favor of the decision? These things look like the cautious patting and petting of a spirited horse preparatory to mounting him, when it is dreaded that he may give the rider a fall. And why the hasty after-endorsement of the decision by the President and others?

We cannot absolutely know that all these exact adaptations are the result of preconcert. But when we see a lot of framed timbers, different portions of which we know have been gotten out at different times and places and by different workmen--Stephen, Franklin, Roger and James, for instance--and when we see these timbers joined together, and see they exactly make the frame of a house or a mill, all the tenons and mortices exactly fitting, and all the lengths and proportions of the different pieces exactly adapted to their respective places, and not a piece too many or too few--not omitting even scaffolding--or, if a single piece be lacking, we see the place in the frame exactly fitted and prepared yet to bring such piece in--in such a case, we find it impossible not to believe that Stephen and Franklin and Roger and James all understood one another from the beginning, and all worked upon a common plan or draft drawn up before the first blow was struck.

It should not be overlooked that, by the Nebraska bill, the people of a *State* as well as Territory, were to be left "perfectly free," "subject only to the Constitution." Why mention a State? They were legislating for Territories, and not for or about States. Certainly the people of a State are and ought to be subject to the Constitution of the United States; but why is mention of this lugged into this merely Territorial law? Why are the people of a Territory and the people of a State therein lumped together, and their relation to the Constitution therein treated as being precisely the same? While the opinion of the Court, by Chief Justice Taney, in the Dred Scott case, and the separate opinions of all the concurring Judges, expressly declare that the Constitution of the United States neither permits Congress nor a Territorial Legislature to exclude Slavery from any United States Territory, they all omit to declare whether or not the same Constitution permits a State, or the people of a State, to exclude it. *Possibly,* this is a mere omission; but who can be quite sure, if McLean or Curtis had sought to get into the opinion a declaration of unlimited power in the people of a State to exclude Slavery from their limits, just as Chase and Mace sought to get such declaration, in behalf of the people of a Territory, into the Nebraska Bill;--I ask, who can be quite sure that it would not have been voted down in the one case as it had been in the other? The nearest approach to the point of declaring the power of a State over Slavery, is made by Judge Nelson. He approaches it more than once, using the precise idea, and almost the language, too, of the Nebraska act. On one occasion, his exact language is, "except in cases where the power is restrained by the Constitution of the United States, the law of the State is supreme over the subject of Slavery within its jurisdiction." In what cases the power of the States is so restrained by the United States Constitution, is left an open question, precisely as the same question, as to the restraint on the power of the territories was left open in the Nebraska act. Put this and that together, and we have another nice little niche, which we may, ere long, see filled with another Supreme Court decision, declaring that the Constitution of the United States does not permit a *State* to exclude slavery from its limits. And this may especially be expected if the doctrine of "care not whether slavery be voted down or voted up," shall gain upon the public mind sufficiently to give promise that such a decision can be maintained when made.

Such a decision is all that slavery now lacks of being alike lawful in all the States. Welcome or unwelcome, such decision is probably coming, and will soon be upon us, unless the power of the present political dynasty shall be met and overthrown. We shall lie down pleasantly dreaming that the people of Missouri are on the verge of making their State free, and we shall awake to the reality instead, that the Supreme Court has made Illinois a slave State. To meet and overthrow the power of that dynasty, is the work now before all those who would prevent that consummation. That is what we have to do. How can we best do it?

There are those who denounce us openly to their own friends, and yet whisper us softly, that Senator Douglas is the aptest instrument there is, with which to affect that object. They wish us to *infer* all, from the fact, that he now has a little quarrel with the present head of the dynasty; and that he has regularly voted with us on a single point, upon which, he and we, have never differed. They remind us that he is a very great man, and that the largest of us are very small ones. Let this be granted. But "a living dog is better than a dead lion." Judge Douglas, if not a dead lion for this work, is at least a caged and toothless one. How can he oppose the advances of slavery? He don't care anything about it. His avowed mission is impressing the "public heart" to *care nothing about* it. A leading Douglas Democratic newspaper thinks Douglas' superior talent will be needed to resist the revival of the African slave trade. Does Douglas believe an effort to revive that trade is approaching? He has not said so. Does he really think so? But if it is, how can he resist it? For years he has labored to prove it a sacred right of white men to take negro slaves into the new territories. Can he possibly show that it is less a sacred right to buy them where they can be bought cheapest? And unquestionably they can be bought cheaper in Africa than in Virginia. He has done all in his power to reduce the whole question of slavery to one of a mere right of property; and as such, how can he oppose the foreign slave trade--how can he refuse that trade in that "property" shall be "perfectly free"--unless he does it as a protection to the home production? And as the home producers will probably not ask the protection, he will be wholly without a ground of opposition.

Senator Douglas holds, we know, that a man may rightfully be wiser to-day than he was yesterday--that he may rightfully change when he finds himself wrong. But, can we for that reason, run ahead, and infer that he will make any particular change, of which he, himself, has given no intimation? Can we safely base our action upon any such vague inference? Now, as ever, I wish not to misrepresent Judge Douglas' position, question his motives, or do aught that can be personally offensive to him. Whenever, if ever, he and we can come together on principle so that our cause may have assistance from his great ability, I hope to have interposed no adventitious obstacle. But clearly, he is not now with us--he does not pretend to be--he does not promise ever to be.

Our cause, then, must be intrusted to, and conducted by, its own undoubted friends--those whose hands are free, whose hearts are in the work--who *do care* for the result. Two years ago the Republicans of the nation mustered over thirteen hundred thousand strong. We did this under the single impulse of resistance to a common danger, with every external circumstance against us. Of strange, discordant, and even hostile elements, we gathered from the four winds, and formed and fought the battle through, under the constant hot fire of a disciplined, proud and pampered enemy. Did we brave all them to falter now?--now; when the same enemy is wavering, dissevered and belligerent? The result is not doubtful. We shall not fail--if we stand firm, we *shall not fail*. Wise counsels may accelerate, or mistakes delay it, but, sooner or later, the victory is sure to come.

"Second Lecture on Inventions and Discoveries"

Jacksonville, Illinois, February 11, 1859

We have all heard Young America. He is the most *current* youth of the age. Some think him conceited, and arrogant; but has he not reason to entertain a rather extensive opinion of himself? Is he not the inventor and owner of the *present*, and sole hope of the *future*? Men, and things, everywhere, are ministering unto him. Look at his apparel, and you shall see cotten fabrics from Manchester and Lowell; flax-linen from Ireland; wool-cloth from Spain; silk from France; furs from the Arctic regions, with a buffalo-robe from the Rocky Mountains, as a general out-sider. At his table, besides plain bread and meat made at home, are sugar from Louisiana; coffee and fruits from the tropics; salt from Turk's Island; fish from New-foundland; tea from China, and spices from the Indies. The whale of the Pacific furnishes his candle-light; he has a diamond-ring from Brazil; a gold-watch from California, and a spanish cigar from Havanna. He not only has a present supply of all these, and much more; but thousands of hands are engaged in producing fresh supplies, and other thousands, in bringing them to him. The iron horse is panting, and impatient, to carry him everywhere, in no time; and the lightening stands ready harnessed to take and bring his tidings in a trifle less than no time. He owns a large part of the world, by right of possessing it; and all the rest by right of *wanting* it, and *intending* to have it. As Plato had for the immortality of the soul, so Young America has "a pleasing hope--a fond desire--a longing after" teritory. He has a great passion--a perfect rage--for the "*new*"; particularly new men for office, and the new earth mentioned in the revelations, in which, being no more sea, there must be about three times as much land as in the present. He is a great friend of humanity; and his

desire for land is not selfish, but merely an impulse to extend the
area of freedom. He is very anxious to fight for the liberation of
enslaved nations and colonies, provided, always, they *have* land, and
have *not* any liking for his interference. As to those who have no
land, and would be glad of help from any quarter, he considers *they*
can afford to wait a few hundred years longer. In knowledge he is
particularly rich. He knows all that can possibly be known; inclines
to believe in spiritual rappings, and is the unquestioned inventor of
"*Manifest Destiny*." His horror is for all that is old, particularly "Old
Fogy"; and if there be any thing old which he can endure, it is only
old whiskey and old tobacco.

   If the said Young America really is, as he claims to be, the
owner of all present, it must be admitted that he has considerable
advantage of Old Fogy. Take, for instance, the first of all fogies,
father Adam. There he stood, a very perfect physical man, as poets
and painters inform us; but he must have been very ignorant, and
simple in his habits. He had had no sufficient time to learn much by
observation; and he had no near neighbors to teach him anything. No
part of his breakfast had been brought from the other side of the
world; and it is quite probable, he had no conception of the world
having any other side. In all of these things, it is very plain, he was
no equal of Young America; the most that can be said is, that
according to his chance he may have been quite as much of a man as
his very self-complaisant descendant. Little as was what he knew, let
the Youngster discard all he has learned from others, and then show,
if he can, any advantage on his side. In the way of *land*, and *live
stock*, Adam was quite in the ascendant. He had dominion over all
the earth, and all the living things upon, and round about it. The
land has been sadly divided out since; but never fret, Young America
will *re-annex* it.

   The great difference between Young America and Old Fogy, is
the result of *Discoveries*, *Inventions*, and *Improvements*. These, in
turn, are the result of *observation*, *reflection* and *experiment*. For
instance, it is quite certain that ever since water has been boiled in
covered vessels, men have seen the lids of the vessels rise and fall a
little, with a sort of fluttering motion, by force of the steam; but so
long as this was not specially observed, and reflected and experimented upon, it came to nothing. At length however, after many thousand
years, some man observes this long-known effect of hot water lifting
a pot-lid, and begins a train of reflection upon it. He says "Why, to
be sure, the force that lifts the pot-lid, will lift any thing else, which
is no heavier than the pot-lid." "And, as man has much hard lifting
to do, can not this hot-water power be made to help him?" He has
become a little excited on the subject, and he fancies he hears a voice
answering "Try me" He does try it; and the *observation*, *reflection*,
and *trial* gives to the world the control of that tremendous, and now

well known agent, called steampower. This is not the actual history in detail, but the general principle.

But was this first inventor of the application of steam, wiser or more ingenious than those who had gone before him? Not at all. Had he not learned much of them, he never would have succeeded-- probably, never would have thought of making the attempt. To be fruitful in invention, it is indispensable to have a *habit* of observation and reflection; and this *habit*, our steam friend acquired, no doubt, from those who, to him, were old fogies. But for the difference in habit of observation, why did yankees, almost instantly, discover gold in California, which had been trodden upon, and over-looked by indians and Mexican greasers, for centuries? Gold-mines are not the only mines overlooked in the same way. There are more mines above the Earth's surface than below it. All nature--the whole world, material, moral, and intellectual,--is a mine; and, in Adam's day, it was a wholly unexplored mine. Now, it was the destined work of Adam's race to develope, by discoveries, inventions, and improvements, the hidden treasures of this mine. But Adam had nothing to turn his attention to the work. If he should do anything in the way of invention, he had first to invent the art of invention--the *instance* at least, if not the *habit* of observation and reflection. As might be expected he seems not to have been a very observing man at first; for it appears he went about naked a considerable length of time, before he even noticed that obvious fact. But when he did observe it, the observation was not lost upon him; for it immediately led to the first of all inventions, of which we have any direct account--*the fig-leaf apron.*

The inclination to exchange thoughts with one another is probably an original impulse of our nature. If I be in pain I wish to let you know it, and to ask your sympathy and assistance; and my pleasureable emotions also, I wish to communicate to, and share with you. But to carry on such communication, some *instrumentality* is indispensable. Accordingly speech--articulate sounds rattled off from the tongue--was used by our first parents, and even by Adam, before the creation of Eve. He gave names to the animals while she was still a bone in his side; and he broke out quite volubly when she first stood before him, the best present of his maker. From this it would appear that speech was not an invention of man, but rather the direct gift of his Creator. But whether Divine gift, or invention, it is still plain that if a mode of communication had been left to invention, *speech* must have been the first, from the superior adaptation to the end, of the organs of speech, over every other means within the whole range of nature. Of the organs of speech the tongue is the principal; and if we shall test it, we shall find the capacities of the tongue, in the utterance of articulate sounds, absolutely wonderful. You can count from one to one hundred, quite distinctly in about forty seconds.

In doing this two hundred and eighty three distinct sounds or syllables are uttered, being seven to each second; and yet there shall be enough difference between every two, to be easily recognized by the ear of the hearer. What other *signs* to represent *things* could possibly be produced so rapidly? or, even, if ready made, could be *arranged* so rapidly to express the sense? *Motions* with the hands, are no adequate substitute. *Marks* for the recognition of the eye--*writing*--although a wonderful auxiliary for speech, is no worthy substitute for it. In addition to the more slow and laborious process of getting up a communication in writing, the materials--pen, ink, and paper--are not always at hand. But one always has his tongue with him, and the breath of his life is the ever-ready material with which it works. Speech, then, by enabling different individuals to interchange thoughts, and thereby to combine their powers of observation and reflection, greatly facilitates useful discoveries and inventions. What one observes, and would himself infer nothing from, he tells to another, and that other at once sees a valuable hint in it. A result is thus reached which neither *alone* would have arrived at.

And this reminds me of what I passed unnoticed before, that the very first invention was a joint operation, Eve having shared with Adam in the getting up of the apron. And, indeed, judging from the fact that sewing has come down to our times as "woman's work" it is very probable she took the leading part; he, perhaps, doing no more than to stand by and thread the needle. That proceeding may be reckoned as the mother of all "Sewing societies"; and the first and most perfect "world's fair" all inventions and all inventors then in the world, being on the spot.

But speech alone, valuable as it ever has been, and is, has not advanced the condition of the world much. This is abundantly evident when we look at the degraded condition of all those tribes of human creatures who have no considerable additional means of communicating thoughts. *Writing*--the art of communicating thoughts to the mind, through the eye--is the great invention of the world. Great in the astonishing range of analysis and combination which necessarily underlies the most crude and general conception of it--great, very great in enabling us to converse with the dead, the absent, and the unborn, at all distances of time and of space; and great, not only in its direct benefits, but greatest help, to all other inventions. Suppose the art, with all conception of it, were this day lost to the world, how long, think you, would it be, before even Young America could get up the letter A. with any adequate notion of using it to advantage? The precise period at which writing was invented, is not known; but it certainly was as early as the time of Moses; from which we may safely infer that it's inventors were very old fogies.

Webster, at the time of writing his Dictionary, speaks of the English Language as then consisting of seventy or eighty thousand words. If so, the language in which the five books of Moses were written must, at that time, now thirtythree or four hundred years ago, have consisted of at least one quarter as many, or, twenty thousand. When we remember that words are *sounds* merely, we shall conclude that the idea of representing those sounds by *marks*, so that whoever should at any time after see the marks, would understand what sounds they meant, was a bold and ingenius conception, not likely to occur to one man of a million, in the run of a thousand years. And, when it did occur, a distinct mark for each word, giving twenty thousand different marks first to be learned, and afterwards remembered, would follow as the second thought, and would present such a difficulty as would lead to the conclusion that the whole thing was impracticable. But the *necessity* still would exist; and we may readily suppose that the idea was conceived, and lost, and reproduced, and dropped, and taken up again and again, until at last, the thought of dividing sounds into parts, and making a mark, not to represent a whole sound, but only a part of one, and then of combining these marks, not very many in number, upon the principles of permutation, so as to represent any and all of the whole twenty thousand words, and even any additional number was somehow conceived and pushed into practice. This was the invention of *phoenetic* writing, as distinguished from the clumsy picture writing of some of the nations. That it was difficult of conception and execution, is apparant, as well by the foregoing reflections, as by the fact that so many tribes of men have come down from Adam's time to ours without ever having possessed it. It's utility may be conceived, by the reflection that, to *it* we owe everything which distinguishes us from savages. Take it from us, and the Bible, all history, all science, all government, all commerce, and nearly all social intercourse go with it.

The great activity of the tongue, in articulating sounds, has already been mentioned; and it may be of some passing interest to notice the wonderful powers of the *eye*, in conveying ideas to the mind from writing. Take the same example of the numbers from *one* to *one hundred*, written down, and you can run your eye over the list, and be assured that every number is in it, in about one half the time it would require to pronounce the words with the voice; and not only so, but you can, in the same short time, determine whether every word is spelled correctly, by which it is evident that every separate letter, amounting to eight hundred and sixty four, has been recognized, and reported to the mind, within the incredibly short space of twenty seconds, or one third of a minute.

I have already intimated my opinion that in the world's history, certain inventions and discoveries occurred, of peculiar value, on account of their great efficiency in facilitating all other inventions and discoveries. Of these were the arts of writing and of printing--the discovery of America, and the introduction of Patent-laws. The date of the first, as already stated, is unknown; but it certainly was as much as fifteen hundred years before the Christian era; the second-- printing--came in 1436, or nearly three thousand years after the first. The others followed more rapidly--the discovery of America in 1492, and the first patent laws in 1624. Though not apposite to my present purpose, it is but justice to the fruitfulness of that period, to mention two other important events--the Lutheran Reformation in 1517, and, still earlier, the invention of negroes, or, of the present mode of using them, in 1434. But, to return to the consideration of printing, it is plain that it is but the *other* half--and in real utility, the *better* half--of writing; and that both together are but the assistants of speech in the communication of thoughts between man and man. When man was possessed of speech alone, the chances of invention, discovery, and improvement, were very limited; but by the introduc- tion of each of these, they were greatly multiplied. When writing was invented, any important observation, likely to lead to a discovery, had at least a chance of being written down, and consequently, a better chance of never being forgotten; and of being seen, and reflected upon by a much greater number of persons; and thereby the chances of a valuable hint being caught, proportionably augmented. By this means the observation of a single individual might lead to an important invention, years, and even centuries after he was dead. In one word, by means of writing, the seeds of invention were more permanently preserved, and more widely sown. And yet, for the three thousand years during which printing remained undiscovered after writing was in use, it was only a small portion of the people who could write, or read writing; and consequently the field of invention, though much extended, still continued very limited. At length printing came. It gave ten thousand copies of any written matter, quite as cheaply as ten were given before; and consequently a thousand minds were brought into the field where there was but one before. This was a great *gain*; and history shows a great *change* corresponding to it, in point of time. I will venture to consider *it*, the true termination of that period called "the dark ages." Discoveries, inventions, and improvements followed rapidly, and have been increasing their rapidity ever since. The effects could not come, all at once. It required time to bring them out; and they are still coming. The *capacity* to read, could not be multiplied as fast as the *means* of reading. Spelling-books just began to go into the hands of the children; but the teachers were not very numerous, or very compe- tent; so that it is safe to infer they did not advance so speedily as they do now-a-days. It is very probable--almost certain--that the great mass of men, at that time, were utterly unconscious, that their *conditions*, or their *minds* were capable of improvement. They not only looked upon the educated few as superior beings; but they supposed themselves to be naturally incapable of rising to equality. To immancipate the mind from this false and under estimate of itself, is the great task which printing came into the world to perform. It is difficult for us, *now* and *here*, to conceive how strong this slavery of the mind was; and how long it did, of necessity, take, to break it's shackles, and to get a habit of freedom of thought, established. It is, in this connection, a curious fact that a new country is most favorable--almost necessary--to the immancipation of thought, and the consequent advancement of civilization and the arts. The human family originated as is thought, somewhere in Asia, and have worked their way princip[al]ly Westward. Just now, in civilization, and the arts, the people of Asia are entirely behind those of Europe; those of the East of Europe behind those of the West of it; while we, here in America, *think* we discover, and invent, and improve, faster than any of them. *They* may think this is arrogance; but they can not deny that Russia has called on us to show her how to build steam-boats and railroads--while in the older parts of Asia, they scarcely know that such things as S.Bs & RR.s. exist. In anciently inhabited countries, the dust of ages--a real downright old-fogyism--seems to settle upon, and smother the intellects and energies of man. It is in this view that I have mentioned the discovery of America as an event greatly favoring and facilitating useful discoveries and inventions.

Next came the Patent laws. These began in England in 1624; and, in this country, with the adoption of our constitution. Before these, any man might instantly use what another had invented; so that the inventor had no special advantage from his own invention. The patent system changed this; secured to the inventor, for a limited time, the exclusive use of his invention; and thereby added the fuel of *interest* to the *fire* of genius, in the discovery and production of new and useful things.

"Cooper Union Address"

New York City, February 27, 1860

Mr. President and Fellow Citizens of New York: The facts with which I shall deal this evening are mainly old and familiar; nor is there anything new in the general use I shall make of them. If there shall be any novelty, it will be in the mode of presenting the facts, and the inferences and observations following that presentation.

In his speech last Autumn, at Columbus, Ohio, as reported in *The New-York Times*, Senator Douglas said:

"Our fathers, when they framed the Government under which we live, understood this question just as well, and even better, than we do now."

I fully indorse this, and I adopt it as a text for this discourse. I so adopt it because it furnishes a precise and an agreed starting point for a discussion between Republicans and that wing of the Democracy headed by Senator Douglas. It simply leaves the inquiry: "What was the understanding those fathers had of the question mentioned?"

What is the frame of Government under which we live?

The answer must be: "The Constitution of the United States." That Constitution consists of the original, framed in 1787 (and under which the present Government first went into operation), and twelve subsequently framed amendments, the first ten of which were framed in 1789.

Who were our fathers that framed the Constitution? I suppose the "thirty-nine" who signed the original instrument may be fairly called our fathers who framed that part of the present Government. It is almost exactly true to say they framed it, and it is altogether true to say they fairly represented the opinion and sentiment of the whole nation at that time. Their names, being familiar to nearly all, and accessible to quite all, need not now be repeated.

I take these "thirty-nine," for the present, as being "our fathers who framed the Government under which we live."

What is the question which, according to the text, those fathers understood just as well, and even better than we do now?

It is this: Does the proper division of local from Federal authority, or anything in the Constitution, forbid our Federal Government to control as to Slavery in our Federal Territories?

Upon this, Douglas holds the affirmative, and Republicans the negative. This affirmative and denial form an issue; and this issue--this question--is precisely what the text declares our fathers understood better than we.

Let us now inquire whether the "thirty-nine" or any of them, ever acted upon this question; and if they did, how they acted upon it--how they expressed that better understanding?

In 1784--three years before the Constitution--the United States then owning the North-Western Territory, and no other--the Congress of the Confederation had before them the question of prohibiting Slavery in that Territory; and four of the "thirty-nine" who afterward framed the Constitution were in that Congress, and voted on that question. Of these, Roger Sherman, Thomas Mifflin, and Hugh Williamson voted for the prohibition--thus showing that, in their understanding, no line dividing local from federal authority, nor any thing else, properly forbade the Federal Government to control as to Slavery in Federal territory. The other of the four--James McHenry--voted against the prohibition, showing that, for some cause, he thought it improper to vote for it.

In 1787, still before the Constitution, but while the Convention was in session framing it, and while the North-Western Territory still was the only territory owned by the United States--the same question of prohibiting Slavery in the Territory again came before the Congress of the Confederation; and three more of the "thirty-nine" who afterward signed the Constitution, were in that Congress, and voted on the question. They were William Blount, William Few, and Abraham Baldwin; and they all voted for the prohibition--thus showing that, in their understanding, no line dividing local from federal authority, nor anything else, properly forbade the Federal Government to control as to Slavery in Federal territory. This time the prohibition became a law, being part of what is now well known as the Ordinance of '87.

The question of Federal control of Slavery in the Territories, seems not to have been directly before the Convention which framed the original Constitution; and hence it is not recorded that the "thirty-nine" or any of them, while engaged on that instrument, expressed any opinion on that precise question.

In 1789, by the first Congress which sat under the Constitution, an act was passed to enforce the Ordinance of '87, including the prohibition of Slavery in the North-Western Territory. The bill for this act was reported by one of the "thirty-nine," Thomas Fitzsimmons, then a Member of the House of Representatives from Pennsylvania. It went through all its stages without a word of opposition, and finally passed both branches without Yeas and Nays, which is equivalent to a unanimous passage. In this Congress there were sixteen of the thirty-nine fathers who framed the original Constitution. They were: John Langdon, Nicholas Gilman, Wm. S. Johnson, Roger Sherman, Robert Morris, Thos. Fitzsimmons, William Few, Abraham Baldwin, Rufus King, William Patterson, George Clymer, Richard Bassett, George Read, Pierce Butler, Daniel Carroll, James Madison.

This shows that, in their understanding, no line dividing local from Federal authority, nor anything in the Constitution, properly forbade Congress to prohibit Slavery in the Federal territory; else both their fidelity to correct principle, and their oath to support the Constitution, would have constrained them to oppose the prohibition.

Again, George Washington, another of the "thirty-nine," was then President of the United States, and, as such, approved and signed the bill, thus completing its validity as a law, and thus showing that, in his understanding, no line dividing local from Federal authority, nor anything in the Constitution, forbade the Federal Government, to control as to Slavery in Federal territory.

No great while after the adoption of the original Constitution, North Carolina ceded to the Federal Government the country now constituting the State of Tennessee; and a few years later Georgia ceded that which now constitutes the States of Mississippi and Alabama. In both deeds of cession it was made a condition by the ceding States that the Federal Government should not prohibit Slavery in the ceded country. Besides this, slavery was then actually in the ceded country. Under these circumstances, Congress, on taking charge of these countries, did not absolutely prohibit Slavery within them. But they did interfere with it--take control of it--even there, to a certain extent. In 1798, Congress organized the Territory of Mississippi. In the act of organization they prohibited the bringing of slaves into the Territory, from any place without the United States, by fine, and giving freedom to slaves so brought. This act passed both branches of Congress without Yeas and Nays. In that Congress were three of the "thirty-nine" who framed the original Constitution. They were John Langdon, George Read and Abraham Baldwin. They all, probably, voted for it. Certainly they would have placed their opposition to it upon record, if, in their understanding, any line dividing local from Federal authority, or anything in the Constitution, properly forbade the Federal Government to Control as to Slavery in Federal territory.

In 1803, the Federal Government purchased the Louisiana country. Our former territorial acquisitions came from certain of our own States; but this Louisiana country was acquired from a foreign nation. In 1804, Congress gave a Territorial organization to that part of it which now constitutes the State of Louisiana. New-Orleans, lying within that part, was an old and comparatively large city. There were other considerable towns and settlements, and Slavery was extensively and thoroughly intermingled with the people. Congress did not, in the Territorial act, prohibit Slavery; but they did interfere with it--take control of it--in a more marked and extensive way than they did in the case of Mississippi. The substance of the provision therein made, in relation to slaves, was:

First: That no slave should be imported into the Territory from foreign parts.

Second: That no slave should be carried into it who had been imported into the United States since the first day of May, 1798.

Third: That no slave should be carried into it, except by the owner, and for his own use as a settler; the penalty in all the cases being a fine upon the violator of the law, and freedom to the slave.

This act also was passed without Yeas and Nays. In the Congress which passed it, there were two of the "thirty-nine." They were Abraham Baldwin and Jonathan Dayton. As stated in the case of Mississippi, it is probable they both voted for it. They would not have allowed it to pass without recording their opposition to it, if, in their understanding, it violated either the line properly dividing local from Federal authority, or any provision of the Constitution.

In 1819-20, came, and passed the Missouri question. Many votes were taken, by Yeas and Nays, in both branches of Congress, upon the various phases of the general question. Two of the "thirty-nine"--Rufus King and Charles Pinckney--were members of that Congress. Mr. King steadily voted for Slavery prohibition and against all compromises, while Mr. Pinckney as steadily voted against Slavery prohibition, and against all compromises. By this Mr. King showed that, in his understanding, no line dividing local from Federal authority, nor anything in the Constitution, was violated by Congress prohibiting Slavery in Federal territory; while Mr. Pinckney, by his votes, showed that in his understanding there was some sufficient reason for opposing such prohibition in that case.

The cases I have mentioned are the only acts of the "thirty-nine," or of any of them, upon the direct issue, which I have been able to discover.

To enumerate the persons who thus acted, as being four in 1784, three in 1787, seventeen in 1789, three in 1798, two in 1804, and two in 1819-20--there would be thirty-one of them. But this would be counting John Langdon, Roger Sherman, William Few, Rufus King, and George Read, each twice, and Abraham Baldwin four times. The true number of those of the "thirty-nine" whom I have shown to have acted upon the question, which, by the text, they understood better than we, is twenty-three, leaving sixteen not shown to have acted upon it in any way.

Here, then, we have twenty-three out of our "thirty-nine" fathers who framed the government under which we live, who have, upon their official responsibility and their corporal oaths, acted upon the very question which the text affirms they "understood just as well, and even better than we do now;" and twenty-one of them--a clear majority of the whole "thirty-nine"--so acting upon it as to make them guilty of gross political impropriety and willful perjury, if, in their understanding, any proper division between local and Federal authority, or anything in the Constitution they had made themselves, and sworn to support, forbade the Federal Government to control as to Slavery in the Federal Territories. Thus the twenty-one acted; and, as actions speak louder than words, so actions under such responsibility speak still louder.

Two of the twenty-three voted against Congressional prohibition of Slavery in the Federal Territories, in the instances in which they acted upon the question. But for what reasons they so voted is not known. They may have done so because they thought a proper division of local from Federal authority, or some provision or principle of the Constitution, stood in the way; or they may, without any such question, have voted against the prohibition, on what appeared to them to be sufficient grounds of expediency. No one who has sworn to support the Constitution, can conscientiously vote for what he understands to be an unconstitutional measure, however expedient he may think it; but one may and ought to vote against a measure which he deems constitutional, if, at the time, he deems it inexpedient. It, therefore, would be unsafe to set down even the two who voted against the prohibition, as having done so because, in their understanding, any proper division of local from Federal authority, or anything in the Constitution, forbade the Federal Government to control as to Slavery in Federal territory.

The remaining sixteen of the "thirty-nine," so far as I have discovered, have left no record of their understanding upon the direct question of Federal control of Slavery in the Federal Territories. But there is much reason to believe that their understanding upon that question would not have appeared different from that of their twenty-three compeers, had it been manifested at all.

For the purpose of adhering rigidly to the text, I have purposely omitted whatever understanding may have been manifested, by any person, however distinguished, other than the thirty-nine fathers who framed the original Constitution; and, for the same reason, I have also omitted whatever understanding may have been manifested by any of the "thirty-nine" even, on any other phase of the general question of Slavery. If we should look into their acts and declarations on those other phases, as the foreign slave-trade, and the morality and policy of Slavery generally, it would appear to us that on the direct question of Federal control of Slavery in Federal Territories, the sixteen, if they had acted at all, would probably have acted just as the twenty-three did. Among that sixteen were several of the most noted anti-

slavery men of those times--as Dr. Franklin, Alexander Hamilton, and Gouverneur Morris--while there was not one now known to have been otherwise, unless it may be John Rutledge of South Carolina.

The sum of the whole is, that of our "thirty-nine" fathers who framed the original Constitution, twenty-one--a clear majority of the whole--certainly understood that no proper division of local from Federal authority, nor any part of the Constitution, forbade the Federal Government to control Slavery in the Federal Territories; while all the rest probably had the same understanding. Such, unquestionably, was the understanding of our fathers who framed the original Constitution; and the text affirms that they understood the question better than we.

But, so far, I have been considering the understanding of the question manifested by the framers of the original Constitution. In, and by, the original instrument, a mode was provided for amending it; and, as I have already stated, the present frame of Government under which we live consists of that original, and twelve amendatory articles framed and adopted since. Those who now insist that Federal control of Slavery in Federal Territories violates the Constitution, point us to the provisions which they suppose it thus violates; and, as I understand, they all fix upon provisions in those amendatory articles, and not in the original instrument. The Supreme Court, in the Dred Scott case, plant themselves upon the fifth amendment, which provides that "no person shall be deprived of property without due process of law;" while Senator Douglas and his peculiar adherents plant themselves upon the tenth amendment, providing that "the powers not granted by the Constitution are reserved to the States respectively, and to the people."

Now, it so happens that these amendments were framed by the first Congress which sat under the Constitution--the identical Congress which passed the act already mentioned, enforcing the prohibition of Slavery in the North-Western Territory. Not only was it the same Congress, but they were the identical, same individual men who, at the same session, and at the same time within the session, had under consideration, and in progress toward maturity, these Constitutional amendements, and this act prohibiting slavery in all the territory the nation then owned. The Constitutional amendments were introduced before and passed after the act enforcing the Ordinanace of '87; to that during the whole pendency of the act to enforce the Ordinance, the Constitutional amendments were also pending.

That Congress, consisting in all of seventy-six members, including sixteen of the framers of the original Constitution, as before stated, were preeminently our fathers who framed that part of the Government under which we live which is now claimed as forbidding the Federal Government to control Slavery in the Federal Territories.

Is it not a little presumptuous in any one at this day to affirm that the two things which that Congress deliberately framed, and carried to maturity at the same time, are absolutely inconsistent with each other? And does not such affirmation become impudently absurd when coupled with the other affirmation, from the same mouth, that those who did the two things, alleged to be inconsistent, understood whether they really were inconsistent better than we--better than he who affirms that they are inconsistent?

It is surely safe to assume that the "thirty-nine" framers of the original Constitution, and the seventy-six members of the Congress which framed the amendments thereto, taken together do certainly include those who may be fairly called "our fathers who framed the Government under which we live." And so assuming, I defy any man to show that any one of them ever in his whole life declared that, in his understanding, any proper division of local from Federal authority or any part of the Constitution, forbade the Federal Government to control as to Slavery in the Federal Territories. I go a step further. I defy any one to show that any living man in the whole world ever did, prior to the beginning of the present century, (and I might almost say prior to the beginning of the last half of the present century), declare that, in his understanding, any proper division of local from Federal authority, or any part of the Constitution, forbade the Federal Government to control as to Slavery in the Federal Territories. To those who now so declare, I give, not only "our fathers who framed the Government under which we live," but with them all other living men within the century in which it was framed, among whom to search, and they shall not be able to find the evidence of a single man agreeing with them.

Now, and here, let me guard a little against being misunderstood. I do not mean to say we are bound to follow implicitly in whatever our fathers did. To do so, would be to discard all the lights of current experience--to reject all progress--all improvement. What I do say is, that if we would supplant the opinions and policy of our fathers in any case, we should do so upon evidence so conclusive, and argument so clear, that even their great authority, fairly considered and weighed, cannot stand; and most surely not in a case where of we ourselves declare they understood the question better than we.

If any man at this day, sincerely believes that a proper division of local from Federal authority, or any part of the Constitution, forbids the Federal Government to control as to Slavery in the Federal Territories, he is right to say so, and to enforce his position by all truthful evidence and fair argument which he can. But he has no right to mislead others, who have less access to history and less leisure to study it, into the false belief that "our fathers, who framed the Government under which we live," were of the same opinion-- thus substituting falsehood and deception for truthful evidence and fair argument. If any man at this day sincerely believes "our fathers, who framed the Government under which we live," used and applied principles, in other cases, which ought to have led them to under-stand that a proper division of local from Federal authority, or some part of the Constitution, forbids the Federal Government to control as to Slavery in the Federal Territories, he is right to say so. But he should, at the same time, brave the responsibility of declaring that, in his opinion, he understands their principles better than they did themselves; and especially should he not shirk that responsibility by asserting that they "understood the question just as well, and even better, than we do now."

But enough: Let all who believe that "our fathers, who framed the Government under which we live, understood this question just as well, and even better than we do now," speak as they spoke, and act as they acted upon it. This is all Republicans ask--all Republicans desire--in relation to Slavery. As those fathers marked it, so let it be again marked, as an evil not to be extended, but to be tolerated and protected only because of and so far as its actual presence among us makes that toleration and protection a necessity. Let all the guaranties those fathers gave it be, not grudgingly, but fully and fairly, maintained. For this Republicans contend, and with this, so far as I know or believe, they will be content.

And now, if they would listen--as I suppose they will not--I would address a few words to the Southern people.

I would say to them: You consider yourselves a reasonable and a just people; and I consider that in the general qualities of reason and justice you are not inferior to any other people. Still, when you speak of us Republicans, you do so only to denounce us as reptiles, or, at the best, as no better than outlaws. You will grant a hearing to pirates or murderers, but nothing like it to "Black Republicans." In all your contentions with one another, each of you deems an uncondi-tional condemnation of "Black Republicanism" as the first thing to be attended to. Indeed, such condemnation of us seems to be an indispensable prerequisite--license, so to speak--among you to be admitted or permitted to speak at all.

Now, can you, or not, be prevailed upon to pause and to consider whether this is quite just to us, or even to yourselves?

Bring forward your charges and specifications, and then be patient long enough to hear us deny or justify.

You say we are sectional. We deny it. That makes an issue; and the burden of proof is upon you. You produce your proof; and what is it? Why, that our party has no existence in your section--gets no votes in your section. The fact is substantially true; but does it prove the issue? If it does, then in case we should, without change of principle, begin to get votes in your section, we should thereby cease to be sectional. You cannot escape this conclusion; and yet, are you willing to abide by it? If you are, you will probably soon find that we have ceased to be sectional, for we shall get votes in your section this very year. You will then begin to discover, as the truth plainly is, that your proof does not touch the issue. The fact that we get no votes in your section, is a fact of your making, and not of ours. And if there be fault in that fact, that fault is primarily yours, and remains until you show that we repel you by any wrong principle or practice. If we do repel you by any wrong principle or practice, the fault is ours; but this brings you to where you ought to have started-- to a discussion of the right or wrong of our principle. If our principle, put in practice, would wrong your section for the benefit of ours, or for any other object, then our principle, and we with it, are sectional, and are justly opposed and denounced as such. Meet us, then, on the question of whether our principle, put in practice, would wrong your section; and so meet it as if it were possible that something may be said on our side. Do you accept the challenge? No? Then you really believe that the principle which our fathers who framed the Government under which we live thought so clearly right as to adopt it, and indorse it again and again, upon their official oaths, is, in fact, so clearly wrong as to demand your condemnation without a moment's consideration.

Some of you delight to flaunt in our faces the warning against sectional parties given by Washington in his Farewell Address. Less than eight years before Washington gave that warning, he had, as President of the United States, approved and signed an act of Congress, enforcing the prohibition of Slavery in the North-Western Territory, which act embodied the policy of the Government upon that subject, up to and at the very moment he penned that warning; and about one year after he penned it he wrote La Fayette that he considered that prohibition a wise measure, expressing in the same connection his hope that we should some time have a confederacy of free States.

Bearing this in mind, and seeing that sectionalism has since arisen upon this same subject, is that warning a weapon in your hands against us, or in our hands against you? Could Washington himself speak, would he cast the blame of that sectionalism upon us, who sustain his policy, or upon you who repudiate it? We respect that warning of Washington, and we commend it to you, together with his example pointing to the right application of it.

But you say you are conservative--eminently conservative-while we are revolutionary, destructive, or something of the sort. What is conservatism? Is it not adherence to the old and tried, against the new and untried? We stick to, contend for, the identical old policy on the point in controversy which was adopted by our fathers who framed the Government under which we live; while you with one accord reject, and scout, and spit upon that old policy, and insist upon substituting something new. True, you disagree among yourselves as to what that substitute shall be. You have considerable variety of new propositions and plans, but you are unanimous in rejecting and denouncing the old policy of the fathers. Some of you are for reviving the foreign slave trade; some for a Congressional Slave-Code for the Territories; some for Congress forbidding the Territories to prohibit Slavery within their limits; some for maintaining Slavery in the Territories through the Judiciary; some for the "gur-reat pur-rinciple" that "if one man would enslave another, no third man should object," fantastically called "Popular Sovereignty;" but never a man among you in favor of Federal prohibition of Slavery in Federal Territories, according to the practice of our fathers who framed the Government under which we live. Not one of all your various plans can show a precedent or an advocate in the century within which our Government originated. Consider, then, whether your claim of conservatism for yourselves, and your charge of destructiveness against us, are based on the most clear and stable foundations.

Again, you say we have made the slavery question more prominent than it formerly was. We deny it. We admit that it is more prominent, but we deny that we made it so. It was not we, but you, who discarded the old policy of the fathers. We resisted, and still resist, your innovation; and thence comes the greater prominence of the question. Would you have that question reduced to its former proportions? Go back to that old policy. What has been will be again, under the same conditions. If you would have the peace of the old times, re-adopt the precepts and policy of the old times.

You charge that we stir up insurrections among your slaves. We deny it; and what is your proof? Harper's Ferry! John Brown!! John Brown was no Republican; and you have failed to implicate a single Republican in his Harper's Ferry enterprise. If any member of our party is guilty in that matter, you know it or you do not know it. If you do know it, you are inexcusable to not designate the man and prove the fact. If you do not know it, you are inexcusable to assert it, and especially to persist in the assertion after you have tried and failed to make the proof. You need not be told that persisting in a charge which one does not know to be true, is simply malicious slander.

Some of you admit that no Republican designedly aided or encouraged the Harper's Ferry affair; but still insist that our doctrines and declarations necessarily lead to such results. We do not believe it. We know we hold to no doctrines, and make no declarations, which were not held to and made by our fathers who framed the Government under which we live. You never dealt fairly by us in relation to this affair. When it occurred, some important State elections were near at hand, and you were in evident glee with the belief that, by charging the blame upon us, you could get an advantage of us in those elections. The elections came, and your expectations were not quite fulfilled. Every Republican man knew that, as to himself at least, your charge was a slander, and he was not much inclined by it to cast his vote in your favor. Republican doctrines and declarations are accompanied with a continual protest against any interference whatever with your slaves, or with you about your slaves. Surely, this does not encourage them to revolt. True, we do, in common with our fathers who framed the Government under which we live, declare our belief that Slavery is wrong; but the slaves do not hear us declare even this. For anything we say or do, the slaves would scarcely know there is a Republican party. I believe they would not, in fact, generally know it but for your misrepresentations of us, in their hearing. In your political contests among yourselves, each faction charges the other with sympathy with Black Republicanism; and then, to give point to the charge, defines Black Republicanism to simply be insurrection, blood and thunder among the slaves.

Slave insurrections are no more common now than they were before the Republican party was organized. What induced the Southampton insurrection, twenty-eight years ago, in which at least three times as many lives were lost as at Harper's Ferry? You can scarcely stretch your very elastic fancy to the conclusion that Southampton was got up by Black Republicanism. In the present state of things in the United States, I do not think a general, or even a very extensive slave insurrection is possible. The indispensable concert of action cannot be attained. The slaves have no means of rapid communication; nor can incendiary freemen, black or white, supply it. The explosive materials are everywhere in parcels; but there neither are, nor can be supplied, the indispensable connecting trains.

Much is said by Southern people about the affection of slaves for their masters and mistresses; and a part of it, at least, is true. A plot for an uprising could scarcely be devised and communicated to twenty individuals before some of them, to save the life of a favorite master or mistress, would divulge it. This is the rule; and the slave-revolution in Hayti was not an exception to it, but a case occurring under peculiar circumstances. The gunpowder plot of British history, though not connected with slaves, was more in point.

In that case, only about twenty were admitted to the secret; and yet one of them, in his anxiety to save a friend, betrayed the plot to that friend, and, by consequence, averted the calamity.   Occasional poisonings from the kitchen, and open or stealthy assassinations in the field, and local revolts extending to a score or so, will continue to occur as the natural results of Slavery; but no general insurrection of slaves, as I think, can happen in this country for a long time. Whoever much fears, or much hopes for such an event, will be alike disappointed.

In the language of Mr. Jefferson, uttered many years ago, "It is still in our power to direct the process of emancipation, and deportation, peaceably, and in such slow degrees, as that the evil will wear off insensibly; and their places be, *pari passu*, filled up by free white laborers. If, on the contrary, it is left to force itself on, human nature must shudder at the prospect held up."

Mr. Jefferson did not mean to say, nor do I, that the power of emancipation is in the Federal Government. He spoke of Virginia; and, as to the power of emancipation, I speak of the slaveholding States only.

The Federal Government, however, as we insist, has the power of restraining the extension of the institution--the power to insure that a slave insurrection shall never occur on any American soil which is now free from Slavery.

John Brown's effort was peculiar. It was not a slave insurrection. It was an attempt by white men to get up a revolt among slaves, in which the slaves refused to participate. In fact, it was so absurd that the slaves, with all their ignorance, saw plainly enough it could not succeed. That affair, in its philosophy, corresponds with the many attempts, related in history, at the assassination of kings and emperors. An enthusiast broods over the oppression of a people, till he fancies himself commissioned by Heaven to liberate them. He ventures the attempt, which ends in little else than in his own execution. Orsini's attempt on Louis Napoleon, and John Brown's attempt on Harper's Ferry were, in their philosophy, precisely the same. The eagerness to cast blame on old England in the one case, and on New-England in the other, does not disprove the sameness of the two things.

And how much would it avail you, if you could, by the use of John Brown, Helper's Book, and the like, break up the Republican organization? Human action can be modified to some extent, but human nature cannot be changed. There is a judgment and a feeling against Slavery in this nation, which cast at least a million and a half of votes. You cannot destroy that judgment and feeling--that sentiment--by breaking up the political organization which rallies around it. You can scarcely scatter and disperse an army which has been formed into order in the face of your heaviest fire, but if you could, how much would you gain by forcing the sentiment which created it out of the peaceful channel of the ballot box, into some other channel? What would that other channel probably be? Would the number of John Browns be lessened or enlarged by the operation?

But you will break up the Union, rather than submit to a denial of your Constitutional rights.

That has a somewhat reckless sound; but it would be palliated, if not fully justified, were we proposing, by the mere force of numbers, to deprive you of some right, plainly written down in the Constitution. But we are proposing no such thing.

When you make these declarations, you have a specific and well-understood allusion to an assumed Constitutional right of yours, to take slaves into the Federal Authorities, and to hold them there as property. But no such right is specifically written in the Constitution. That instrument is literally silent about any such right. We, on the contrary, deny that such a right has any existence in the Constitution, even by implication.

Your purpose, then, plainly stated, is, that you will destroy the Government, unless you be allowed to construe and enforce the Constitution as you please, on all points in dispute between you and us. You will rule or ruin in all events.

This, plainly stated, is your language to us. Perhaps you will say the Supreme Court has decided the disputed Constitutional question in your favor. Not quite so. But, waiving the lawyer's distinction between dictum and decision, the Court have decided the question for you in a sort of way. The Court have substantially said, it is your Constitutional right to take slaves into the Federal Territories, and to hold them there as property.

When I say the decision was made in a sort of way, I mean it was made in a divided Court by a bare majority of the Judges, and they not quite agreeing with one another in the reasons for making it; that it is so made as that its avowed supporters disagree with one another about its meaning; and that it was mainly based upon a mistaken statement of fact--the statement in the opinion that "the right of property in a slave is distinctly and expressly affirmed in the Constitution."

An inspection of the Constitution will show that the right of property in a slave is not distinctly and expressly affirmed in it. Bear in mind the Judges do not pledge their judicial opinion that such right is impliedly affirmed in the Constitution; but they pledge their veracity that it is distinctly and expressly affirmed there--"distinctly"---that is, not mingled with anything else-- "expressly"--that is, in words meaning just that, without the aid of any inference, and susceptible of no other meaning.

If they had only pledged their judicial opinion that such right is affirmed in the instrument by implication, it would be open to others to show that neither the word "slave" nor "Slavery" is to be found in the Constitution, nor the word "property" even, in any connection with language alluding to the things slave, or Slavery, and that wherever in that instrument the slave is alluded to, he is called a "person;" and wherever his master's legal right in relation to him is alluded to, it is spoken of as "service or labor due," as a "debt" payable in service or labor. Also, it would be open to show, by contemporaneous history, that this mode of alluding to slaves and Slavery, instead of speaking of them, was employed on purpose to exclude from the Constitution the idea that there could be property in man.

To show all this is easy and certain.

When this obvious mistake of the Judges shall be brought to their notice, is it not reasonable to expect that they will withdraw the mistaken statement; and reconsider the conclusion based upon it?

And then it is to be remembered that "our fathers, who framed the Government under which we live"--the men who made the Constitution--decided this same Constitutional question in our favor, long ago--decided it without a division among themselves, when making the decision; without division among themselves about the meaning of it after it was made, and, so far as any evidence is left without basing it upon any mistaken statement of facts.

Under all these circumstances, do you really feel yourselves justified to break up this Government, unless such a court decision as yours is shall be at once submitted to as a conclusive and final rule of political action? But you will not abide the election of a Republican President. In that supposed event, you say, you will destroy the Union; and then, you say, the great crime of having destroyed it will be upon us!

That is cool. A highwayman holds a pistol to my ear, and mutters through his teeth, "stand and deliver, or I shall kill you, and then you will be a murderer!"

To be sure, what the robber demanded of me--my money--was my own; and I had a clear right to keep it; but it was no more my own than my vote is my own; and the threat of death to me, to extort my money, and the threat of destruction to the Union, to extort my vote, can scarcely be distinguished in principle.

A few words now to Republicans. It is exceedingly desirable that all parts of this great Confederacy shall be at peace, and in harmony, one with another. Let us Republicans do our part to have it so. Even though much provoked, let us do nothing through passion and ill temper. Even though the Southern people will not so much as listen to us, let us calmly consider their demands, and yield to them if, in our deliberate view of our duty, we possibly can. Judging by all they say and do, and by the subject and nature of their controversy with us, let us determine, if we can, what will satisfy them?

Will they be satisfied if the Territories be unconditionally surrendered to them? We know they will not. In all their present complaints against us, the Territories are scarcely mentioned. Invasions and insurrections are the rage now. Will it satisfy them if, in the future, we have nothing to do with invasions and insurrections? We know it will not. We so know because we know we never had anything to do with invasions and insurrections; and yet this total abstaining does not exempt us from the charge and the denunication.

The question recurs, what will satisfy them? Simply this: We must not only let them alone, but we must, somehow, convince them that we do let them alone. This, we know by experience, is no easy task. We have been so trying to convince them, from the very beginning of our organization, but with no success. In all our platforms and speeches, we have constantly protested our purpose to let them alone; but this has had no tendency to convince them. Alike unavailing to convince them is the fact that they have never detected a man of us in any attempt to disturb them.

These natural, and apparently adequate means all failing, what will convince them? This, and this only: cease to call slavery *wrong*, and join them in calling it *right*. And this must be done thoroughly-- done in *acts* as well as in *words*. Silence will not be tolerated--we must place ourselves avowedly with them. Senator Douglas's new sedition law must be enacted and enforced, suppressing all declarations that slavery is wrong, whether made in politics, in presses, in pulpits, or in private. We must arrest and return their fugitive slaves with greedy pleasure. We must pull down our Free-State constitutions. The whole atmosphere must be disinfected from all taint of opposition to Slavery, before they will cease to believe that all their troubles proceed from us.

I am quite aware they do not state their case precisely in this way. Most of them would probably say to us, "Let us alone, do nothing to us, and say what you please about Slavery." But we do let them alone--have never disturbed them--so that, after all, it is what we say, which dissatisfies them. They will continue to accuse us of doing, until we cease saying.

I am also aware they have not, as yet, in terms, demanded the overthrow of our Free-State Constitutions. Yet those Constitutions declare the wrong of Slavery, with more solemn emphasis, than do all other sayings against it; and when all these other sayings shall have been silenced, the overthrow of these Constitutions will be demanded, and nothing be left to resist the demand. It is nothing to the contrary, that they do not demand the whole of this just now. Demanding what they do, and for the reason they do, they can voluntarily stop nowhere short of this consummation. Holding as they do, that Slavery is morally right, and socially elevating, they cannot cease to demand a full national recognition of it, as a legal right, and a social blessing.

Nor can we justifiably withhold this, on any ground save our conviction that Slavery is wrong. If Slavery is right, all words, acts, laws, and Constitutions against it, are themselves wrong, and should be silenced, and swept away. If it is right, we cannot justly object to its nationality--its universality; if it is wrong, they cannot justly insist upon its extension--its enlargement. All they ask, we could readily grant, if we thought Slavery right; all we ask, they could as readily grant, if they thought it wrong. Their thinking it right, and our thinking it wrong, is the precise fact upon which depends the whole controversy. Thinking it right, as they do, they are not to blame for desiring its full recognition, as being right; but, thinking it wrong, as we do, can we yield to them? Can we cast our votes with their view, and against our own? In view of our moral, social, and political responsibilities, can we do this?

Wrong as we think Slavery is, we can yet afford to let alone where it is, because that much is due to the necessity arising from its actual presence in the nation; but can we, while our votes will prevent it, allow it to spread into the National Territories, and to overrun us here in these Free States? If our sense of duty forbids this, then let us stand by our duty, fearlessly and effectively. Let us be diverted by none of those sophistical contrivances wherewith we are so industriously plied and belabored--contrivances such as groping for some middle ground between the right and the wrong, vain as the search for a man who should be neither a living man nor a dead man--such as a policy of "don't care" on a question about which all true men do care--such as Union appeals beseeching true Union men to yield to Disunionists, reversing the divine rule, and calling, not the sinners, but the righteous to repentance--such as invocations to Washington, imploring men to unsay what Washington said, and undo what Washington did.

Neither let us be slandered from our duty by false accusations against us, nor frightened from it by menaces of destruction to the Government, nor of dungeons to ourselves. Let us have faith that right makes might, and in that faith, let us, to the end, dare to do our duty, as we understand it.

"Farewell to Springfield"

Springfield, Illinois, February 11, 1861

Friends, no one who has never been placed in a like position, can understand my feelings at this hour, nor the oppressive sadness I feel at this parting. For more than a quarter of a century I have lived among you, and during all that time I have received nothing but kindness at your hands. Here I have lived from my youth until now I am an old man. Here the most sacred ties of earth were assumed; here all my children were born; and here one of them lies buried. To you, dear friends, I owe all that I have, all that I am. All the strange, chequered past seems to crowd now upon my mind. Today I leave you; I go to assume a task more difficult than that which devolved upon General Washington. Unless the great God who assisted him, shall be with and aid me, I must fail. But if the same omniscient mind, and the same Almighty arm that directed and protected him, shall guide and support me, I shall not fail, I shall succeed. Let us all pray that the God of our fathers may not forsake us now. To him I commend you all--permit me to ask that with equal security and faith, you all will invoke His wisdom and guidance for me. With these few words I must leave you--for how long I know not. Friends, one and all, I must now bid you an affectionate farewell.

"First Inaugural Address"

Washington, D. C., March 4, 1861

Fellow-Citizens of the United States:

In compliance with a custom as old as the Government itself, I appear before you to address you briefly, and to take in your presence the oath prescribed by the Constitution of the United States to be taken by the President before he enters on the execution of his office. I do not consider it necessary at present for me to discuss those matters of administration about which there is no special anxiety or excitement.

Apprehension seems to exist among the people of the Southern States that by the accession of a Republican Administration, their property, and their peace and personal security are to be endangered. There has never been any reasonable cause for such apprehension. Indeed, the most ample evidence to the contrary has all the while existed, and been open to their inspection. It is found in nearly all the published speeches of him who now addresses you. I do but quote from one of those speeches when I declare that "I have no purpose, directly or indirectly, to interfere with the institution of Slavery in the States where it exists. I believe I have no lawful right to do so, and I have no inclination to do so." Those who nominated and elected me did so with full knowledge that I had made this and many similar declarations, and had never recanted them. And more than this, they placed in the platform, for my acceptance, and as a law to themselves and to me, the clear and emphatic resolution which I now read:

"*Resolved*, That the maintenance inviolate of the rights of the States, and especially the right of each State to order and control its own domestic institutions according to its own judgment exclusively, is essential to that balance of power on which the perfection and endurance of our political fabric depend; and we denounce the lawless invasion by armed force of the soil of any State or Territory, no matter under what pretext, as among the gravest of crimes."

I now reiterate these sentiments, and in doing so, I only press upon the public attention the most conclusive evidence of which the case is susceptible, that the property, peace and security of no section are to be in any wise endangered by the now incoming Administration. I add, too, that all the protection which, consistently with the Constitution and the laws, can be given, will be cheerfully given to all the States when lawfully demanded, for whatever cause, as cheerfully to one section as to another.

There is much controversy about the delivering up of fugitives from service or labor. The clause I now read is as plainly written in the Constitution as any other of its provisions:

"No person held to service or labor in one State under the laws thereof escaping into another, shall, in consequence of any law or regulation therein, be discharged from such service or labor, but shall be delivered up on claim of the party to whom such service or labor may be due."

It is scarcely questioned that this provision was intended by those who made it, for the reclaiming of what we call fugitive slaves, and the intention of the law-giver is the law. All members of Congress swear their support to the whole Constitution; to this provision as well as any other. To the proposition, then, that slaves whose cases come within the terms of this clause "shall be delivered up," their oaths are unanimous. Now, if they would make the effort in good temper, could they not, with nearly equal unanimity, frame and pass a law by means of which to keep good that unanimous oath. There is some difference of opinion whether this clause should be enforced by national or by State authority, but surely that difference is not a very material one. If the slave is to be surrendered, it can be of but little consequence to him or to others, by which authority it is done, and should any one, in any case, be content that his oath shall go unkept on a merely unsubstantial controversy as to how it shall be kept? Again, in any law upon this subject, ought not all the safeguards of liberty known in the civilized and humane jurisprudence to be introduced, so that a free-man be not, in any case, surrendered as a slave, and might it not be well at the same time to provide by law for the enforcement of that clause in the Constitution which guarantees that "the citizens of each State shall be entitled to all the privileges and immunities of citizens in the several States." I take the official oath to-day with no mental reservations, and with no purpose to construe the Constitution or laws, by any hypercritical rules; and while I do not choose now to specify particular acts of Congress as proper to be enforced, I do suggest that it will be much safer for all, both in official and private stations, to conform to and abide by all those acts which stand unrepealed, than to violate any of them, trusting to find impunity in having them held to be unconstitutional.

It is seventy-two years since the first inauguration of a President under our National Constitution. During that period fifteen different and very distinguished citizens have in succession administered the Executive branch of the Government. They have conducted it through many perils, and generally with great success. Yet, with all this scope for precedent, I now enter upon the same task for the brief Constitutional term of four years, under great and peculiar difficulty. A disruption of the Federal Union, heretofore only menaced, is now formidably attempted. I hold, that in contemplation of universal law and of the Constitution, the Union of these States is perpetual. Perpetuity is implied if not expressed in the fundamental law of all National Governments. It is safe to assert that no Government proper ever had a provision in its organic law for its own termination. Continue to execute all the express provisions of our National Constitution, and the Union will endure forever, it being impossible to destroy it except by some action not provided for in the instrument itself. Again, if the United States be not a government proper, but an association of States in the nature of a contract merely, can it as a contract be peaceably unmade by less than all the parties who made it. One party to a contract may violate it, break it, so to speak, but does it not require all to lawfully rescind it? Descending from these general principles, we find the proposition that, in legal contemplation, the Union is perpetual, confirmed by the history of the Union itself. The Union is much older than the Constitution. It was formed, in fact, by the articles of association in 1774. It was matured and continued in the Declaration of Independence in 1776. It was further matured, and the faith of all the then thirteen States expressly plighted and engaged that it should be perpetual by the Articles of Confederation in 1778, and finally in 1787 one of the declared objects for ordaining and establishing the Constitution was to form a more perfect Union.

But if the destruction of the Union by one or by a part only of the States be lawfully possible, the Union is less than before, the Constitution having lost the vital element of perpetuity. It follows from these views that no State, upon its own mere motion, can lawfully get out of the Union; that resolves and ordinances to that effect are legally void, and that acts of violence within any State or States against the authority of the United States are insurrectionary or revolutionary, according to circumstances. I, therefore, consider that, in view of the Constitution and the laws, the Union is unbroken, and, to the extent of my ability, I shall take care, as the Constitution itself expressly enjoins upon me, that the laws of the Union be faithfully executed in all the States. Doing this I deem to be only a simple duty on my part. I shall perform it so far as is practicable, unless my rightful masters, the American people, shall withhold the requisition, or in some authoritative manner direct the contrary. I trust this will not be regarded as a menace, but only as the declared purpose of the Union, that it will constitutionally defend and maintain itself. In doing this there need be no bloodshed or violence, and there shall be none unless it is forced upon the national authority. The power confided to me will be used to hold, occupy, and possess the property and places belonging to the Government, and collect the duties and imports, but beyond what may be necessary for these objects, there will be no invasion, no using of force against or among the people anywhere. Where hostility to the United States shall be so great and so universal as to prevent competent resident citizens from holding the Federal offices, there will be no attempt to force obnoxious strangers among the people that object. While the strict legal right may exist of the Government to enforce the exercise of these offices, the attempt to do so would be so irritating, and so nearly impracticable with all, that I deem it better to forego for the time the uses of such offices. The mails, unless repelled, will continue to be furnished in all parts of the Union. So far as possible, the people every where shall have that sense of perfect security which is most favorable to calm thought and reflection. The course here indicated will be followed, unless current events and experience shall show a modification or change to be proper, and in every case and exigency my best discretion will be exercised according to the circumstances actually existing, and with a view and hope of a peaceful solution of the national troubles and the restoration of fraternal sympathies and affections. That there are persons in one section or another who seek to destroy the Union at all events, and are glad of any pretext to do it, I will neither affirm nor deny. But, if there be such, I need address no word to them. To those, however, who really love the Union, may I not speak? Before entering upon so grave a matter as the destruction of our national fabric, with all its benefits, its memories, and its hopes, would it not be wise to ascertain precisely why we do it? Will you hazard so desperate a step while any portion of the ills you fly from have no real existence? Will you while the certain ills you fly to are greater than all the real ones you fly from? Will you risk the commission of so fearful a mistake? All profess to be content in the Union, if all Constitutional rights can be maintained. Is it true then, that any right plainly written in the Constitution has been denied? I think not. Happily the human mind is so constituted that no party can reach to the audacity of doing this. Think, if you can, of a single instance in which a plainly-written provision of the Constitution has ever been denied. If, by the mere force of numbers, a majority should deprive a minority of any clearly-written constitutional right, it might in a moral point of view, justify revolution; certainly would, if such right were a vital one. But such is not our case. All the vital rights of minorities and of individuals are so plainly assured to them by affirmations and negations, guaranties and prohibitions, in the Constitution, that controversies never arise concerning them. But no organic law can ever be framed with a provision specifically applicable to every question which may occur in practical administration. No foresight can anticipate, nor any document of reasonable length contain express provisions for all possible questions. Shall fugitives from labor be surrendered by National or by State authority? The Constitution does not expressly say. Must Congress prohibit Slavery in the Territories? The Constitution does not expressly say. From questions of this class spring all our constitutional controversies, and we divide upon them into majorities and minorities. If the minority will not acquiesce the majority must, or the Government must cease. There is no alternative for continuing the Government but acquiescence on the one side or the other. If a minority in such a case will secede rather than acquiesce, they make a precedent which in turn will divide and ruin them, for a minority of their own will secede from them whenever a majority refuses to be controlled by such a minority. For instance, why may not any portion of a new Confederacy a year or two hence arbitrarily secede again, precisely as portions of the present Union now claim to secede from it? All who cherish disunion sentiments are now being educated to the exact temper of doing this. Is there such perfect identity of interests among the States to compose a new Union as to produce harmony only and prevent renewed secession? Plainly, the central idea of secession is the essence of anarchy. A majority, held in restraint by constitutional checks and limitations, and always changing easily with deliberate changes of popular opinions and sentiments, is the only true sovereign of a free people. Whoever rejects it, does, of necessity, fly to anarchy or to despotism. Unanimity is impossible. The rule of a minority, as a permanent arrangement, is wholly inadmissible, so that, rejecting the majority principle, anarchy or despotism in some form is all that is left.

I do not forget the position assumed by some, that Constitutional questions are to be decided by the Supreme Court, nor do I deny that such decisions must be binding in any case upon the parties to a suit, as to the object of that suit, while they are also entitled to very high respect and consideration in all parallel cases by all other Departments of the Government, and while it is obviously possible that such decision may be erroneous in any given case, still the evil effect following it, being limited to that particular case, with the chance that it may be overruled, and never become a precedent for other cases, can better be borne than could the evils of a different practice. At the same time the candid citizen must confess that if the policy of the Government upon the vital questions affecting the whole people is to be irrevocably fixed by the decisions of the Supreme Court, the instant they are made in ordinary litigation between parties in personal actions, the people will have ceased to be their own masters, having to that extent practically resigned their government into the hands of that eminent tribunal. Nor is there in this view any assault upon the Court or the Judges. It is a duty from which they may not shrink to decide cases properly brought before them, and it is no fault of theirs if others seek to turn their decisions to political purposes. One section of our country believes Slavery is right and ought to be extended, while the other believes it is wrong and ought not to be extended. This is the only substantial dispute; and the Fugitive Slave clause of the Constitution, and the law for the suppression of the foreign slave-trade, are each as well enforced, perhaps, as any law can ever be in a community where the moral sense of the people imperfectly supports the law itself. The great body of the people abide by the dry legal obligation in both cases, and a few break over in each. This, I think, cannot be perfectly cured, and it would be worse in both cases after the separation of the sections than before. The foreign slave-trade, now imperfectly suppressed, would be ultimately revived, without restriction in one section, while fugitive slaves, now only partially surrendered, would not be surrendered at all by the other.

Physically speaking, we cannot separate--we cannot remove our respective sections from each other, nor build an impassable wall between them. A husband and wife may be divorced and go out of the presence and beyond the reach of each other, but the different parts of our country cannot do this. They cannot but remain face to face, and intercourse, either amicable or hostile, must continue between them. Is it possible, then, to make that intercourse more advantageous or more satisfactory after separation than before? Can aliens make treaties easier than friends can make laws? Can treaties be more faithfully enforced between aliens than laws can among friends? Suppose you go to-day, you cannot fight always, and when, after much loss on both sides and no gain on either, you cease fighting, the identical questions as to terms of intercourse are again upon you.

This country, with its institutions, belongs to the people who inhabit it. Whenever they shall grow weary of the existing Government, they can exercise their constitutional right of amending, or their revolutionary right to dismember or overthrow it. I cannot be ignorant of the fact that many worthy and patriotic citizens are desirous of having the national Constitution amended. While I make no recommendation of amendment, I fully recognize the full authority of the people over the whole subject, to be exercised in either of the modes prescribed in the instrument itself, and I should, under existing circumstances, favor rather than oppose a fair opportunity being afforded the people to act upon it. I will venture to add that to me the Convention mode seems preferable, in that it allows amendments to originate with the people themselves, instead of only permitting them to take or reject propositions originated by others not especially chosen for the purpose, and which might not be precisely such as they would wish either to accept or refuse. I understand that a proposed amendment to the Constitution, which amendment however, I have not seen, has passed Congress, to the effect that the Federal Government shall never interfere with the domestic institutions of States, including that of persons held to service. To avoid misconstruction of what I have said, I depart from my purpose, not to speak of particular amendments, so far as to say that, holding such a provision to now be implied constitutional law, I have no objection to its being made express and irrevocable.

The Chief-Magistrate derives all his authority from the people, and they have conferred none upon him to fix the terms for the separation of the States. The people themselves also can do this if they choose, but the Executive, as such, has nothing to do with it. His duty is to administer the present Government as it came to his hands, and to transmit it unimpaired by him to his successor. Why should there not be a patient confidence in the ultimate justice of the people? Is there any better or equal hope in the world? In our present differences, is either party without faith of being in the right? If the Almighty Ruler of nations, with his eternal truth and justice, be on your side of the North, or on yours of the South, that truth and that justice will surely prevail by the judgment of this great tribunal, the American people. By the frame of the Government under which we live, this same people have wisely given their public servants but little power for mischief, and have with equal wisdom provided for the return of that little to their own hands at very short intervals. While the people retain their virtue and vigilence, no Administration, by any extreme wickedness or folly, can very seriously injure the Government in the short space of four years.

My countrymen, one and all, think calmly and well upon this whole subject. Nothing valuable can be lost by taking time. If there be an object to hurry any of you, in hot haste, to a step which you would never take deliberately, that object will be frustrated by taking time--but no good object can be frustrated by it. Such of you as are now dissatisfied still have the old Constitution unimpaired, and on the sensitive point, the laws of your own framing under it, while the new Administration will have no immediate power, if it would, to change either. If it were admitted that you who are dissatisfied hold the right side in the dispute, there is still no single reason for precipitate action. Intelligence, patriotism, Christianity, and a firm reliance on Him who has never yet forsaken this favored land, are still competent to adjust, in the best way, all our present difficulty. In your hands, my dissatisfied fellow-countrymen, and not in mine, is the momentous issue of civil war. The Government will not assail you. You can have no conflict without being yourselves the aggressors. You have no oath registered in Heaven to destroy the Government, while I shall have the most solemn one to "preserve, protect and defend" it. I am loth to close. We are not enemies, but friends. We must not be enemies. Though passion may have strained, it must not break our bonds of affection. The mystic chords of memory streching from every battle-field and patriot grave to every living heart and hearthstone all over this broad land, will yet swell the chorus of the Union, when again touched, as surely they will be, by the better angels of our nature.

"Gettysburg Address"

Gettysburg, Pennsylvania, November 19, 1863

Fourscore and seven years ago, our fathers brought forth upon this continent a new nation, conceived in liberty and dedicated to the proposition that all men are created equal.

Now we are engaged in a great civil war, testing whether that nation--or any nation, so conceived and so dedicated--can long endure.

We are met on a great battle-field of that war. We are met to dedicate a portion of it as the final resting-place of those who have given their lives that that nation might live.

It is altogether fitting and proper that we should do this.

But, in a larger sense, we cannot dedicate, we cannot consecrate, we cannot hallow, this ground. The brave men, living and dead, who struggled here, have consecrated it, far above our power to add or to detract.

The world will very little note nor long remember what we say here; but it can never forget what they did here.

It is for us, the living, rather, *to be dedicated*, here, to the unfinished work that they have thus far so nobly carried on. It is rather for us to be here dedicated to the great task remaining before us; that from these honored dead we take increased devotion to that cause for which they *here* gave the last full measure of devotion; that we here highly resolve that these dead shall not have died in vain; that the nation shall, under God, have a new birth of freedom, and that government of the people, by the people, for the people, shall not perish from the earth.

"Second Inaugural Address"

Washington, D. C., March 4, 1865

Fellow-Countrymen: At this second appearing to take the oath of the Presidential office, there is less occasion for an extended address than there was at the first. Then a statement somewhat in detail of a course to be pursued seemed fitting and proper. Now, at the expiration of four years, during which public declarations have been constantly called forth on every point and phase of the great contest which still absorbs the attention and engrosses the energies of the Nation, little that is new could be presented. The progress of our arms, upon which all else chiefly depends, is as well known to the public as to myself, and it is, I trust, reasonably satisfactory and encouraging to all. With high hope for the future, no prediction in regard to it is ventured.

On the occasion corresponding to this four years ago, all thoughts were anxiously directed to an impending civil war. All dreaded it; all sought to avoid it. While the Inaugural Address was being delivered from this place, devoted altogether to *saving* the Union without war, insurgent agents were in this city seeking to *destroy* it without war--seeking to dissolve the Union and divide its effects, by negotiation. Both parties deprecated war, but one of them would *make* war rather than let the nation survive, and the other would *accept* war rather than let it perish, and the war came.

One eighth of the whole population were colored slaves, not distributed generally over the Union, but localized in the Southern part of it. These slaves constituted a peculiar and powerful interest. All knew that this interest was somehow the cause of the war. To strengthen, perpetuate and extend this interest was the object for which the insurgents would rend the Union even by war, while the

Government claimed no right to do more than to restrict the territorial enlargement of it.

Neither party expected for the war the magnitude or the duration, which it has already attained. Neither anticipated that the *cause* of the conflict might cease with or even before the conflict itself should cease. Each looked for an easier triumph and a result less fundamental and astounding.

Both read the same Bible and pray to the same God, and each invokes His aid against the other. It may seem strange that any men should dare to ask a just God's assistance in wringing their bread from the sweat of other men's faces, but let us judge not that we be not judged. The prayers of both could not be answered--that of neither has been answered fully. The Almighty has His own purposes. Woe unto the world because of offenses, for it must needs be that offenses come; but woe to that man by whom the offense. If we shall suppose that American Slavery is one of these offenses, which in the providence of God must needs come, but which having continued through His appointed time He now wills to remove, and that He gives to both North and South this terrible war as the woe due to those by whom the offense came, shall we discern therein any departure from those Divine attributes which the believers in a living God always ascribe to Him?

Fondly do we hope, fervently do we pray, that this mighty scourge of war may speedily pass away. Yet, if God wills that it continue until all the wealth piled by the bondman's two hundred and fifty years of unrequited toil shall be sunk, and until every drop of blood drawn with the lash shall be paid by another drawn with the sword, as was said three thousand years ago, so still it must be said, that the judgments of the Lord are true and righteous altogether.

With malice toward none, with charity for all, with firmness in the right, as God gives us to see the right, let us strive on to finish the work we are in, to bind up the nation's wounds, to care for him who shall have borne the battle, and for his widow and his orphans; to do all which may achieve and cherish a just and lasting peace among ourselves and with all nations.

Notes

PART I

PREFACE

1. Theodore C. Blegen, *Lincoln's Imagery: A Study in Word Power* (La Crosse, WI: Sumac Press, 1954), p. 31; William Jennings Bryan, "Lincoln as an Orator," in *Building the Myth: Selected Speeches Memorializing Lincoln*, ed. Waldo W. Braden (Urbana, IL: University of Illinois Press, 1990), p. 141; and Henry Clay Whitney, *Life on the Circuit with Lincoln*, 1892, Introduction and notes by Paul M. Angle (Caldwell, ID: Caxton Printers, 1940), p. 200.

ACKNOWLEDGMENTS

1. The quotation from Lincoln comes from a letter to his friend Joseph Gillespie, Abraham Lincoln, *The Collected Works of Abraham Lincoln*, (hereafter *CW*), ed. Roy P. Basler, Marion D. Pratt, and Lloyd A. Dunlap (New Brunswick, NJ: Rutgers University Press, 1953, vol. 2, p. 57.

INTRODUCTION

1. "Lost Speech," Bloomington, Illinois, [May 29, 1856].
2. Herbert Mitgang, ed., *Abraham Lincoln: A Press Portrait* (Chicago, IL: Quadrangle Books, 1971), p. xv; Horace White, "Introduction," in William H. Herndon and Jesse W. Weik, *Abraham Lincoln: The True Story of a Great Life*, ed. Horace White (New York: D. Appleton and Co., 1892), vol. 1, pp. xix-xx.

3. Roy P. Basler, "Lincoln's Development as a Writer," in *Abraham Lincoln: His Speeches and Writings*, ed. Roy P. Basler (Cleveland, OH: The World Publishing Company, 1946), p. 28.

4. Matlon, Ronald, J. and Peter C. Facciola, eds., *Index to Journals in Communication Studies Through 1985* (Annandale, VA: Speech Communication Association, 1987).

5. Bernard Mayo, *Myths and Men: George Washington, Patrick Henry, Thomas Jefferson* (Athens, GA: University of Georgia Press, 1959), p. 2.

6. Herbert A. Wichelns, "The Literary Criticism of Oratory," in *The Rhetorical Idiom*, ed. Donald C. Bryant (Ithaca, NY: Cornell University Press, 1958) p. 35. I used the following sources for each of the speech texts in the Selected Speeches section: "Lyceum Address," *Sangamo Journal*, February 3, 1838; "Temperance Address," *Sangamo Journal*, March 25, 1842; "'House Divided' Speech," *Chicago Tribune*, June 19, 1858; "Second Lecture on Discoveries and Inventions," *Illinois State Journal*, February 14, 1959; "Cooper Union Address," *New-York Daily Tribune*, February 28, 1860; "Farewell to Springfield," *Illinois State Journal*, February 12, 1861; "First Inaugural Address, *New-York Daily Tribune*, March 5, 1861; "Gettysburg Address," *Boston Advertiser* (Hale version); and "Second Inaugural Address," *New-York Daily Tribune*, March 6, 1865.

7. *CW*, 9 vols.

8. *New-York Daily Tribune*, February 28, 1860, p. 1; Earl W. Wiley, "Lincoln the Speaker, 1830-1837," *Quarterly Journal of Speech* 21 (1935): 305-22.

9. Information on illiteracy was not obtained by the Bureau of the Census until 1870. In 1870, twenty percent of the population in the United States was illiterate. See *Historical Statistics of the United States: Colonial Times to 1970*, Part I (Washington, D.C.: Bureau of the Census, 1975), pp. 364-65.

10. Michael Leff, "Rhetorical Timing in Lincoln's 'House Divided' Speech," The Van Zelst Lecture in Communication (Evanston, IL: Northwestern University School of Speech, May 1983), p. 4. The phrase "literary artist" is used in many works; this particular reference comes from Herbert Joseph Edwards and John Erskine Hankins, *Lincoln the Writer: The Development of His Literary Style* (Orono, ME: University of Maine, 1962), pp. 61 and 72.

11. The seven Lincoln-Douglas debates took place in Illinois in 1858: (1) Ottawa, August 21; (2) Freeport, August 27; (3) Jonesboro, September 15; (4) Charleston, September 18; (5) Galesburg, October 7; (6) Quincey, October 13; and (7) Alton, October 15.

12. *CW*, vol. 1, p. xv.

1: LINCOLN SPEAKS ABOUT SPEAKING

1. Richard Weaver, *The Ethics of Rhetoric* (Chicago, IL: Henry Regnery Company, 1953), p. 105.

2. The quotation from Lincoln's "Autobiography" may be found in *CW*, vol. 4, p. 62.

3. Lincoln used the term "political religion" in his "Lyceum Address" (see Selected Speeches). For an excellent discussion of what Lincoln meant by "political religion," see Glen E. Thurow, *Abraham Lincoln and American Political Religion* (Albany, NY: State University of New York Press, 1976) and Glen E. Thurow, "Abraham Lincoln and American Political Religion," in *The Historian's Lincoln*, ed. Gabor S. Boritt and Norman O. Forness (Urbana, IL: University of Illinois Press, 1988), pp. 125-43. The quotation comes from *CW*, vol. 4, p. 24.

4. *CW*, vol. 1, p. 8 and *CW*, vol. 2, p. 124.

5. *CW*, vol. 1, p. 509.

6. Francis Carpenter, *The Inner Life of Abraham Lincoln: Six Months at the White House* (Boston: Houghton Mifflin, 1883), pp. 312-13; Herndon and Weik, vol. 2, pp. 301-302.

7. For a discussion of Lincoln's "Lectures on Discoveries and Inventions," see James Frank Vickrey, Jr., "The Lectures on 'Discoveries and Inventions'--A Neglected Aspect of the Public Speaking Career of Abraham Lincoln," *Central States Speech Journal* 21 (1970): 181-90. The other quotation comes from *CW*, vol. 4, pp. 480-81.

8. Herndon and Weik, vol. 1, pp. 102 and 41.

9. Herndon and Weik, vol. 2, pp. 302 and 1.

10. James Hurt, "All the Living and the Dead: Lincoln's Imagery," *American Literature* 52 (1980): 357.

11. *CW*, vol. 3, p. 344.

12. Richard Whately, *Elements of Rhetoric*, ed. Douglas Ehninger, 7th ed. (1846; rpt., Carbondale, IL: Southern Illinois University Press, 1963); p. 112.

13. Chauncey M. DePew in *Reminiscences of Abraham Lincoln, By Distinguished Men of His Time*, ed. Allen Thorndyke Rice (New York: North American Review, 1888), pp. 427-28.

14. Quintilian, *Institutes of Oratory*, trans. J. S. Watson (London: George Bell and Sons, 1875).

15. *CW*, vol. 2, p. 81.

16. *CW*, vol. 2, p. 126; *CW*, vol. 7, p. 234; Herndon and Weik, vol. 2, pp. 1-29.

17. Herndon and Weik, vol. 2, p. 307.

18. *CW*, vol. 1, p. 134; *CW*, vol. 4, p. 433; and Carpenter, pp. 126-27.

19. Quoted in Albert J. Beveridge, *Abraham Lincoln, 1809-1858* (Boston, MA: Houghton Mifflin, 1928), p. 81; *CW*, vol. 1, p. 509; *CW*, vol. 1, p. 165.

20. *CW*, vol. 2, p. 248; Herndon and Weik, vol. 1, p. 325.

21. *CW*, vol. 1, p. 62; and Mort Reis Lewis, "Abraham Lincoln: Storyteller," in *Lincoln for the Ages*, ed. Ralph G. Newman (Garden City, NY: Doubleday & Company, 1960), p. 132.

22. *CW*, vol. 2, p. 81.

23. *CW*, vol. 4, p. 209; *CW*, vol. 7, p. 17.

2. DID LINCOLN PRACTICE WHAT HE PREACHED? CHARACTERISTICS AND DEVELOPMENT OF LINCOLN'S SPEAKING

1. William Jennings Bryan, in Braden, p. 144; T. Harry Williams, ed. *Selected Writings and Speeches of Abraham Lincoln* (New York: Hendricks House, 1943), pp. xviii-liii; Herbert Joseph Edwards and John Erskine Hankins, "Lincoln the Writer: The Development of His Literary Style," *University of Maine Bulletin* 64 (10 April 1962): 81; and Marie Hochmuth Nichols, "Lincoln's First Inaugural," in *American Speeches*, ed. Wayland Maxfield Parrish and Marie Hochmuth Nichols (New York: Longmans, Green and Company, 1954).

2. Mark Van Doren, *New York Herald Tribune Book Review* (8 February 1953): 6.

3. Herndon and Weik, vol. 2, p. 307. For contemporary reactions to Lincoln's speeches, see Howard Cecil Perkins, ed. *Northern Editorials on Secession*, 2 vols. (New York: D. Appleton-Century, 1942); Dwight Lowell Dumond, ed. *Southern Editorials on Secession* (New York: The Century Company, 1931); and Mitgang.

4. *CW*, vol. 4, p. 226; *CW*, vol. 4, p. 24; *CW*, vol. 2, p. 506; *CW*, vol. 4, p. 236; and Richard Hofstadter, "Abraham Lincoln and the Self-Made Myth," *The American Political Tradition* (New York: Vintage Books, 1948), p. 94.

5. Herndon and Weik, vol. 2, p. 318; DePew in Rice, pp. 427-28.

6. Eliade, Mircea, *The Myth of the Eternal Return: Or Cosmos and History* (Princeton, NJ: Princeton University Press, 1971).

7. Weaver, p. 109.

8. *CW*, vol. 7, p. 512; and Weaver, p. 110.

9. George B. Forgie, *Patricide in the House Divided: A Psychological Interpretation of Lincoln and His Age* (New York: W. W. Norton, 1979), p. 267.

10. All Biblical quotations in this book come from *The Holy Bible Containing the Old and New Testaments in the King James Version, Self-pronouncing Red Letter Edition* (New York: Thomas

Nelson Publishers, 1984). For help in locating Biblical words and passages, I used Robert Young, *Young's Analytical Concordance to the Bible Based upon the King James Version* (New York: Thomas Nelson Publishers, 1982).

11. Herndon and Weik, vol. 2, p. 67.

12. James M. McPherson, "How Lincoln Won the War with Metaphors." The Eighth Annual R. Gerald McMurty Lecture. Fort Wayne, IN: Louis A. Warren Lincoln Library and Museum, 1985. This lecture is reprinted in James M. McPherson, *Abraham Lincoln and the Second American Revolution* (New York: Oxford University Press, 1990): 93-112.

13. Blegen, p. 21; Michael Osborn, "The 'Seven Spheres' of Interpreting the Rhetoric in Metaphor," unpublished paper, fall 1988, p. 2; Michael Osborn, "Archetypal Metaphor in Rhetoric: The Light-Dark Family." *Quarterly Journal of Speech* 53 (1967): 115-26; Michael Osborn, "The Evolution of the Archetypal Sea in Rhetoric and Poetic," *Quarterly Journal of Speech* 63 (1977): 346-63; and Michael Osborn and Douglas Ehninger, "The Metaphor in Public Address," *Speech Monographs* 29 (1962): 223-34.

14. Blegen, p. 21; *CW*, vol. 4, p. 15; *CW*, vol. 4, p. 11; *CW*, vol. 3, p. 313; and Osborn, "Archetypal Metaphor in Rhetoric," p. 116.

15. Forgie, p. 16 and p. 55.

16. *CW*, vol. 4, p. 195.

17. Forgie, p. 104.

18. *CW*, vol. 6, pp. 409-10.

19. Carroll C. Arnold, *Criticism of Oral Rhetoric* (Columbus, OH: Bell and Howell Company, 1974), pp. 168-69.

20. Nichols, p. 98.

21. Herndon and Weik, vol. 2, p. 302.

22. Blegen, p. 26.

23. For instances where Lincoln referred to his anxiety about speaking, see *CW*, vol. 1, p. 159 and *CW*, vol. 3, p. 438.

24. Mildred Freburg Berry, "Abraham Lincoln: His Development in the Skills of the Platform." In *A History and Criticism of American Public Address*, ed. William Norwood Brigance, vol. 2 (New York: Russell and Russell, 1960), p. 851.

25. *CW*, vol. 4, p. 209; *CW*, vol. 5, p. 450.

26. *CW*, vol. 7, p. 17.

27. Lord Charnwood, *Abraham Lincoln* (Garden City, NY: Doubleday, 1917), p. 439.

28. Roy P. Basler, "Abraham Lincoln's Rhetoric," *American Literature* 11 (May 1939): 167.

29. Joshua F. Speed, in Herndon and Weik, vol. 2, pp. 234-35.

30. Herndon and Weik, vol. 1, p. 181 and Hunt, p. 364 describe the "Lyceum Address" as "highly sophomoric." The Basler quotation

comes from Roy P. Basler, "Abraham Lincoln--Artist," *North American Review* 245 (Spring 1938): 144.

3. NO LAUGHING MATTER: LINCOLN'S USE OF HUMOR AS A RHETORICAL DEVICE

1. The story about the Quaker ladies may be found in "Mint of Lincoln's Wit," *Magazine of History* 32 (1926): 44; Herndon and Weik, vol. 2, p. 301.
2. William D. Howells, *Life of Abraham Lincoln* (Springfield, IL: Abraham Lincoln Association, 1938), p. 20.
3. Carl Sandburg, *Abraham Lincoln: The War Years* (New York: Harcourt Brace and World, 1939), vol. 3, p. 306.
4. Quoted in Rufus R. Wilson, *Lincoln Among His Friends* (Caldwell, ID: Caxton Printers, 1942), p. 26.
5. Sandburg, *The War Years*, vol. 3, p. 367; Judge David Davis, quoted in Reinhard H. Luthin, *The Real Abraham Lincoln* (Englewood Cliffs, NJ: Prentice-Hall, 1960), p. 116.
6. James G. Randall, *Lincoln the President: Midstream* (New York: Dodd, Mead, 1953), p. 67; Mark E. Neely, Jr., Director of the Lincoln Museum, made the same argument. See his "Commentary on 'Abe Lincoln Laughing.'" in *The Historian's Lincoln*, p. 28. Lincoln's comment about stories may be found in Anthony Gross, *Lincoln's Own Stories* (New York: Harpers, 1912), p. 210.
7. Sandburg, *The War Years*, vol. 3, p. 300; DePew in *Reminiscences*, pp. 427-28; *New York Herald*, 21 November 1863; and Alexander K. McClure, *Abe Lincoln's Yarns and Stories* (Philadelphia, PA: Times Publishing Company, 1892), Preface, A, B.
8. Story told by Judge Beckwith, quoted in McClure, p. 93.
9. Mort Reis Lewis, "Lincoln's Humor." In *Lincoln: A Contemporary Portrait*, ed. Allan Nevins and Irving Stone (Garden City, NY: Doubleday and Company, 1962), p. 168.
10. P. M. Zall, *Abe Lincoln Laughing* (Berkeley, CA: University of California Press, 1982). For some Irish stories not included in Zall's book, see *CW*, vol. 1, pp. 177-78 and *CW*, vol. 4, p. 217.
11. Jules Feiffer, quoted in *Getting Angry Six Times a Week--A Portfolio of Political Cartoons*, ed. Alan F. Westin (Boston, MA: Beacon Press, 1970), p. vii; *CW*, vol. 1, p. 509.
12. W. A. Dahlberg, "Lincoln the Wit," *Quarterly Journal of Speech* 31 (1945): 425; and *CW*, vol. 3, p. 17. The phrase "wit lash" comes from Dahlberg, p. 426.
13. *CW*, vol. 1, pp. 509-10.
14. *CW*, vol. 3, p. 279 and *CW*, vol. 3, p. 184.
15. *CW*, vol. 3, p. 412.
16. *CW*, vol. 3, p. 278.
17. *CW*, vol. 4, p. 233.

18. Aristotle, *The Rhetoric and the Poetics of Aristotle*, trans. W. Rhys Roberts, ed. Friedrich Solmsen (New York: Random House, 1954), p. 216.

19. *The New York Herald*, quoted in Sandburg, *War Years*, vol. 3, p. 303.

20. *New York Herald*, 19 February 1864; Robert Hitt interview in Stewart Scrapbook, Huntington Library, accession 151179, 5: 64, quoted in P. M. Zall, "Abe Lincoln Laughing," in *The Historian's Lincoln*, p. 10; Sandburg, *The War Years*, vol. 3, pp. 321 and 316.

21. Zall, "Abe Lincoln Laughing," p. 3.

4. LINCOLN'S FIRST INAUGURAL: PEACE AND SWORD

1. Nichols, p. 95. When I presented a draft of this chapter at the Eastern Communication Association Convention (Pittsburgh, PA: 28 April 1991), historian Gabor S. Boritt said in his "Response" that Lincoln's "First Inaugural Address" set "just about the right tone."

2. Perkins; Dumond; and Mitgang.

3. Judd Stewart, *Lincoln's First Inaugural: Original Draft and Its Final Form* (privately printed, 1920).

4. Gabor S. Boritt, "The Voyage to the Colony of Linconia: The Sixteenth President, Black Colonization, and the Defense Mechanism of Avoidance," *The Historian* 37 (1975): 619-32.

5. *CW*, vol. 4, p. 423; Gabor S. Boritt, "Abraham Lincoln: War Opponent and War President," The Inaugural Lecture of the First Robert C. Fluhrer Professor of Civil War Studies (Gettysburg, PA: 28 March 1987).

6. *CW*, vol. 4, p. 230. For a detailed discussion of this twelve-day journey, see Victor Searcher, *Lincoln's Journey to Greatness, A Factual Account of the Twelve-Day Inaugural Trip* (New York: Holt, Rinehart and Winston, 1960).

7. *CW*, vol. 4, p. 226; *CW*, vol. 4, p. 210; and *CW*, vol. 4, p. 231.

8. *Daily Missouri Republican*, 21 November 1860, quoted in Dumond, p. 260.

9. *New York Journal of Commerce* and *Albany Evening Journal* (5 March 1861), quoted in Perkins, vol. 2, pp. 631 and 629.

10. *The Richmond Times Dispatch* (5 March 1861), quoted in Dumond, p. 475.

11. *CW*, vol. 1, p. 48; *CW*, vol. 3, p. 453; *CW*, vol. 4, p. 240; *CW*, vol. 4, p. 226; and *CW*, vol. 4, p. 199.

5. EVOLVING RHETORICAL STANCES ON EMANCIPATION

1. *CW*, vol. 3, p. 315; and *CW*, vol. 3, pp. 145-46.

2. *CW*, vol. 7, p. 281; *CW*, vol. 3, p. 312; and *CW*, vol. 3, p. 315.

3. *CW*, vol. 2, p. 532; *CW*, vol. 2, pp. 222-23; and *CW*, vol. 5, p. 537.

4. *CW*, vol. 4, p. 18.

5. The speech Lincoln referred to in his "First Inaugural Address" was his "Reply to Douglas" in the first debate at Ottawa. See *CW*, vol. 3, p. 16. *CW*, vol. 4, p. 11.

6. *CW*, vol. 6, p. 64.

7. *CW*, vol. 3, p. 220.

8. *CW*, vol. 3, p. 16; *CW*, vol. 3, p. 249; *CW*, vol. 4, p. 240; *CW*, vol. 4, p. 438; G. S. Boritt, *Lincoln and the Economics of the American Dream* (Memphis, TN: Memphis State University Press, 1978).

9. *CW*, vol. 3, p. 249.

10. *CW*, vol. 3, pp. 145-46.

11. *CW*, vol. 2, p. 498; *CW*, vol. 3, p. 249.

12. *CW*, vol. 3, p. 27; *CW*, vol. 2, p. 256.

13. *CW*, vol. 4, p. 27.

14. Weaver, pp. 97 and 112.

15. *CW*, vol. 8, p. 405.

16. Leff, p. 15; and Matthew 7: 24-27.

17. *CW*, vol. 2, p. 547; and *CW*, vol. 4, p. 240.

18. The phrase "the last best hope of earth" comes from Lincoln's "Annual Message to Congress," 1 December 1862 (*CW*, vol. 5, p. 537).

19. Benjamin P. Thomas, "Abe Lincoln, Country Lawyer," *The Atlantic Monthly* 193 (February 1954): 61.

20. *CW*, vol. 2, p. 406 and *CW*, vol. 3, p. 301; Weaver, p. 112. David Zarefsky and Glen E. Thurow also argued that Lincoln considered the equality pronouncement in the Declaration of Independence a proposition rather than a fact. See David Zarefsky, *Lincoln, Douglas, and Slavery: In the Crucible of Public Debate* (Chicago, IL: University of Chicago Press, 1990) and Thurow, *Abraham Lincoln*.

21. *CW*, vol. 5, p. 388; *CW*, vol. 5, pp. 433-34. Examples by historians of the argument that Lincoln used the Greeley letter rhetorically may be found in Don E. Fehrenbacher, *Lincoln in Text and Context: Collected Essays* (Stanford, CA: Stanford University Press, 1987), p. 109 and Benjamin P. Thomas, *Abraham Lincoln: A Biography* (New York: Alfred A. Knopf, 1952), p. 342.

22. For a summary of both sides of the argument see Gabor S. Boritt, "Introduction: Looking for Lincoln," in *The Historian's Lincoln*, pp. xv-xvi.

23. *CW*, vol. 4, pp. 432-33.

24. *CW*, vol. 3, p. 254; Herndon and Weik, vol. 2, pp. 303, 6, and 315.

25. Charles E. Schutz, *Political Humor from Aristophanes to Sam Ervin* (Rutherford, NJ: Farleigh Dickinson University Press,

1977); Norman A. Graebner, "Commentary" to "Abe Lincoln Laughing," in *The Historian's Lincoln*, ed. Gabor S. Boritt (Urbana, IL: University of Illinois Press, 1988), pp. 19-25.

26. Zarefsky, p. 164. The phrase "in God's good time" comes from Zarefsky.

27. Weaver, pp. 108-11.

28. *CW*, vol. 5, pp. 370-75; *CW*, vol. 5, p. 318; *CW*, vol. 5, p. 223; and *CW*, vol. 5, p. 145.

29. The Preliminary Emancipation Proclamation is reprinted in *CW*, vol. 5, pp. 433-36; the official Emancipation Proclamation is reprinted in *CW*, vol. 6, pp. 28-31. Lincoln's explanation comes from *CW*, vol. 6, pp. 48-49.

30. F. B. Carpenter, *Six Months at the White House with Lincoln*, ed. John Crosby Freeman (Watkins Glen, NY: Century House, 1961), pp. 21-22; *CW*, vol. 7, pp. 281-82.

31. *CW*, vol. 6, p. 156.

32. Amy R. Slagell, "A Textual Analysis of Abraham Lincoln's Second Inaugural Address," Unpublished M.A. Thesis, University of Wisconsin-Madison, 1986, p. 17.

33. Slagell, p. 28.

34. See, for example, *CW*, vol. 5, p. 537.

6. LINCOLN'S GETTYSBURG ADDRESS: IMMEDIATE FAILURE AND LASTING SUCCESS

1. Ronald F. Reid, "Newspaper Response to the Gettysburg Addresses," *Quarterly Journal of Speech* 53 (1967): 50-60.

2. Stephen E. Lucas, "The Renaissance of American Public Address: Text and Context in Rhetorical Criticism," *Quarterly Journal of Speech* 74 (1988): 247. For rhetorical analyses of the "Gettysburg Address," see Waldo W. Braden, "The Lasting Qualities of the Gettysburg Address," paper presented at the Gettysburg Conference on Rhetorical Transactions, Gettysburg College, 25 June 1983; Lane Cooper, "Introduction," *The Rhetoric of Aristotle* (Englewood Cliffs, NJ: Prentice-Hall, Inc., 1932), pp. xxxi-xxxv; Harold Zyskind, "A Rhetorical Analysis of the Gettysburg Address," *Journal of General Education* 4 (1949): 202-12; Earl W. Wiley, "Buckeye Criticism of the Gettysburg Address," *Speech Monographs* 23 (1956): 1-8; Gilbert Highet, "The Gettysburg Address," in *Readings in Speech*, ed. Haig A. Bosmajian (New York: Harper and Row, 1971), pp. 221-27; Herbert L. Carson, "So Long Remembered," *Today's Speech* 12 (November 1964): 19-21; and Mrs. Corinne K. Flemings, "Gettysburg Revisited," *Today's Speech* 14 (April 1966): 26-30. None of these works, however, thoroughly evaluates the "Gettysburg Address" as a <u>speech</u> delivered to a <u>specific</u> audience at a <u>specific</u> time and place.

3. William E. Barton, *Lincoln at Gettysburg* (New York: Peter Smith, 1950), p. 114.

4. The text of Wills' letter to Lincoln is quoted in Louis A. Warren, *Lincoln's Gettysburg Declaration* (Fort Wayne, IN.: Lincoln National Life Foundation, 1964), pp. 45-46.

5. Lincoln probably did not give an advance copy of his speech to the press because although he wrote at least half of the speech in Washington, he did not complete writing it until after he reached Gettysburg. It is also plausible that Lincoln did not give out a copy of the text because he thought of his <u>message</u> as incidental to the <u>acts</u> of remembering the dead and dedicating a national cemetery. For an excellent discussion of Lincoln's preparation of the "Gettysburg Address," see David C. Mearns and Lloyd A. Dunlap, *Long Remembered: The Gettysburg Address in Facsimile* (Washington, D.C.: The Library of Congress, 1963).

6. Allan Nevins, ed., *Lincoln and the Gettysburg Address* (IL: Board of Trustees of the University of Illinois, 1964), pp. 446-47.

7. Genesis 16:16; Joshua 14: 10; Psalms 90:10; and Luke 2:37.

8. Roy P. Basler, *A Touchstone for Greatness: Essays, Addresses, and Occasional Pieces about Abraham Lincoln* (Westport, CT: Greenwood Press, Inc., 1973), pp. 94-95.

9. *CW*, vol. 6, p. 319.

10. Warren, p. 111.

11. Barton, p. 132.

12. For an excellent discussion of the reasons why Lincoln probably emphasized the word "people," see Louis A. Warren, *Abraham Lincoln's Gettysburg Address: An Evaluation* (Columbus, OH: Charles E. Merrill Publishing Company, 1968), pp. 23-24.

13. Zyskind, pp. 202-12.

14. *CW*, vol. 8, pp. 116-17.

15. Pericles, "Funeral Speech," in *The Speaker's Resource Book*, eds. Carroll C. Arnold, Douglas Ehninger, and John C. Gerber (Glenview, IL.: Scott, Foresman and Co., 1966), pp. 194-95.

16. G.P. Mohrmann and A.W. Staub, "Rhetoric and Poetic: A New Critique," in *Contemporary Rhetoric*, ed. Douglas Ehninger (Glenview, IL.; Scott, Foresman and Co., 1972), p. 114.

17. Robert Gunning, *The Technique of Clear Writing* (New York: McGraw-Hill Book Company, 1968) and Rudolf Flesch, *The Art of Readable Writing* (New York: Harper and Row, Publishers, 1974). Interestingly, both Gunning and Flesch gave readability scores for the "Gettysburg Address" to support their claims that Lincoln's message is an example of great literature. Gunning did not count the eighty-two word last sentence of the speech because it consists of a list and most lists, he argued, make easy reading (pp. 58 and 277-82). What makes easy reading does not necessarily make easy listening. Flesch determined the speech's readability, but not its human interest (p.

234). In applying the two indices to the "Gettysburg Address," I counted thought units rather than sentences because speakers talk in units of thought rather than in sentences. To check the fairness of my method, I recalculated the scores using sentences, and on both scales, the "Gettysburg Address" scored <u>more</u> difficult using sentences than it did using thought units.

18. For the exact places where the words appear in the Bible, see Young.

CONCLUSION: THE MAKING OF A LEGEND

1. *CW*, vol. 7, p. 366.
2. Richard M. Ohmann, *Shaw: The Style and the Man* (Middletown, CT: Wesleyan University Press, 1962), p. xv.

HISTORY IN MOTION:
SELECTED BIBLIOGRAPHY ON LINCOLN

1. Carl Sandburg, *Abraham Lincoln: The Prairie Years.* New York: Harcourt, Brace and World, 1926, vol. 1, p. 71.
2. *CW*, vol. 4, p. 121.

Chronology of Selected Major Speeches

Speech in the Illinois Legislature, Springfield, Illinois, January 11, 1837.

The Perpetuation of Our Political Institutions: Address Before the Young Men's Lyceum, Springfield, Illinois, January 27, 1838.

Speech on the Sub-Treasury, Springfield, Illinois, December 26, 1839.

Address to the Washington Temperance Society, Springfield, Illinois, February 22, 1842.

Speech in the U.S. House of Representatives on the War with Mexico, Washington, D.C., January 12, 1848.

Speech in the U.S. House of Representatives on Internal Improvements, Washington, D.C., June 20, 1848.

Speech in the U.S. House of Representatives on the Presidential Question, Washington, D.C., July 27, 1848.

Eulogy on Zachary Taylor, Chicago, Illinois, July 25, 1850.

Eulogy on Henry Clay, Springfield, Illinois, July 6, 1852.

The Repeal of the Missouri Compromise and the Propriety of Its Restoration, Peoria, Illinois, October 16, 1854.

Fremont, Buchanan, and the Extension of Slavery, Kalamazoo, Michigan, August 27, 1856.

Speech at Republican Banquet, Chicago, Illinois, December 10, 1856.

Speech on the Dred Scott Decision, Springfield, Illinois, June 26, 1857.

"House Divided" Speech, Springfield, Illinois, June 16, 1858.

Speech in Reply to Douglas, Chicago, Illinois, July 10, 1858.

Speech in Reply to Douglas, Springfield, Illinois, July 17, 1858.

First Lincoln-Douglas Debate, Ottawa, Illinois, August 21, 1858.

Second Lincoln-Douglas Debate, Freeport, Illinois, August 27, 1858.

Speech, Edwardsville, Illinois, September 11, 1858.

Third Lincoln-Douglas Debate, Jonesboro, Illinois, September 15, 1858.

Fourth Lincoln-Douglas Debate, Charleston, Illinois, September 18, 1858.

Fifth Lincoln-Douglas Debate, Galesburg, Illinois, October 7, 1858.

Sixth Lincoln-Douglas Debate, Quincy, Illinois, October 13, 1858.

Seventh Lincoln-Douglas Debate, Alton, Illinois, October 15, 1858.

Last Speech in Campaign of 1858, Springfield, Illinois, October 30, 1858.

Second Lecture on Discoveries and Inventions, Jacksonville, Illinois, February 11, 1859.

Address to the Wisconsin State Agricultural Society, Milwaukee, Wisconsin, September 30, 1859.

Address at Cooper Institute, New York City, February 27, 1860.

Speech, New Haven, Connecticut, March 6, 1860.

Remarks at Republican Rally, Springfield, Illinois, August 8, 1860.

Farewell Address, Springfield, Illinois, February 11, 1861.

Speech at Indianapolis, Indiana, February 11, 1861.

Speech to Germans at Cincinnati, Ohio, February 12, 1861.

Address to the New Jersey Senate, Trenton, New Jersey, February 21, 1861.

Address to the New Jersey General Assembly, Trenton, New Jersey, February 21, 1861.

Speech at Independence Hall, Philadelphia, Pennsylvania, February 22, 1861.

First Inaugural Address, Washington, D.C., March 4, 1961.

Message to Congress in Special Session, Washington, D.C., July 4, 1861.

Annual Message to Congress, Washington, D.C., December 3, 1861.

Appeal to Border-State Representatives for Compensated Emancipation, Washington, D.C., July 12, 1862.

Address on Colonization to a Committee of Colored Men, Washington, D.C., August 14, 1862.

Remarks to the Army of the Potomac, Frederick, Maryland, October 4, 1862.

Annual Message to Congress, Washington, D.C., December 1, 1862.

Speech to Indian Chiefs, Washington, D.C., March 27, 1863.

Response to Serenade, Washington, D.C., July 7, 1863.

Reply to Sons of Temperance, Washington, D.C., September 29, 1863.

Remarks to Baltimore Presbyterian Synod, Washington, D.C., October 24, 1863.

Address Delivered at the Dedication of the Cemetery at Gettysburg, Gettysburg, Pennsylvania, November 19, 1863.

Annual Message to Congress, Washington, D.C., December 8, 1863.

Address at Sanitary Fair, Baltimore, Maryland, April 18, 1864.

Speech at Great Central Sanitary Fair, Philadelphia, Pennsylvania, June 16, 1864.

Speech to the 164th Ohio Regiment, Washington, D.C., August 18, 1864.

Speech to the 166th Ohio Regiment, Washington, D.C., August 22, 1864.

Annual Message to Congress, Washington, D.C., December 6, 1864.

Second Inaugural Address, Washington, D.C., March 4, 1865.

Speech to the 140th Indiana Regiment, Washington, D.C., March 17, 1865.

Speech on Reconstruction [last public address], Washington, D.C., April 11, 1865.

This photograph, ultimately used for the engraving on the five dollar bill, presents Lincoln's Presidential image. Photo courtesy of Leib Image Archives.

History in Motion:
Selected Bibliography
on Lincoln

The things I want to know are in books; my best friend is the man who'll git me a book I ain't read.

Lincoln to his cousin Dennis Hanks

Get the books, and read, and study them carefully.

Lincoln's advice on how to study law

Anyone who wants to read about Lincoln need not look far. His own words--extant speeches, letters, and state papers--total more words than are in the entire Bible. At least two of his speeches--the "Gettysburg Address" and "Second Inaugural Address"--have been translated into almost every foreign language. In addition to his own words, there supposedly has been more written in English about Lincoln than about any other person with the exception of Jesus Christ. This interest in Lincoln shows no sign of declining; new works about him appear on the average of one a week.[1]

On almost every aspect of Lincoln's life and speaking, scholars disagree. Was he an eloquent orator or a literary artist but second-rate speaker? Did he precipitate the Civil War? Was the "Gettysburg Address" the greatest speech of all time or was it a failure as a speech? Was Lincoln a "great emancipator" or a White supremacist? Was he a bumbling buffoon or a savvy storyteller? The list of questions goes on as new works continually refine, challenge, and change the Lincoln image.

The purpose of this bibliography is to suggest sources that provide a foundation for understanding Lincoln's speaking. The material is divided into the following sections: primary sources;

research collections; bibliographies, indexes, and historiographical essays; historical landmarks; and secondary sources.

With so many sources available, compiling a bibliography of works by and about Lincoln inevitably involves selection. I have used the following guidelines in making my choices: (1) Since this is a book on "Abraham Lincoln the Orator," I included all studies about Lincoln that have appeared in speech/communication journals and all works that I know of by speech/communication scholars appearing in other publication outlets. (2) I included all works that I found especially useful, works that, in my opinion, contribute significantly to understanding Lincoln as a speaker. My choices are necessarily personal. Ralph G. Newman wrote in the introduction to his bibliography, "No two students or collectors could or would compile identical lists which is as it should be, and explains in part why there always will be new Lincoln books. We each seek our own Lincoln." (3) I included classic works about Lincoln, even if outdated, because they contribute to the historiography of the Lincoln image. (4) I included material for Lincoln enthusiasts both inside and outside of the academic world. (5) I included controversial works (even ones with which I vehemently disagree) to show the range and diversity of views and to allow readers of this book to participate in the debates about numerous aspects of Lincoln's life and speaking. In Lincoln's words, "Get the books, and read, and study them carefully." To this I add, "Then decide for yourself."[2]

PRIMARY SOURCES

Anderson, David D., ed. *The Literary Works of Abraham Lincoln.* Columbus, OH: Charles E. Merrill Publishing, 1970.

Angle, Paul M., ed. *Abraham Lincoln's Speeches and Letters, 1832-1865.* New York: E. P. Dutton, 1957.

---, ed. *The Complete Lincoln-Douglas Debates of 1858.* Chicago, IL: University of Chicago Press, 1990.

---, ed. *Created Equal? The Complete Lincoln-Douglas Debates of 1858.* Chicago, IL: University of Chicago Press, 1958.

--- and Earl Scheck Miers, eds. *The Living Lincoln, the Man, His Mind, His Times, and the War He Fought.* Reconstructed from his own writings. New Brunswick, NJ: Rutgers University Press, 1955.

---, ed. *New Letters and Papers of Lincoln.* Boston, MA: Houghton Mifflin Company, 1930.

Basler, Roy P., ed. *Abraham Lincoln: His Speeches and Writings.* Cleveland, OH: World Publishing Company, 1946.

---, ed. with Marion D. Pratt and Lloyd A. Dunlap. *The Collected Works of Abraham Lincoln.* 9 vols. New Brunswick, NJ: Rutgers University Press, 1953.

---, ed. *The Collected Works of Abraham Lincoln Supplement 1832-1865*. Westport, CT: Greenwood Press, 1974.

--- and Basler, Christian, eds. *The Collected Works of Abraham Lincoln, 1848-1865*. Vol. II, 2nd supplement. New Brunswick, NJ: Rutgers University Press, 1990.

Cuomo, Mario M. and Harold Holzer, eds. *Lincoln on Democracy*. New York: Harper/Collins, 1990.

Current, Richard N., ed. *The Political Thought of Abraham Lincoln*. Indianapolis, IN: Bobbs-Merrill, 1967.

Dumond, Dwight Lowell, ed. *Southern Editorials on Secession*. New York: The Century Company, 1931.

Fehrenbacher, Don E., ed. *Abraham Lincoln: A Documentary Portrait Through His Speeches and Writings*. New York: New American Library of World Literature, 1964.

---, ed. *Abraham Lincoln: Speeches and Writings, 1832-1858*. New York: Library of America, 1989.

---, ed. *Abraham Lincoln: Speeches and Writings, 1859-1865*. New York: Library of America, 1989.

Jaffa, Harry V. and Robert W. Johannsen, eds. *In the Name of the People: Speeches and Writings of Lincoln and Douglas in the Ohio Campaign of 1859*. Columbus, OH: The Ohio State University Press, 1959.

Johannsen, Robert W., ed. *The Letters of Stephen Douglas*. Urbana, IL: University of Illinois Press, 1961.

---, ed. *The Lincoln-Douglas Debates of 1858*. New York: Oxford University Press, 1965.

McClure, James Baird, ed. *Abraham Lincoln's Speeches Complete*. Chicago, IL: Rhodes, and McClure Publishing, 1891.

Mearns, David C., ed. *The Lincoln Papers*. 2 vols. New York: Doubleday and Company, 1948.

--- and Lloyd C. Dunlap, eds. *Long Remembered: Facsimiles of the Five Versions of the Gettysburg Address in the Handwriting of Abraham Lincoln*. Washington, D.C.: The Library of Congress, 1963.

Mitgang, Herbert, ed. *Abraham Lincoln: A Press Portrait*. Chicago, IL: Quadrangle Books, 1971.

Nicolay, John G. and John Hay, eds. *The Complete Works of Abraham Lincoln*. 10 vols. Harrogate, TN: Lincoln Memorial University, 1894.

Perkins, Howard Cecil, ed. *Northern Editorials on Secession*. 2 vols. New York: D. Appleton-Century, 1942.

Sparks, Edwin Erle, ed. *The Lincoln-Douglas Debates of 1858*. Collections of the Illinois State Historical Society. Springfield, IL: Illinois State Historical Library, 1908, Vol. 3.

Tracy, Gilbert A. *Uncollected Letters of Abraham Lincoln*. Boston, MA: Houghton Mifflin, 1917.

U.S. War Department. *War of the Rebellion: A Compilation of the Official Records of the Union and Confederate Armies.* Washington, D.C.: U.S. Printing Office, 1880-1901.

Williams, T. Harry, ed. *Selected Writings and Speeches of Abraham Lincoln.* New York: Hendricks House, 1943.

RESEARCH COLLECTIONS

Abraham Lincoln Association Papers (Lincoln reference file), Illinois State Historical Library

Abraham Lincoln Mss., Chicago Historical Society

Abraham Lincoln Papers, Library of Congress

Albert J. Beveridge Papers, Library of Congress

Herndon-Lamon Papers, Huntington Library

Herndon-Weik Papers, Library of Congress

Horace Greeley Mss., Library of Congress

Horace Greeley Mss., New York Historical Society

Horace Greeley Mss., New York Public Library

Jefferson Davis Papers, Duke University

John G. Nicolay Papers, Library of Congress

John Hay Correspondence, Huntington Library

Lincoln Collection, Huntington Library

Lincoln Collection, University of Chicago Library

Lincoln Memorial University, Harrogate, Tennessee

The Lincoln Museum (formerly the Louis A. Warren Lincoln Library and Museum), Fort Wayne, Indiana, has published *Lincoln Lore*, a monthly leaflet, since 1929

Miscellaneous Mss. Collection, Lincoln National Life Foundation

The New York Public Library Newspaper Annex

Papers of Lincoln's Cabinet Members, Lincoln National Life Foundation

Robert Todd Lincoln Collection of the Papers of Abraham Lincoln, Library of Congress

Salmon P. Chase Mss., Library of Congress

Stephen A. Douglas Mss., Library of Congress

Stephen A. Douglas Mss., University of Chicago Library

Unpublished Lincoln Papers, Illinois State Historical Library

William H. Herndon Papers, Massachusetts Historical Society

BIBLIOGRAPHIES, INDEXES, AND HISTORIOGRAPHICAL ESSAYS

Angle, Paul M. *A Shelf of Lincoln Books: A Critical Selective Bibliography of Lincolniana.* New Brunswick, NJ: Rutgers University Press, 1946.

Basler, Roy P. "A Survey of Lincoln Literature." In his *The Lincoln Legend: A Study in Changing Conceptions.* Boston, MA: Houghton Mifflin Company, 1935, pp. 3-51.

Booker, Richard. *Abraham Lincoln in Periodical Literature, 1860-1940.* Chicago, IL: Fawley-Brost, 1941.

Boritt, G. S. "Historiographical Essay: Lincoln, God and Man." In his *Lincoln and the Economics of the American Dream.* Memphis, TN: Memphis State University Press, 1978, pp. 289-311.

---. "Introduction: Looking for Lincoln." In *The Historian's Lincoln: Pseudohistory, Psychohistory, and History.* Ed. Gabor S. Boritt and Norman O. Forness. Urbana, IL: University of Illinois Press, 1988, pp. xv-xxviii.

Current, Richard N. "Bibliographical Essay." In his *The Lincoln Nobody Knows.* New York: Hill and Wang, 1958, pp. 288-304.

Dunlap, Leslie W., comp. "Materials on Display in the University of Illinois Library, February, 1959." In *The Enduring Lincoln*, ed. Norman A. Graebner. Urbana, IL: The Board of Trustees of the University of Illinois, 1959, pp. 95-121.

Donald, David. "Bibliographical Essay." In his *Lincoln Reconsidered.* New York: Alfred A. Knopf, 1972, pp. 237-50.

Fehrenbacher, D. E. *The Changing Image of Lincoln in American Historiography.* Oxford, Great Britain: Clarendon Press, 1968.

---. "The Changing Image of Lincoln in American Historiography." In his *Lincoln in Text and Context.* Stanford, CA: Stanford University Press, 1987), pp. 181-96.

Index to the Abraham Lincoln Papers, Manuscript Division, Library of Congress. Washington, D.C.: U.S. Government Printing Office, 1960.

Monaghan, Jay, comp. *Lincoln Bibliography, 1830-1939.* 2 vols. Springfield, IL: Illinois State Historical Library Association, 1945.

Potter, David M. "The Lincoln Theme and American National Historiography." Inaugural Lecture. Oxford, Great Britain: Clarendon Press, 1948.

Searcher, Victor. *Lincoln Today: An Introduction to Modern Lincolniana.* New York: Thomas Yoseloff, n.d.

Squire, Dick. *The "Best" Lincoln Biography: Results of a Survey.* Bedford, OH: The Lincoln Press, 1955.

Thomas, Benjamin P. "The Lincoln Literature." In his *Abraham Lincoln.* New York: The Modern Library, 1952, pp. 523-48.

HISTORICAL LANDMARKS

Abraham Lincoln Birthplace National Historic Site, Hodgenville, Kentucky

Abraham Lincoln Book Shop, Chicago, Illinois
Ford's Theatre National Historic Site, Washington, D.C.
Gettysburg National Military Park, Gettysburg, Pennsylvania
Lincoln Boyhood National Memorial and Lincoln State Park, Lincoln
    City, Indiana
Lincoln-Herndon Law Offices, Springfield, Illinois
Lincoln Home National Historic Site, Springfield, Illinois
Lincoln Memorial, Washington, D.C.
Lincoln Tomb State Historic Site, Springfield, Illinois
Lincoln's Boyhood Home, Hodgenville, Kentucky
Lincoln's New Salem State Park, Petersburg, Illinois
Old State Capitol, Springfield, Illinois

SECONDARY SOURCES

Abzug, Robert H. and Stephen E. Maizlish, eds. *New Perspectives on Race and Slavery in America: Essays in Honor of Kenneth M. Stampp.* Lexington, KY: University Press of Kentucky, 1986.
Alisky, Marvin. "White House Wit: Presidential Humor to Sustain Politicies, from Lincoln to Reagan." *Presidential Studies Quarterly* 20 (1990): 373-81.
Anderson, David D. *Abraham Lincoln.* New York: Twayne Publishers, 1970.
Anderson, Dwight G. *Abraham Lincoln: The Quest for Immortality.* New York: Alfred A. Knopf, 1982.
Angle, Paul M. "Four Lincoln Firsts." *Papers of the Bibliographical Society of America* 36 (1942): 1-17.
---. *Here I Have Lived.* New Brunswick, NJ: Rutgers University Press, 1935.
---, ed. *Herndon's Life of Lincoln.* New York: Da Capo Press, 1983.
---. *Lincoln, 1854-1861; Being the Day-by-Day Activities of Abraham Lincoln from January 1, 1854 to March 4, 1861.* Springfield, IL: Abraham Lincoln Association, 1933.
---, ed. *The Lincoln Reader.* New Brunswick, NJ: Rutgers University Press, 1947.
---. "Lincoln's Power with Words." *Papers of the Abraham Lincoln Association.* Springfield, IL: 1981, pp. 9-23.
Arnold, Carroll C. "The Senate Committee of Thirteen, December 6-31, 1860." In *Antislavery and Disunion, 1858-1861.* Ed. J. Jeffery Auer. New York: Harper and Row, 1963, pp. 310-30.
Auer, J. Jeffery, ed. *Antislavery and Disunion, 1858-1861: Studies in the Rhetoric of Compromise and Conflict.* New York: Harper and Row, 1963.
---. "Cooper Institute: Tom Corwin and Abraham Lincoln." *New York History* 32 (1951): 399-413.

Aune, James Arnt. "Lincoln and the American Sublime." *Communication Reports* 1 (1988): 14-19.

Baringer, William E. *A House Dividing: Lincoln as President Elect.* Springfield, IL: The Abraham Lincoln Association, 1945.

Barker, Thoburn V. "Lincoln: Rhetorical Copycat?" *Communication Quarterly* 15 (1967): 29-30.

Barondess, Benjamin. *Three Lincoln Masterpieces.* Charleston, WV: Educational Foundation of West Virginia, 1954.

Barton, William E. *Abraham Lincoln and His Books.* Chicago, IL: Marshall Field and Company, 1920.

---. *The Life of Abraham Lincoln.* 2 vols. Indianapolis, IN: Bobbs-Merrill, 1925.

---. *Lincoln at Gettysburg: What He Intended to Say; What He Said; What He Was Reported to Have Said; What He Wished He Had Said.* New York: Peter Smith, 1950.

Barzun, Jacques. *Lincoln the Literary Genius.* Evanston, IL: Evanston Publishing Company, 1960.

---. *On Writing, Editing, and Publishing.* 2nd ed. Chicago, IL: University of Chicago Press, 1986. 65-81.

Basler, Roy P. "Abraham Lincoln--Artist." *North American Review* 245 (Spring 1938): 144-53.

---. "Abraham Lincoln's Rhetoric." *American Literature* 11 (May 1939): 167-82.

---. *The Lincoln Legend: A Study in Changing Conceptions.* Boston, MA: Houghton Mifflin, 1935.

---. *A Touchstone for Greatness: Essays and Occasional Pieces about Abraham Lincoln.* Westport, CT: Greenwood Press, 1973.

Bauer, Marvin G. "The Influence of Lincoln's Audience on His Speeches." *Quarterly Journal of Speech* 11 (1925): 225-29.

---. "Persuasive Methods in the Lincoln-Douglas Debates." *Quarterly Journal of Speech* 13 (1927): 29-39.

---. "The Rhetorical Practice of Abraham Lincoln." Unpublished M.A. thesis, Cornell University, 1924.

Bennet, Lerone, Jr. "Was Abe Lincoln a White Supremacist?" *Ebony* (February 1968): 35, 40, 43.

Berry, Mildred Freburg. "Abraham Lincoln: His Development in the Skills of the Platform." In *A History and Criticism of American Public Address,* ed. William Norwood Brigance. Vol. II. New York: Russell and Russell, 1960, pp. 828-58.

---. "Lincoln--The Speaker (Part I)" and "Lincoln--The Speaker (Part II)," *Quarterly Journal of Speech* 17 (1931): 25-40 and 177-90.

Beveridge, Albert J. *Abraham Lincoln, 1809-1858.* 4 vols. Boston, MA: Houghton Mifflin, 1928.

Beveridge, John W. "Lincoln's Views on Slavery and Blacks as Expressed in the Debates with Stephen A. Douglas." *Lincoln Herald* 83 (1981): 791-800.

Black, Edwin. *Rhetorical Criticism: A Study in Method*. Madison, WI: The University of Wisconsin Press, 1978.

Blankenship, Jane. "State Legislator as Debater: Lincoln, 1834-1842." *Journal of the American Forensic Association* 2 (1965): 28-32.

Blegen, Theodore C. *Lincoln's Imagery: A Study in Word Power*. La Crosse, WI: Sumac Press, 1954.

Boase, Paul H. "Cartwright Meets Lincoln." *Central States Speech Journal* 2 (1951): 26-34.

Borah, William E. "Lincoln the Orator." In William E. Borah. *American Problems: A Selection of Speeches and Prophecies*. Ed. Horace Green. New York: Duffield, 1924, pp. 31-42.

Boritt, Gabor S. "Abraham Lincoln: War Opponent and War President." The Inaugural Lecture of the First Robert C. Fluhrer Professor of Civil War Studies. Gettysburg, Pennsylvania, Gettysburg College, 28 March 1987.

---, ed. *The Historian's Lincoln: Pseudohistory, Psychohistory, and History*. Urbana, IL: University of Illinois Press, 1988.

---, ed. *The Historian's Lincoln: Rebuttals*. Gettysburg, PA: Civil War Studies, Gettysburg College, 1988.

---. *Lincoln and the Economics of the American Dream*. Memphis, TN: Memphis State University Press, 1978.

---. "A Question of Political Suicide: Lincoln's Opposition to the Mexican War." *Journal of the Illinois State Historical Society* 67 (1974): 79-100.

---. "The Voyage to the Colony of Linconia." *The Historian* 37 (1975): 619-32.

Bormann, Ernest G. "Fetching Good Out of Evil: A Rhetorical Use of Calamity." *Quarterly Journal of Speech* 63 (1977): 130-39.

---. *The Force of Fantasy*. Carbondale, IL: Southern Illinois University Press, 1985.

Braden, Waldo W. "Abraham Lincoln." In *American Orators Before 1900: Critical Studies and Sources*. Ed. Bernard K. Duffy and Halford R. Ryan. Westport, CT: Greenwood Press, 1987, pp. 259-70.

---. *Abraham Lincoln, Public Speaker*. Baton Rouge, LA: Louisiana State University Press, 1988.

---, ed. *Building the Myth: Selected Speeches Memorializing Abraham Lincoln*. Urbana, IL: University of Illinois Press, 1990.

---. "The Lasting Qualities of the Gettysburg Address." Paper delivered at the Gettysburg Conference on Rhetorical Transactions in the Civil War Era. Gettysburg, PA: June 1983.

Bradford. M. E. *A Better Guide Than Reason: Studies in the American Revolution*. La Salle, IL: Sherwood Sugden and Company, 1979, pp. 29-57 and 185-203.

---. "Dividing the House: The Gnosticism of Lincoln's Political Rhetoric." *Modern Age* 23 (1979): 10-24.

---. "The Lincoln Legacy: A Long View" *Modern Age* 24 (1980): 355-63.

Bradley, Bert E. "North Carolina Newspaper Accounts of Lincoln's First Inaugural." *The North Carolina Historical Review* 46 (1969): 271-80.

Branham, Robert J. and W. Barnett Pearce. "Between Text and Context: Toward a Rhetoric of Contextual Reconstruction." *Quarterly Journal of Speech* 71 (1985): 19-36.

Brooks, Noah. *Abraham Lincoln and the Downfall of American Slavery.* New York: G. P. Putnam's Sons, 1894.

---. *Men of Achievement - Abraham Lincoln.* New York: Scribner's, 1893.

Browne, Ray B., ed. *Lincoln Lore--Lincoln in the Popular Mind.* Bowling Green, OH: Popular Press, 1974.

Bruce, Robert V. "The Shadow of a Coming War." 28th Annual Robert Fortenbaugh Memorial Lecture. Gettysburg, Pennsylvania, 1989.

Bryan, William Jennings. "Lincoln as an Orator." In *Building the Myth: Selected Speeches Memorializing Abraham Lincoln.* Ed. Waldo W. Braden. Urbana, IL: University of Illinois Press, 1990, pp. 141-44.

Campbell, Karlyn Kohrs and Kathleen Hall Jamieson. *Deeds Done in Words: Presidential Rhetoric and the Genres of Governance.* Chicago, IL: University of Chicago Press, 1990.

---. "Inaugurating the Presidency." *Presidential Studies Quarterly* 15 (1985): 394-411.

Carmichael, Orton H. *Lincoln's Gettysburg Address.* New York: Abingdon Press, 1917.

Carpenter, Francis B. *Six Months at the White House with Lincoln: The Story of a Picture.* Watkins Glen, NY: Century House, 1961.

Carson, Herbert L. "So Long Remembered." *Today's Speech* 12 (November 1964): 19-21.

Carter, Hodding. *Their Words Were Bullets: The Southern Press in War, Reconstruction, and Peace.* Athens, GA: University of Georgia Press, 1969.

Charnwood, Lord. *Abraham Lincoln.* Garden City, NY: Doubleday, 1917.

Chu, James C. Y. "Horace White: His Association with Abraham Lincoln, 1854-60." *Journalism Quarterly* 49 (1972): 51-60.

Collins, Bruce W. "The Lincoln-Douglas Contest of 1858 and the Illinois Electorate." *Journal of American Studies* 20 (1986): 391-420.

Conwell, Russell H. *Why Lincoln Laughed.* New York: Harper and Brothers, 1922.

Cooper, Lane, ed. *The Rhetoric of Aristotle.* Englewood Cliffs, NJ: Prentice-Hall, 1932, pp. xxxi-xxxv.

Cooper, William J., Jr. *The South and the Politics of Slavery ,1828-1856.* Baton Rouge, LA: Louisiana State University Press, 1978.

Cox, LaWanda. *Lincoln and Black Freedom: A Study in Presidential Leadership.* Columbia, SC: University of South Carolina Press, 1981.

Cox, J. Robert. "The Die is Cast: Topical and Ontological Dimensions of the *Locus* of the Irreparable." *Quarterly Journal of Speech* 68 (1982): 227-39.

Crissey, Elwell. *Lincoln's Lost Speech.* New York: Hawthorn Books, 1967.

Crocker, Lionel. *An Analysis of Lincoln and Douglas as Public Speakers and Debaters.* Springfield, IL: Charles C. Thomas, 1968.

---. "Lincoln and Beecher." *Southern Speech Communication Journal* 26 (1960): 149-59.

Current, Richard N. "Lincoln and Daniel Webster." *Journal of the Illinois State Historical Society* 47 (1955): 307-21.

---. *The Lincoln Nobody Knows.* New York: Hill and Wang, 1958.

---. *Speaking of Abraham Lincoln: The Man and His Meaning for Our Times.* Urbana, IL: University of Illinois Press, 1983.

Dahlberg, Walfred A. "A Critical Analysis of Lincoln's Use of Wit and Humor for Persuasive Effect." Unpublished M.A. thesis, Northwestern University, 1931.

---. "Lincoln the Wit." *Quarterly Journal of Speech* 31 (1945): 424-27.

Davis, Cullom, Charles B. Strozier, Rebecca Monroe Veach, and Geoffrey C. Ward. *The Public and Private Lincoln: Contemporary Perspectives.* Carbondale, IL: Southern Illinois University Press, 1979.

Davis, Michael. *The Image of Lincoln in the South.* Knoxville, TN: The University of Tennessee Press, 1971.

DeAlvarez, Leo Paul S., ed. *Abraham Lincoln, The Gettysburg Address, and American Constitutionalism.* Irving, TX: University of Dallas, 1976.

Denton, Robert E., Jr. *The Symbolic Dimensions of the American Presidency: Description and Analysis.* Prospect Heights, IL: Waveland Press, 1982.

Depoe, Steve. "Lincoln's Irreparable Vision of a House Divided." Paper delivered at the Gettysburg Conference on Rhetorical Transactions in the Civil War Era. Gettysburg, PA: June 1983.

Devlin, Lee. "Lincoln's Ethos: Viewed and Practiced." *Central States Speech Journal* 16 (1965): 99-105.

Dodge, Daniel K. *Abraham Lincoln: The Evolution of His Literary Style*. Urbana, IL: University of Illinois Studies, 1900.

---. *Abraham Lincoln, Master of Words*. New York: Appleton, 1924.

Donald, David. *Lincoln's Herndon*. New York: Alfred A. Knopf, 1948.

---. *Lincoln Reconsidered*. New York: Alfred A. Knopf, 1972.

Duncan, Kunigunde and D. F. Nickols. *Mentor Graham, The Man Who Taught Lincoln*. Chicago, IL: University of Chicago Press, 1944.

Edwards, Herbert Joseph and John Erskine Hankins. "Lincoln, the Writer: The Development of His Literary Style." *University of Maine Bulletin* 64 (10 April 1962).

Emrich, Richard S., Rev. "The Greatness of Lincoln." In *The Congressional Record*, 105:A (2 February 1959): 694-95.

Emsley, Bert. "Phonetic Structure in Lincoln's Gettysburg Address." *Quarterly Journal of Speech* 24 (1938): 281-87.

Fehrenbacher, Don E. "The Historical Significance of the Lincoln-Douglas Debates." *Wisconsin Magazine of History* 42 (1959): 193-99.

---. *The Leadership of Abraham Lincoln*. New York: John Wiley and Sons, 1970.

---. "In Quest of Psychohistorical Lincoln." *Reviews in American History* 11 (1983): 12-19.

---. *Lincoln in Text and Context: Collected Essays*. Stanford, CA: Stanford University Press, 1987.

---. "The Origins and Purpose of Lincoln's 'House Divided' Speech." *Mississippi Valley Historical Review* 46 (1960): 615-46.

---. *Prelude to Greatness: Lincoln in the 1850's*. Stanford, CA: Stanford University Press, 1962.

Fields, Wayne D. "The Making of an Issue: A Rhetorical Analysis of the Lincoln-Douglas Debates." Unpublished Ph.D. dissertation, University of Chicago, 1972.

Finkelman, Paul. *An Imperfect Union: Slavery, Federalism, and Comity*. Chapel Hill, NC: University of North Carolina Press, 1981.

Fischer, Roger A. "The Republican Presidential Campaigns of 1856 and 1860: Analysis Through Artifacts." *Civil War History* 27 (1981): 123-37.

Fisher, Walter R. "Reaffirmation and Subversion of the American Dream." *The Quarterly Journal of Speech* 59 (1973): 160-67.

Flemmings, Mrs. Corinne K. "Gettysburg Revisited." *Today's Speech* 14 (April 1966): 26-28 and 30.

Floyd, James J. and W. Clifton Adams. "A Content Analysis Test of Richard M. Weaver's Critical Methodology." *Southern Speech Communication Journal* 41 (1976): 374-87.

Foner, Eric. *Free Soil, Free Labor, Free Men: The Ideology of the Republican Party Before the Civil War.* New York: Oxford University Press, 1970.

--- and Olivia Mahoney. *A House Divided: America in the Age of Lincoln.* New York: W.W. Norton, 1990.

---. *Politics and Ideology in the Age of the Civil War.* New York: Oxford University Press, 1980.

Forgie, George B. *Patricide in the House Divided: A Psychological Interpretation of Lincoln and His Age.* New York: W. W. Norton, 1979.

Frank, John P. *Lincoln as a Lawyer.* Urbana, IL: University of Illinois Press, 1961.

Fredrickson, George M. "A Man but Not a Brother: Abraham Lincoln and Racial Equality." *Journal of Southern History* 41 (1975): 39-58.

Freedman, Russell. *Lincoln: A Photobiography.* New York: Clarion Books, 1987.

Garfinkle, Norton, ed. *Lincoln and the Coming of the Civil War.* Boston, MA: D. C. Heath, 1959.

Garner, Wayne Lee. "Abraham Lincoln and the Uses of Humor." Unpublished Ph.D. dissertation, State University of Iowa, 1963.

Germino, Dante. *The Inaugural Addresses of American Presidents: The Public Philosophy and Rhetoric.* New York: Lanham, 1984.

Gibson, Mary B. "A Study of the Background, Occasion, and Growing Significance of Abraham Lincoln's Gettysburg Address." Unpublished M.A. thesis, University of Michigan, 1947.

Goldwin, Robert A., ed. *100 Years of Emancipation.* Chicago, IL: Rand McNally, 1964.

Goodman, Florence Jeanne. "Pericles at Gettysburg." *The Midwest Quarterly* 6 (1965): 317-36.

Goodnight, G. Thomas and John Poulakos. "Conspiracy Rhetoric: From Pragmatism to Fantasy in Public Discourse." *Western Journal of Speech Communication* 45 (1981): 299-316.

Graebner, Norman A. "Commentary" to "Abe Lincoln Laughing." In *The Historian's Lincoln.* Ed. Gabor S. Boritt. Urbana, IL: University of Illinois Press, 1988. 19-25.

---. *The Enduring Lincoln.* Urbana, IL: University of Illinois Press, 1959.

Gross, Anthony. *Lincoln's Own Stories.* New York: Harpers, 1912.

Gunderson, Robert G. "Lincoln and the Policy of Eloquent Silence: November, 1860, to March, 1861." *Quarterly Journal of Speech* 47 (1961): 1-9.

---. "Lincoln's Rhetorical Style." *Vital Speeches* 27 (15 February 1961): 273-75.

---. *The Log-Cabin Campaign.* Lexington, KY: University of Kentucky Press, 1957.

---. *Old Gentleman's Convention: The Washington Peace Conference of 1861.* Madison, WI: University of Wisconsin Press, 1961.

---. "Reading Lincoln's Mail." *Indiana Magazine of History* 55 (1959).

Hahn, Dan F. and Anne Morlando. "A Burkean Analysis of Lincoln's Second Inaugural Address." *Presidential Studies Quarterly* 9 (1979): 376-79.

Hamilton, Charles and Lloyd Ostendorf. *Lincoln in Photographs: An Album of Every Known Pose.* Dayton, OH: Morningside, 1985.

Handlin, Oscar and Lilian. *Abraham Lincoln and the Union.* Boston, MA: Little, Brown and Company, 1980.

Harper, Robert S. *Lincoln and the Press.* New York: McGraw-Hill, 1951.

Harris, B. W. "A Study of Outstanding Interest-Producing Sentences Employed in Lincoln's Speeches." Unpublished M.A. thesis, University of Southern California, 1931.

Harris, Leon A. *The Fine Art of Political Wit.* New York: E. P. Dutton, 1964.

Heckman, Richard Allen. "The Lincoln-Douglas Debates: A Case Study in 'Stump Speaking.'" *Civil War History* 12 (1966): 54-66.

---. *Lincoln vs Douglas: The Great Debates Campaign.* Washington, D. C.: Public Affairs Press, 1967.

Herndon, William H. and Jesse W. Weik. *Abraham Lincoln: The True Story of a Great Life.* 2 vols. New York: D. Appleton and Company, 1892.

Hertz, Emanuel. *Abraham Lincoln, A New Portrait.* New York: H. Liveright, 1931.

---. *The Hidden Lincoln.* New York: Viking, 1938.

Highet, Gilbert. "The Gettysburg Address." In *Readings in Speech.* Ed. Haig A. Bosmajian. New York: Harper and Row, 1971, pp. 221-27.

Hill, Frederick Trevor. *Lincoln the Lawyer.* New York: The Century Company, 1906.

---. *Lincoln the Emancipator of the Nation.* New York: D. Appleton Company, 1928.

Hochmuth, Marie. "Lincoln's First Inaugural." In *American Speeches.* Ed. Wayland Maxfield Parrish and Marie Hochmuth. New York: Longmans, Green and Company, 1954, pp. 21-71.

Hofstadter, Richard. "Abraham Lincoln and the Self-Made Myth." *The American Political Tradition*. New York: Vintage Books, 1948, pp. 93-136.

---. *The Paranoid Style in American Politics*. New York: Random House, 1964.

Holland, Josiah Gilbert. *The Life of Abraham Lincoln*. Springfield, MA: Gurdon Bill, 1866.

Holtman, Robert B. "The Negro from North to South." *Southern Speech Communication Journal* 15 (1950): 263-69.

Holzer, Harold. "'A Few Appropriate Remarks.'" *American History Illustrated* 23 (1988): 37-46.

---, Gabor S. Boritt, and Mark E. Neely, Jr. *Changing the Lincoln Image*. Fort Wayne, IN: Louis A. Warren Lincoln Library and Museum, 1985.

---, Gabor S. Boritt, and Mark E. Neely, Jr. *The Lincoln Image: Abraham Lincoln and the Popular Print*. New York: Charles Scribner's Sons, 1984.

Howe, Beverly W. *Two Hours and Two Minutes, or Lincoln and Everett at Gettysburg*. n.p.: 1933.

Hunt, Everett Lee. "Lincoln's Rhetorical Triumph at Cooper Union." In *Rhetoric of the People*. Ed. Harold Barrett. Amsterdam: Rodopi NV, 1974, pp. 303-10.

Hurt, James. "All the Living and the Dead: Lincoln's Imagery." *American Literature* 52 (1980): 351-80.

Ingersoll, Robert G. *Abraham Lincoln, a Lecture*. New York: C. P. Farrell, 1895.

Jacobs, Henry Eyster. *Lincoln's Gettysburg World-Message*. Philadelphia, PA: The United Lutheran Publication House, 1917.

Jaffa, Harry V. *Crisis of the House Divided: An Interpretation of the Issues in the Lincoln-Douglas Debates*. Garden City, NY: Doubleday, 1959.

---. *Equality and Liberty*. New York: Oxford University Press, 1965.

---. "Expediency and Morality in the Lincoln-Douglas Debates." *The Anchor Review* 2 (1957): 179-204.

Jamieson, Kathleen Hall and David S. Birdsell. *Presidential Debates*. New York: Oxford University Press, 1988.

Jennison, Keith, W. *The Humorous Mr. Lincoln*. Woodstock, VT: The Countryman Press, 1988.

Johannsen, Robert W. "The Lincoln-Douglas Campaign of 1858: Background and Perspective." *Journal of the Illinois State Historical Society* 73 (1980): 242-62.

Jones, Alfred Haworth. "Roosevelt and Lincoln: The Political Uses of a Literary Image." Unpublished Ph.D. dissertation, Yale University, 1967.

Jordan, Harriet Patricia. "The Lincoln-Douglas Debates of 1858: A Presentation of the Rhetorical Scene and Setting with a Pilot

Film Script of the Ottawa Debate." Unpublished Ph.D. dissertation, University of Illinois, 1958.

Kekes, John. "Essentially Contested Concepts: A Reconsideration." *Philosophy and Rhetoric* 10 (1977): 71-89.

Kemp, Robert L. *Lincoln-Douglas Debating.* Clayton, MD: The Alan Company, 1984.

Kincaid, Robert L. "Abraham Lincoln: The Speaker." *Southern Speech Communication Journal* 16 (1951): 241-50.

Kunhardt, Philip B., Jr. *A New Birth of Freedom: Lincoln at Gettysburg.* Boston, MA: Little, Brown and Company, 1983.

Lambert, William H. "The Gettysburg Address: When Written; How Received; Its True Form." *Pennsylvania Magazine of History and Biography* 33 (1909): 385-408.

Lamon, Ward H. *The Life of Abraham Lincoln.* Boston, MA: James R. Osgood and Company, 1872.

---. *Recollections of Abraham Lincoln.* Ed. Dorothy Lamon Teillard. Cambridge: The University Press, 1911.

Lang, H. Jack, ed. *The Wit and Wisdom of Abraham Lincoln.* Cleveland, OH: World Publishing Company, 1942.

Leckie, Robert. *None Died in Vain: The Saga of the American Civil War.* New York: Harper Collins, 1990.

Leff, Michael. "Dimensions of Temporality in Lincoln's Second Inaugural." *Communication Reports* 1 (1988): 26-31.

--- and G. P. Mohrmann. "Lincoln at Cooper Union: A Rhetorical Analysis of the Text." *Quarterly Journal of Speech* 60 (1974): 346-58.

---. "Rhetorical Timing in Lincoln's 'House Divided' Speech." The Van Zelst Lecture in Communication. Evanston, Illinois, Northwestern University School of Speech, May 1983.

Lewis, Lloyd. *Myths After Lincoln.* New York: Harcourt, Brace and Company, 1929.

Lewis, Mort Reis. "Abraham Lincoln: Storyteller." In *Lincoln for the Ages.* Ed. Ralph G. Newman. Garden City, NY: Doubleday and Company, 1960, pp. 130-34.

---. "Lincoln's Humor." In *Lincoln: A Contemporary Portrait.* Ed. Allan Nevins and Irving Stone. Garden City, NY: Doubleday and Company, 1962, pp. 163-83.

Linkugel, Wil A. "Lincoln, Kansas, and Cooper Union." *Speech Monographs* 37 (1970): 172-79.

Lorant, Stefan. *Lincoln, a Picture Story of His Life.* New York: Harper and Brothers, 1952.

Luthin, Reinhard H. *The Real Abraham Lincoln.* Englewood Cliffs, NJ: Prentice-Hall, 1960.

Maizlish, Stephen E. and John J. Kushma, eds. *Essays on American Antebellum Politics, 1840-1860.* College Station, TX: Texas A&M University Press, 1982.

Masters, Edgar Lee. *Lincoln the Man*. New York: Dodd, Mead and Company, 1931.

McClure, Alexander K. *Abe Lincoln's Yarns and Stories*. Philadelphia, PA: Times Publishing Co., 1892.

McMurtry, Gerald. "The Different Editions of the 'Debates of Lincoln and Douglas.'" *Journal of the Illinois State Historical Society* 27 (1934): 95-107.

McPherson, James M. *Abraham Lincoln and the Second American Revolution*. New York: Oxford University Press, 1990. The book includes the lecture listed below.

---. "How Lincoln Won the War with Metaphors." The Eighth Annual R. Gerald McMurtry Lecture. Fort Wayne, IN: Louis A. Warren Lincoln Library and Museum, 1985.

Mellon, James, comp. and ed. *The Face of Lincoln*. New York: Viking, 1979.

Meserve, Frederick Hill and Carl Sandburg. *The Photographs of Abraham Lincoln*. New York: Harcourt, Brace and Company, 1944.

Miers, E. S., W. E. Baringer, and C. P. Powell, eds. *Lincoln Day by Day, A Chronology, 1809-1865*. 3 vols. Washington, D.C.: Lincoln Sesquicentennial Commission, 1960.

Miller, William Lee. "Lincoln's Second Inaugural: The Zenith of Statecraft." *The Center Magazine* (July/August 1980): 53-64.

"Mint of Lincoln's Wit." *Magazine of History*, 32 (1926): 44.

Mitgang, Herbert. *Lincoln as They Saw Him*. New York: Rinehart and Company, 1956.

Mohrmann, G. P. and Michael C. Leff. "Lincoln at Cooper Union: A Rationale for Neo-Classical Criticism." *Quarterly Journal of Speech* 60 (1974): 459-67.

Moore, Charles. *Abraham Lincoln's Gettysburg Address and Second Inaugural*. Boston, MA: Houghton Mifflin, 1927.

Murray, Byron D. "Lincoln Speaks." *Contemporary Review* 208 (1966): 250-61.

Neely, Mark E., Jr. *The Abraham Lincoln Encyclopedia*. New York: McGraw-Hill, 1982.

---. "American Nationalism in the Image of Henry Clay: Abraham Lincoln's Eulogy of Henry Clay in Context." *Register of the Kentucky Historical Society* 73 (January 1973): 31-60.

---. "Commentary" to "Abe Lincoln Laughing." In *The Historian's Lincoln*. Ed. Gabor S. Boritt. Urbana, IL: University of Illinois Press, 1988, pp. 26-30.

---. *The Fate of Liberty: Abraham Lincoln and Civil Liberties*. New York: Oxford University Press, 1991.

Nelson, Larry E. *Bullets, Ballots, and Rhetoric: Confederate Policy for the United States Presidential Contest of 1864*. University, AL: The University of Alabama Press, 1980.

Nevins, Allan. *The Emergence of Lincoln*. 2 vols. New York: Charles Scribner's Sons, 1950.

--- and Irving Stone, eds. *Lincoln: A Contemporary Portrait*. Garden City, NY: Doubleday and Company, 1962.

---, ed. *Lincoln and the Gettysburg Address: Commemorative Papers*. Urbana, IL: University of Illinois Press, 1964.

---. *The Statesmanship of the Civil War*. New York: The Macmillan Company, 1953.

---. *The War for the Union*. New York: Charles Scribner's Sons, 1959.

Newman, Ralph G., ed. *Lincoln for the Ages*. Garden City, NY: Doubleday and Company, 1960.

Nicolay, John G. and John Hay. *Abraham Lincoln: A History*. 10 vols. New York: Century Company, 1890.

---. "Lincoln's Gettysburg Address," *The Century* 47 (1893-94): 596-608.

---. "Lincoln's Literary Experiments," *The Century* 47 (1893-94): 823-32.

Oates, Stephen B. *Abraham Lincoln: The Man Behind the Myths*. New York: Harper and Row, 1984.

---. "Builders of the Dream: Abraham Lincoln and Martin Luther King, Jr." The Fifth Annual R. Gerald McMurtry Lecture. Fort Wayne, IN: 1982.

---. *With Malice Toward None*. New York: Harper and Row, 1977.

Oliver, Robert T. *History of Public Speaking in America*. Boston, MA: Allyn and Bacon, 1965.

Petersen, Sven. *The Gettysburg Addresses, The Story of Two Orations*. New York: Frederick Ungar Publishing, 1963.

Phillips, Issac N. *Abraham Lincoln By Some Men Who Knew Him*. Bloomington, IL: Pantagraph Printing and Stationary Company, 1910.

Potter, David, M. *The Impending Crisis*. Completed by Don Fehrenbacher. New York: Harper and Row, 1976.

---. *Lincoln and His Party in the Secession Crisis*. New Haven, CT: Yale University Press, 1942.

Randall, James G. *Lincoln: The Liberal Statesman*. New York: Dodd, Mead and Company, 1947.

---. *Lincoln the President: Midstream*. New York: Dodd, Mead and Company, 1953.

---. *Lincoln the President, Springfield to Gettysburg*. 2 vols. New York: Dodd, Mead and Company, 1945-1946.

--- and Richard N. Current. *Lincoln the President: Last Full Measure*. New York: Dodd, Mead and Company, 1955.

---. *Lincoln and the South*. Baton Rouge, LA: Louisiana State University Press, 1946.

Reid, Ronald F. "Newspaper Response to the Gettysburg Addresses." *Quarterly Journal of Speech* 53 (1967): 50-60.

Reilly, Tom. "Early Coverage of a President-Elect: Lincoln at Springfield 1860." *Journalism Quarterly* 49 (1972): 469-79.

---. "Lincoln-Douglas Debates of 1858 Forced New Role on the Press." *Journalism Quarterly* 56 (1979): 734-43.

Rice, Allen Thorndike, comp. and ed. *Reminiscences of Abraham Lincoln by Distinguished Men of His Time.* New York: North American Review, 1888.

Richards, John T. *Abraham Lincoln, the Lawyer-Statesman.* Boston, MA: Houghton Mifflin, 1916.

Riddle, Donald W. *Congressman Abraham Lincoln.* Urbana, IL: University of Illinois Press, 1957.

---. *Lincoln Runs for Congress.* New Brunswick, NJ: Rutgers University Press, 1948.

Robinson, Luther E. *Abraham Lincoln as a Man of Letters.* New York: G. P. Putnam's Sons, 1923.

Roosevelt, Theodore. *Abraham Lincoln.* Rpt., n.p.: E. C. Patterson, 1909.

Safire, William. *Freedom: A Novel of Abraham Lincoln and the Civil War.* New York: Doubleday, 1987.

Sandburg, Carl. *Abraham Lincoln: The Prairie Years.* 2 vols. New York: Harcourt, Brace and World, 1926.

---. *Abraham Lincoln: The War Years.* 4 vols. New York: Harcourt, Brace and World, 1939.

Schouler, James. *Abraham Lincoln at Tremont Temple in 1848.* Proceedings of the Massachusetts Historical Society, January-February, 1909.

Schutz, Charles E. *Political Humor from Aristophanes to Sam Ervin.* Rutherford, NJ: Farleigh Dickinson University Press, 1977.

Selby, Paul. *The Anecdotal Lincoln Speeches, Stories and Yarns.* Chicago, IL: Thompson and Thomas, 1900.

Sewall, Richard H. *Ballots for Freedom: Antislavery Politics in the United States, 1837-1860.* New York: Oxford University Press, 1976.

Shaw, Albert. *Abraham Lincoln: His Path to the Presidency.* New York: The Review of Reviews Corporation, 1930.

Shopen, Timothy and Joseph M. Williams. *Style and Variables in English.* Cambridge, MA: Winthrop Publishers, 1981.

Sigelschiffer, Saul. *The American Conscience: The Drama of the Lincoln-Douglas Debates.* New York: Horizon Press, 1973.

Simonton, Dean Keith. *Why Presidents Succeed: A Political Psychology of Leadership.* New Haven, CT: Yale University Press, 1987.

Slagell, Amy R. "A Textual Analysis of Abraham Lincoln's Second Inaugural Address." Unpublished M.A. Thesis, University of Wisconsin-Madison, 1986.

Smiley, C. M. "Lincoln and Gorgias." *Classical Journal* 13 (1917): 124-28.

Smith, R. Franklin. "A Night at Cooper Union." *Central States Speech Journal* 13 (1962): 270-75.

Solomon, Martha. "'With Firmness in the Right': The Creation of Moral Hegemony in Lincoln's Second Inaugural." *Communication Reports* 1 (1988): 32-37.

Somkin, Fred. "Scripture Notes to Lincoln's Second Inaugural." *Civil War History* 27 (1981): 172-73.

Staub, A. W. and G. P. Mohrmann. "Rhetoric and Poetic: A Critique." *Southern Speech Communication Journal* 28 (1962): 131-41.

Stewart, Charles J. "Lincoln's Assassination and the Protestant Clergy of the North." *Journal of the Illinois State Historical Society* 54 (Autumn 1961): 268-93.

---. "The Pulpit and the Assassination of Lincoln." *Quarterly Journal of Speech* 50 (1964): 299-307.

---. "The Pulpit in Time of Crisis: 1865 and 1963." *Speech Monographs* 32 (1965): 427-34.

---. "A Rhetorical Study of the Reaction of the Protestant Pulpit in the North to Lincoln's Assassination." Unpublished Ph.D. diss., University of Illinois at Urbana-Champaign, 1963.

Stewart, Judd. *Lincoln's First Inaugural: Original Draft and Its Final Form.* Privately printed, 1920.

Strozier, Charles B. *Lincoln's Quest for Union: Public and Private Meanings.* New York: Basic Books, 1982.

Tarbell, Ida M. *In the Footsteps of the Lincolns.* New York: Harper and Brothers, 1924.

---. *The Life of Abraham Lincoln.* 2 vols. New York: McClure, Phillips and Company, 1900.

Teeter, Junella. "A Study of the Homely Figures of Speech Used by Abraham Lincoln in His Speeches." Unpublished M.A. thesis, Northwestern University, 1931.

Thomas, Benjamin P. "Abe Lincoln, Country Lawyer," *The Atlantic Monthly, 193* (February, 1954): 57-61.

---. *Abraham Lincoln: A Biography.* New York: Alfred A. Knopf, 1952.

---. "Lincoln's Humor: An Analysis." *Abraham Lincoln Association Papers.* Springfield, IL: Abraham Lincoln Association, 1936, pp. 61-90.

---. *Portrait for Posterity: Lincoln and His Biographers.* New Brunswick, NJ: Rutgers University Press, 1947.

Thurow, Glen E. *Abraham Lincoln and American Political Religion.* Albany, NY: State University of New York Press, 1976.

Trueblood, Elton. *Abraham Lincoln: Theologian of American Anguish.* New York: Harper and Row, 1973.

Tulis, Jeffrey K. *The Rhetorical Presidency.* Princeton, NJ: Princeton University Press, 1987.

Vickrey, James Frank, Jr. "The Lectures on 'Discoveries and Inventions'--A Neglected Aspect of the Public Speaking Career of Abraham Lincoln." *Central States Speech Journal* 21 (1970): 181-90.

Vidal, Gore. *Lincoln: A Novel.* New York: Random House, 1984.

Villard, Henry. *Lincoln on the Eve of '61: A Journalist's Story.* Ed. Harold G. and Oswald Garrison Villard. New York: Alfred A. Knopf, 1941.

Warren, Louis A. *Abraham Lincoln's Gettysburg Address: An Evaluation.* Columbus, OH: Charles E. Merrill, 1968.

---. "Biblical Influences in the Second Inaugural Address." *Lincoln Lore*, No. 1226 (October 6, 1952).

---. *Lincoln's Gettysburg Declaration: "A New Birth of Freedom."* Fort Wayne, IN: Lincoln National Life Foundation, 1964.

---. "Sources of the Second Inaugural Address." *Lincoln Lore*, No. 1352 (March 7, 1955).

Weaver, Richard. *The Ethics of Rhetoric.* Chicago, IL: Henry Regnery Company, 1953, pp. 85-114.

White, Horace. *The Lincoln and Douglas Debates.* Chicago, IL: The University of Chicago Press, 1914.

Whitney, Henry Clay. *Life on the Circuit with Lincoln, 1892.* Introduction and notes by Paul M. Angle. Caldwell, ID: Caxton Printers, 1940.

Wichelns, Herbert A. "The Literary Criticism of Oratory." In *The Rhetorical Idiom.* Ed. Donald C. Bryant. Ithaca, NY: Cornell University Press, 1958.

Wiley, Earl W. "Abraham Lincoln: His Emergence as the Voice of the People." In *A History and Criticism of American Public Address.* Ed. William Norwood Brigance, Vol. 2. New York: Russell and Russell, 1960, pp. 859-77.

---. *Abraham Lincoln: Portrait of a Speaker.* New York: Vantage Press, 1970.

---. "Buckeye Criticism of the Gettysburg Address." *Speech Monographs* 23 (1956): 1-8.

---. "Eloquence at Gettysburg and Daniel Webster." *Dartmouth Alumni Magazine* (April 1967): 11-12.

---. "A Footnote on the Lincoln-Douglas Debates." *Quarterly Journal of Speech* 18 (1932): 216-24.

---. *Four Speeches by Lincoln, Hitherto Unpublished and Unknown.* Columbus, OH: Ohio State University Press, 1927.

---. "Lincoln and the Freedom Riders of the 1930's." *Lincoln Herald* (Summer 1967): 60-69.

---. "Lincoln the Speaker: 1816-1830." *Quarterly Journal of Speech* 20 (1934): 1-15.

---. "Lincoln the Speaker: 1830-1837." *Quarterly Journal of Speech* 21 (1935): 305-22.

---. "Motivation as a Factor in Lincoln's Rhetoric." *Quarterly Journal of Speech* 24 (1938): 615-21.

Williams, Joseph. "Lincoln's Second Inaugural: Benevolent Double-speak." Paper presented at the Speech Communication Association Convention, Chicago, IL, November 2, 1984.

Williams, T. Harry. *Lincoln and the Radicals.* Madison, WI: University of Wisconsin Press, 1941.

Wills, John W. "Abraham Lincoln's Speech Textbooks." *Southern Speech Communication Journal* 27 (1962): 220-25.

Wills, Garry. *Inventing America.* Garden City, NY: Doubleday & Company, Inc., 1978, pp. xiv-xxiv, 309, 357, and 368.

Wilson, Edmund. "Abraham Lincoln." In his *Patriotic Gore: Studies in the Literature of the American Civil War.* New York: Oxford University Press, 1962, pp. 99-130.

Wilson, Rufus Rockwell and R. Gerald McMurtry. *Lincoln in Caricature.* New York: Horizon Press, 1953.

Wilson, Woodrow. "Abraham Lincoln: A Man of the People." In *Selected Literary and Political Papers and Addresses of Woodrow Wilson.* Vol. 1. New York: Grosset, 1925, p. 234.

Windt, Theodore. "Lincoln's Presidential Rhetoric." Address delivered at the Gettysburg Conference on Rhetorical Transactions in the Civil War Era. Gettysburg, PA: June 1983.

Wolf, William J. *The Almost Chosen People.* Garden City, NY: Doubleday, 1959.

Woodward, C. Vann. "Gilding Lincoln's Lily." *The New York Review of Books*, vol. 34, no. 14 (September 24, 1987): 23-26.

Wright, John S. *Lincoln and the Politics of Slavery.* Reno, NE: University of Nevada Press, 1970.

Zall, P. M., ed. *Abe Lincoln Laughing.* Berkeley, CA: University of California Press, 1982.

Zall, P. M. "Abe Lincoln Laughing." In *The Historian's Lincoln.* Ed. Gabor S. Boritt. Urbana, IL: University of Illinois Press, 1988, pp. 3-18.

Zarefsky, David. "Approaching Lincoln's Second Inaugural Address." *Communication Reports* 1 (1988): 9-13.

---. "Conspiracy Arguments in the Lincoln-Douglas Debates." *Journal of the American Forensic Association* 21 (1984): 63-75.

---. "In Search of the Founding Fathers: Historical Argument in the Lincoln-Douglas Debates." In *Argument and Social Practice: Proceedings of the Fourth SCA/AFA Conference on Argumenta-*

tion.   Ed. J. Robert Cox, et al.   Annandale, VA: Speech
    Communication Association, 1985, pp. 179-92.
---. "The Lincoln-Douglas Debates Revisited: The Evolution of Public
    Argument." *Quarterly Journal of Speech* 72 (1986): 162-84.
---. *Lincoln, Douglas, and Slavery: In the Crucible of Public Debate.*
    Chicago, IL: University of Chicago Press, 1990.
Zyskind, Harold. "A Rhetorical Analysis of the Gettysburg Address."
    Journal of General Education 4 (1950): 202-12.

Index

Abe Lincoln Laughing, 48
Abolitionists, 60, 68, 76, 79, 82, 103
Abraham Lincoln: A Press Portrait, 56
Aesop's Fables, 14, 28, 32, 45, 46, 52
African slave trade, 73
American Dream, 81
Archetypal images, 28-33
Arguments from: definition, 78-79, 83, 84; principles, 67, 68, 69, 71, 73, 79-83, 91
Aristotle, 17-18, 52
Arnold, Carroll C., 33
Audiences of Lincoln's speeches, 5, 6, 20, 26, 36, 41-42, 60, 68, 76, 95-96, 101, 104-106, 110, 111
"Autobiography," 12, 27

Barton, William E., 94
Barzun, Jacques, 40
Basler, Roy P., 4, 8, 38, 42, 98
Battle of Gettysburg, 94-95, 108
Berry, Mildred Freburg, 36
Biblical references, 27-28, 34-35, 37-38, 40, 84, 87-90, 96-100, 108-110, 111, 184-185
Bixby, Letter to Mrs., 106-107
Blegen, Theodore, xvii, 28, 35
Books read, 14-15
Boritt, Gabor S., 57, 74
Brevity, 33-35, 36, 104-105, 110
Browne, Sir Thomas, 46
Bryan, William Jennings, xvii, 23-24
Buchanan, James, 30-31, 59, 90
Burden of proof, 15-16
Burke, Kenneth, 25-26

Carlyle, Thomas, 113
Carpenter, Francis B., 13
Characteristics of speaking, xvii, 4, 6-7, 21-42, 43-53, 73, 84-85
Charnwood, Lord, 38
Childhood, influence of on speaking, 12-15, 21, 24-25
"Chosen People" theme, 67
Churchill, Winston, 4
Civil War, 26, 31, 38, 43, 45, 57, 63, 77, 82, 85-91, 94-95, 98, 100, 102, 104, 105, 111, 197

Clarity, 13, 16, 20, 33-34, 109
Clay, Henry, 17, 36
Collected Works, 5, 8
Colonization, 57, 77, 85
Communication: importance of,
    xvii, 3-4, 8, 11, 23-24,
    113, 197; study of, 6, 7-8,
    11-21, 83
Conciseness, 20, 33-35
Confederacy, 34, 64-65, 197
Conservatism, 7, 34, 62-63, 71,
    77-85, 91
Conspiracy argument, 30
Constitution, 14, 24, 62, 65, 66,
    73, 74, 78, 80, 86
Contract argument, 64-65
Cooper Union Address, 5, 6, 8,
    24-25, 26, 27, 32-33, 49-
    50, 77-78, 80, 84, 151-
    166
Corwin, Tom, 52-53
Cosmic perspective, 26-33, 41,
    84
Courtroom rhetoric, 15, 21, 47-
    48

Dahlberg, W. A., 49
Davis, Judge David, 45
Davis, Jefferson, 43, 64-65
Declaration of Independence,
    14, 26, 35, 67, 73, 74, 75-
    76, 77, 78, 79, 80-82, 98-
    99
Deliberative speaking, 37, 41,
    106
Delivery, 13, 35-36, 41, 51-52,
    110-111
Democratic Party, 30, 75, 77-
    78, 87-88
DePew, Chauncey M., 16
Detachment, 4, 27-28, 37-38,
    41, 84, 87-90, 108-111
Development of speaking, 7,
    23, 25, 26-27, 33, 36-42,
    49-52

Discoveries and inventions,
    Second lecture on, 3, 7-8,
    13-14, 23, 26, 30, 31, 74-
    75, 143-149, 183
Dialogue, 47, 51
Douglas, Stephen A., debates
    against, 8, 15-16, 22, 32-
    33, 49, 51, 71, 72, 74, 75-
    76, 77, 81, 83, 84; oppo-
    sition to, 4, 8, 15-16, 22,
    30-31, 32-33, 49-52, 71,
    73, 74, 75-76, 79-80, 81,
    84; on popular sovereign-
    ty, 51, 73, 79-80
Dred Scott decision, 79

Editing, 5, 13, 27-28
Education, 12-15, 19, 21, 24
Edwards, Herbert Joseph, 23,
    40
Elements of Rhetoric, 15
Eliade, Mircea, 26
Emancipation, 70-91, 111
Emancipation Proclamation,
    52, 70, 71, 77, 82, 84, 85-
    86, 90-91
Emancipation with compensa-
    tion, 85, 86
Epideictic speaking, 37, 41, 97,
    106
Equality of opportunity, 74-75
Ethics, 17-18
Ethnic humor, 48
Ethos, 17-18, 25, 63, 108
Euclid, 15
Eulogy on Henry Clay, 17
Everett, Edward, 41, 93-96,
    101, 103, 108
Evolution of Lincoln's speak-
    ing, 7, 23, 25, 26-27, 33,
    36-42, 49-52

Farewell to Springfield Speech,
    8, 31, 167
Fehrenbacher, Don E., 76, 90
Feiffer, Jules, 49

Figurative language, 14, 19-20, 28-35, 37, 40, 50-51, 72-73, 74-75, 76, 85
First Inaugural Address, 7, 8, 18, 23-24, 27-28, 29-30, 34, 37, 38, 39, 40-42, 55-69, 73, 78, 84, 88, 90, 169-176
Flesch, Rudolf, 64, 109, 190
Fog index of readability, 64, 109
Forensic speaking, 37
Forgie, George B., 27, 29, 30
Founding Fathers, 24, 29, 32, 35, 73, 74, 78, 96-97, 99
Fragment on Slavery, 72
Frontier life, 12-15, 26, 32, 45, 46-47, 49-51
Frost, Robert, 97
Fugitive Slave Law, 61, 62

Gettysburg Address, 5, 7, 8, 26, 37-38, 39, 40, 41-42, 76, 81, 93-112, 177, 197
God, references to, 5, 27-28, 67, 86-90, 103, 108-109
Godby, Russell, 14
Government, views on, 12, 63, 65, 72-73, 79-82, 90-91, 97-99, 103-104
Gradual emancipation, 73, 77, 82, 84-86, 90-91
Graebner, Norman A., 83-84
Graham, Mentor William, 3
Great American Dream, 12
Great Emancipator, 84, 90-91, 113, 197
Grant, Ulysses S., 17
Greeley, Horace, 82
Gunning, Robert, 109, 190

Hankins, John Erskine, 23, 40
Hanks, Dennis, 45, 197
Hayne, Robert, 103
Herndon, William, 13, 14-15, 18-19, 20, 24-25, 43, 83

Hodges, Albert G., 85-86
Hofstadter, Richard, 25
"House," used as an image, 30, 49, 79-80
"House Divided" Speech, 7, 8, 10, 11, 27, 28, 50, 73, 79, 100, 135-141
Humble man appeal, 25, 36, 51, 101
Humor, 4, 7, 8, 37, 43-53, 76, 83-84, 197
Hurt, James, 15

Ideas on speaking, 6, 7-8, 11-21, 83, 113
Identification, 4, 20, 21, 25-26, 28-33, 35, 46-48, 51, 53, 87, 108, 113
Illinois State Legislature, 19, 24, 79
Illiteracy rate, 6, 95, 182
Imagery, 15, 46-47, 50-51; sensory, 33, 37, 107-108, 109; intellectual, 33, 34, 37, 109
Immigration, 48
Inauguration in 1861, 7, 58, 65, 69
Index to Journals in Communication Through 1985, 4
Irish jokes, 48

Jesus, "Sermon on the Mount," 80

Kennedy, John F., 97
King James Bible, 14, 27, 28, 38, 45, 46, 88, 89, 96-104, 108-110, 197

Law: how to study, 15, 197; importance of, 15-16; influence of, 15-16; training in, 12, 15-16, 21
Lawyer, Lincoln as, 15-16, 17, 83

Lecture on Discoveries and Inventions, 3, 7-8, 13-14, 23, 26, 30, 31, 74-75, 143-149, 183

Lee, Robert E., 94

Leff, Michael, 7, 79-80

Lincoln, Abraham: books read, 14-15; characteristics of speeches, 4, 6-7, 22-42, 43-53, 73, 84-85; childhood, 12-15; cosmic perspective, 26-33, 41, 84; delivery of speeches, 13, 35-36, 41, 51-52, 110-111; development of speaking, 7, 23, 25, 26-27, 33, 36-42, 49-52; editing changes made, 5, 13, 27-28; education, 12-15, 19, 21, 24; emotional detachment, 4, 27-28, 37-38, 41, 84, 87-90, 108-111; humble man image, 25, 36, 51, 101; humor, 4, 7, 8, 37, 43-53, 76, 83-84, 197; legend, 4-5, 7, 12, 25, 53, 115, 196, 197; as literary artist, 7-8, 23, 40-42, 197; preparation of speeches, 5, 13, 20-21, 190; as public speaker, 7-8, 23-24, 40-42, 197; reactions to speeches, 7, 8, 25, 40-42, 55-69, 93-94; strategic silence, 7, 8, 13, 21, 58-59, 69; views on government, 12, 63, 65, 72-73, 79-82, 90-91, 97-99, 103-104; views on racial equality, 7, 71, 74-77, 82, views on slavery, 7, 20, 21, 24, 29, 64, 66-67, 71-91

Lincoln Address Memorial, 92

Lincoln legend, 4-5, 7, 12, 25, 53, 113-115, 196, 197

Lincoln Memorial, 114

Lincoln, Thomas, 15, 45

Logan, Stephen T., 47-48

"Lost Speech," 3

Lovejoy, Owen, 113

Lucas, Stephen E., 93-94

Lyceum Address, 7, 18, 26, 27, 29, 30, 32, 33, 35, 41-42, 84, 119-126

McClure, Colonel Alexander, 46

McPherson, James M., 28

Metaphors, 28-33, 40, 50-51, 72-73, 74-75, 85

Mitgang, Herbert, 3

Moderate positions, 59, 77-85, 91

Mohrmann, Gerald P., 108

Myth of the eternal return, 26

Myths about Lincoln, 4, 24

Newman, Ralph G., 198

New-York Daily Tribune, 6

New York Herald, 46, 52

New York Tribune, 82

Nichols, Marie Hochmuth, 23-24, 34, 55-56, 60

Norms in the nineteenth century, 6, 11-12, 27-28, 34, 58-59, 66, 67, 76-77, 80, 87, 90, 97, 104-105

Northern Editorials on Secession, 56

Northwest Ordinance of 1787, 73-74

Ohmann, Richard M., 113-115

Oral to written style, 7, 40-42, 109-110

Oratorical vs. literary excellence, 7-8, 23-24, 40-42, 93-112, 197

Osborn, Michael, 28

Parables, 14, 45, 46

Parker, Theodore, 103
Peoria Address, 20, 35, 77
Perorations, 27-28, 39, 40, 56, 60, 61-62, 68, 90, 104, 108
Pericles, 107-198
Personality, 6, 7, 38, 45-46, 49, 77, 83, 84-85, 91
Political religion, 12
Popular lecturer, 8, 36
Popular sovereignty, 51, 73, 79-80
Pragmatism, 11-12, 20, 21, 46, 52, 57, 81-82, 85-86
Precision, 13, 15-16, 19, 21, 24, 33-35, 111
Preliminary Emancipation Proclamation, 82, 85-86
Preparation of speeches, 5, 13, 20-21, 190
Presidential election: in 1860, 7, 21, 45, 57-58, 69, 79; in 1864, 52-53
Presumption, 15-16
Proclamation Appointing a National Fast Day, 86-87

Quintilian, 16

Racial equality, 7, 71, 74-77, 82, 197
Randall, James G., 46
Reactions to Lincoln's speeches: at times of delivery, 7, 8, 25, 40-42, 55-69, 93-94; today, 7, 8, 40-42, 55-56, 93-94
Readability indexes, 64, 109
Reading: ideas on, nature of, 14-15, 74; importance of, 14-15; reading aloud, 15
Reason, emphasis on, 15-19, 24-25, 49, 64
Reconstruction, 90
References to God, 5, 27-28, 67, 86-90, 103, 108-109

Refutation, 7, 16
Reid, Ronald F., 93
Repetition, 32, 33, 38, 39, 40, 100, 102
Republican Party, 64, 75, 77-78, 87-88
Revolutionary War, 31-32, 33, 94, 99
Rhetoric: definition of, 3, 5, 8, 24; history of, 3-4, 46; importance of, xvii, 3-4, 8, 11, 23-24, 113-115, 197
Rhetorical criticism, definition of, 5-6, 23-24; compared to other types of criticism, 5, 8, 23-24, 55-56, 69, 93-112, 189
Rhetorical techniques: alliteration, 38, 39, 40, 84; analogy, 40, 47, 50, 83; anaphora, 39, 40; antithesis, 38-39, 40, 110; assonance, 39, 40; metaphor, 28-33, 40, 50-51, 72-73, 74-75, 85; parallelism, 38-39, 40, 84, 88, 110; religious language and imagery, 27-28, 34-35, 37-38, 40, 84, 87-90, 96-104, 108-110, 111, 184-185; repetition, 32, 33, 38, 39, 40, 100, 102; rhyme, 39, 40, 110; story, 14, 16, 19-20, 27, 34, 83, 84, 197; tricolon, 40, 110
Rhythm, 40, 110
Ridicule, 20, 32, 37, 49-52, 76

Sandburg, Carl, 40, 45, 46, 53, 93
Schutz, Charles E., 83-84
Second Inaugural Address, 8, 27, 34, 37-38, 39, 40, 41-

42, 76, 81, 84, 86-90, 179-180, 197
Second Lecture on Inventions and Discoveries, 3, 7-8, 13-14, 23, 26, 30, 31, 74-75, 143-149, 183
Secession, 21, 30, 34, 59, 61, 62, 64-65, 68, 82, 83
Self-deprecation, 51
Seward, William, 27-28, 56, 103
Shakespeare, William, 14, 28, 43
Silence, 7, 8, 13, 21, 58-59, 69
Simplicity, 28, 33-35, 40, 46-47, 109, 111
Slagell, Amy R., 87-88, 89
Slavery, 7, 20, 21, 24, 29, 64, 66-67, 71-91; preventing the extension of, 20, 68, 72-73, 79-80, 81-82
Southern Editorials on Secession, 56
Speaking: characteristics of, 4, 6-7, 22-42, 43-53, 73, 84-85; delivery, 13, 35-36, 41, 51-52, 110-111; development of, 7, 23, 25, 26-27, 33, 36-42, 49-52
Speaking, ideas on: have listeners' best interests at heart, 17-18; keep passion under control of reason, 18-19; prepare diligently, 20-21; speak for practical effect, 17; include stories and analogies, 19-20; values and limitations of, 16-17, 101
Speech anxiety, 36, 41, 185
Speeches by Lincoln: Cooper Union Address, 5, 6, 8, 24-25, 26, 27, 32-33, 49-50, 77-78, 80, 84, 151-166; debates against Douglas, 8, 15-16, 22, 32-33, 49, 51, 71, 72, 74, 75, 76, 77, 81, 83, 84; Farewell to Springfield, 8, 31, 167; First Inaugural Address, 7, 8, 18, 23-24, 27-28, 29-30, 34, 37, 38, 39, 40-42, 55-69, 73, 78, 84, 88, 90, 113, 169-176; Gettysburg Address, 5, 7, 8, 26, 37-38, 39, 40, 41-42, 76, 81, 93-112, 113, 177, 197; "House Divided" Speech, 7, 8, 10, 11, 27, 28, 50, 73, 79, 100, 135-141; Lyceum Address, 7, 18, 26, 27, 29, 30, 32, 33, 35, 41-42, 84, 119-126; Second Inaugural Address, 8, 27, 34, 37-38, 39, 40, 41-42, 76, 81, 84, 86-90, 113, 179-180, 197; Second Lecture on Inventions and Discoveries, 3, 7-8, 13-14, 23, 26, 30, 31, 74-75, 143-149, 183; Temperance Address, 7, 18, 26, 30, 31-32, 48, 75, 127-134
Speed, Joshua F., 41
Squatter sovereignty, 79
Staub, August W., 108
Stewart, Judd, 56
Stories, 14, 16, 19-20, 27, 34, 83, 84, 197

Temperance Address, 7, 18, 26, 30, 31-32, 48, 75, 127-134
Text, choice of, 5-6, 7
Thirteenth Amendment, 90
Thomas, Benjamin, 81
Truth: definition of, 18-19; will triumph in the end, 18-19, 49, 73

Union, preserving the, 30, 50, 61, 65, 68, 73, 79, 81-82, 84-91, 98, 107

Van Doren, Mark, 24
Village Voice, 49

Washington, George, 66, 103
Weaver, Richard, 11, 26, 78, 81
Webster, Daniel, 96-97, 103
Weems, Mason L., 103
Whately, Richard, 15
White, Horace, 4

Whitney, Henry Clay, xvii
Wichelns, Herbert A., 5
Widmer, John H., 15
Wiley, Earl W., 6
Williams, T. Harry, 23
Wills, David, 94-95
Writing, ideas on, 7-8, 11-21

Young America, 30

Zall, P. M., 48, 53
Zarefsky, David, 84
Zyskind, Harold, 106

About the Author

LOIS J. EINHORN is Associate Professor of Rhetoric at the State University of New York at Binghamton. She has written at length on public address and rhetorical theory and criticism. She is also a co-author of *Effective Employment Interviewing: Unlocking Human Potential* (1982).

Great American Orators

Defender of the Union: The Oratory of Daniel Webster
Craig R. Smith

Harry Emerson Fosdick: Persuasive Preacher
Halford R. Ryan

Eugene Talmadge: Rhetoric and Response
Calvin McLeod Logue

The Search of Self-Sovereignty: The Oratory of Elizabeth Cady Stanton
Beth M. Waggenspack

Richard Nixon: Rhetorical Strategist
Hal W. Bochin

Henry Ward Beecher: Peripatetic Preacher
Halford R. Ryan

Edward Everett: Unionist Orator
Ronald F. Reid

Theodore Roosevelt and the Rhetoric of Militant Decency
Robert V. Friedenberg

Patrick Henry, The Orator
David A. McCants

Anna Howard Shaw: Suffrage Orator and Social Reformer
Wil A. Linkugel and Martha Solomon

William Jennings Bryan: Orator of Small-Town America
Donald K. Springen

Robert M. La Follette, Sr.: the Voice of Conscience
Carl R. Burgchardt

Ronald Reagan: The Great Communicator
Kurt Ritter and David Henry

Clarence Darrow: The Creation of an American Myth
Richard J. Jensen

"Do Everything" Reform: The Oratory of Frances E. Willard
Richard W. Leeman

CPSIA information can be obtained at www.ICGtesting.com
Printed in the USA
LVOW06*1503180315

431076LV00005B/71/P